White Blaze Fever

Georgia to Maine on the
Appalachian Trail

*A rare blend of Appalachian Trail adventure and
"Hiker Tips"*

The views and opinions in this book are solely the opinion of the author as formulated during his thru-hike of the Appalachian Trail. Some names, places and/or events may have been altered to protect the privacy of those involved.

"White Blaze Fever: Georgia to Maine on the Appalachian Trail," by William Schuette" ISBN 1-58939-429-1 (softcover), 1-58939-430-5 (hardcover).

Manufactured in the United States of America.

To Keith, a brother-like friend and fellow hiker who shared the best of times with me on the Appalachian Trail. May the courage and perseverance you exhibited in the Mahoosucs see you through the challenges before you.

Acknowledgements:

In an effort to avoid leaving someone out I have elected to refrain from the naming of specific individuals and simply thank all the many friends and family who assisted me in my thru-hike and the writing of my book.

There is one individual who I do need to acknowledge specifically, my wife Connie, for without her indefatigable support and unending assistance, neither my thru-hike nor book would have come to fruition.

Last but not least, I would be remiss if I didn't acknowledge all the wonderful people along the Appalachian Trail, hikers and non-hikers, who, without their affability and wonderful stories, my book would not have been possible.

CONTENTS

Foreword

It's called "White Blaze Fever," and although you will not find the fever mentioned in any medical journal, have no doubt in your mind – it does exist and no one is immune. Only the most casual, most minute contact with the Appalachian Trail is needed to catch the fever. I speak from experience, having caught the fever while on a vacation with my family many years ago.

Although I had heard of the Appalachian Trail, it was not until our family visit to the A.T. in the Shenandoah National Park that I came to understand that it was not just another trail meandering for a few miles through the mountains. Rather, the Appalachian Trail, affectionately referred to as simply the A.T. by hikers, was a continuous footpath that extends all the way from Springer Mountain in Georgia to Mount Katahdin in Maine, a total of roughly 2,100 miles.

It was during this time in the park that I began to seriously consider the possibility of hiking the trail in one continuous journey. It was also at this time that I had my very first, be it ever so brief, encounter with an Appalachian Trail thru-hiker. It was a pathetic-looking soul that staggered off the A.T. into the Skyline Lodge while my wife and I were checking on a room. Dirt from head to toe, hair a tangled, matted mess, a smell that knocked your socks off, and the look of "What the hell did I get myself into?" written across the face all told me instantly this was a thru-hiker.

Consequently, with the simple act of taking a leisurely family walk along the Appalachian Trail in the Shenandoah National Park, "White Blaze Fever" was in my blood! And as I eventually found out, once you get the fever, it is next to impossible to get rid of. Wherever you go, whatever you do, the fever remains within you. Oh, it may lie dormant, hidden deep within your soul, but just when you think you may be over it, Wham! Back it comes! A drive through the wooded countryside, a scenic mountain picture, or the sweet smell of the azalea is all it takes to bring the fever roaring back! Yes, for many years after that first walk along the Appalachian Trail, I was a victim of "White Blaze Fever" and it had a terminal grip on me.

The desire to strike out with a pack on my back and head into the unknown for an extended time continued to flicker deep within my soul. But family, job, and time constraints required that I alter and limit my quest for adventure to an assortment of short summer excursions.

Eventually, with my three grown children off pursuing their own goals in life, and my wife, cognizant of the burning in my gut to thru-hike the A.T., giving me her total support, I opted to retire from public education after thirty years; and at the tender age of 51, I followed my dream of thru-hiking the Appalachian Trail.

So on a cool, clear August morning, I found myself atop the 5,267-foot peak of Mount Katahdin, a combined sense of joy, relief, and sadness engulfing me. For five months I incessantly followed the white blazes of the Appalachian Trail from Springer Mountain, Georgia, to Mount Katahdin, Maine, covering more than 2,167 miles. My hike and adventure then over, the memories collected while following the white blazes north would never be forgotten and were as fortified in my mind as the granite mountains I had hiked!

I now welcome you to be my vicarious hiking partner as we pursue the two-inch by six-inch white blazes from Springer Mountain, Georgia, to Mount Katahdin, Maine. Through my daily journal entries – revised only a little – you will share encounters with bear, moose, snakes and other wildlife, as well as gain a sense of the toll taken on both the body and mind that accompanies the carrying of a thirty-six-pound pack while hiking rigorous mountains from sunup to sundown. You will feel the thrill of viewing the most magnificent vistas east of the Mississippi and come to know a unique collection of individuals guaranteed to bring a smile to your face and warmth to your heart.

And last but not least, for the stalwart hikers who not only enjoy reading of hiking adventure but are also looking for specific information on hiking the Appalachian Trail, I have infused over one hundred informative and essential "Hiker Tips" throughout my book for your assistance and benefit.

Enough talk! Find that favorite easy chair and prepare yourself for an experience of a lifetime as together we follow the white blazes north on the Appalachian Trail!

Chapter 1
Springer Mt. to
Damascus

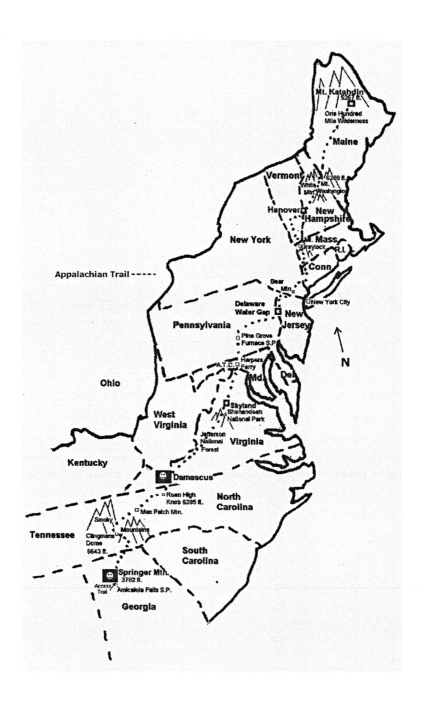

———————

"Badger, look---!" is all I could get out of my mouth. He was gone! It all happened so fast that I couldn't do anything but watch with horror as he and his backpack went tumbling like a box turtle over the side of the mountain! Afraid to look and expecting the worst, I took my pack off and slowly crawled to the mountain edge. There, to my great relief, was Badger, lying face up like a spider in a web, in what appeared to be the branches of a small tree about ten feet below. With a grimace on his face and a slow, wary hand check of his extremities, my dazed but undaunted hiking partner shouted up, "I think I'm still in one piece!"

He untangled himself from the branches and crawled back up to the trail. He was bruised and scratched but otherwise appeared to be all right, considering he had just rolled over the side of a mountain.

It was May 27th and I had been hiking north on the Appalachian Trail for the last fifty-nine days. With more than eight hundred A.T. miles under my boots I thought I had seen it all, but Badger's little tumble over the mountainside immediately reinforced what I had already come to realize early on: every day on the A.T. was an adventure like no other!

But, I've gotten ahead of myself. Let us now go back to the very beginning: Springer Mountain, Georgia, on a beautiful March 28th morning...

———————

March 28, Amicalola Falls State Park, Georgia

The anxious young hiker in front of me struggled to control his rapid breathing and appeared to be hyperventilating as he nervously attempted to answer the rapid-fire questions of the park official: "Name? Address? How many in your hiking party? Destination? Date? Pack weight?" All these questions had to be repeated several times before his answers were forthcoming, and I found my own anxiety diminishing somewhat with an inner laugh as his attempt at the very simple question of the day's date left him with a tortured, bewildered, blank look on his face. "It's March the 27th, no wait – the 28th. Hell, I'm so nervous I'm not sure what day it is," he blurted. "All I know: I'm headed to Maine!"

So began my adventure on the Appalachian Trail.

With my excitement and anticipation running at a fever pitch, my wife and I arrived at Amicalola Falls State Park Georgia, on a sunny 65-degree spring day. The drive from our home just outside Versailles, Ohio, was about 550 miles and required a stopover in Chattanooga,

Tennessee, to allow for a pleasant drive and late morning arrival time at the park. Upon our arrival, we immediately stopped at the visitor center for directions to the lodge where we planned to spend the evening before the start of my thru-hike the next morning. After a quick glance around the center, I found it not only offered the typical visitor center cards and souvenirs, but also had a few last-minute supply items for the trail, not the least of which was toilet paper, which seemed like a good idea. Somehow the thought of oak leaves against the tender skin of the buttocks did not have the same appeal as the soft texture of Mr. Whipple's Charmin!

After picking up a park map, we left the center and drove up a steep mountain grade to the rustic hilltop lodge, just visible above the highest treetops. I had made reservations back in November, both in anticipation of a throng of thru-hikers and to take advantage of the "Mountain Dew" special, which included a breakfast buffet. I could only assume that the "Mountain Dew" special would be my last hearty breakfast for awhile, as pop tarts and granola bars would be my breakfast of necessity on the trail. Our room had a spectacular view of the Georgia mountains, and directly above, the impressive Amicalola Falls. Amicalola, a Cherokee word meaning "tumbling waters," was an appropriate name for the 729-foot falls, tallest in Georgia. The leaves of the trees were just opening up, and many spring flowers had exploded into full bloom.

After quickly unpacking at the lodge, I was eager to see if any thru-hikers were headed out on the trail. Back at the visitor center, a number of hikers were prepared to leave on the approach trail to the top of Springer Mountain, and I instantly tried to determine if they were thru-hikers. Most were young hikers in their early twenties, and, without much success, I found myself anxiously scanning the various groups for any hint of gray hair or similar indicators. I was 51, and I began to wonder, "Am I the only old man beginning a thru-hike?" Picture-taking accompanied last-minute hugs and quite a few tears. From the display of emotions, it seemed obvious that most of these hikers were potential thru-hikers, and as I quickly surveyed the wide assortment of individuals (in particular the young fellow in the skirt?), I could not help but wonder how many I would come to know along the way. Most hikers took advantage of the restroom facilities before heading out; trees, a hole in the ground, or an occasional outhouse would constitute restroom amenities for the next five to six months!

(In preparation for my thru-hike, I had read a number of books and articles by previous thru-hikers and appreciated the information they shared with their readers. Therefore, from time to time, I will share my thoughts – presented in italics – on the various aspects of my hike for the benefit of future thru-hikers and others just interested in hiking.)

Hiker tips: To assist in hiking the A.T., there are many resources available, most of which can be found at or ordered from the Appalachian Trail Conference Center in Harpers Ferry, West Virginia. The three I have found most beneficial are: "Appalachian Trail Thru-Hikers' Companion" by Henry Edwards/Stacy Mikkalsen, the "Appalachian Trail Data Book" by Daniel D. Chazin, and "The Thru-Hiker's Handbook" by Dan "Wingfoot" Bruce.

One of my first objectives at the visitors' center was to weigh my pack. Hoisting it onto the hook of the "meat market" type scales, I was very happy to see that my agonies over what to bring and what to leave at home had paid off with a pack weight of thirty-six pounds. This included a liter and half of water and food for three days.

I did not plan to add anything else, so I was very pleased with the weight. Pack weight had been a major concern of mine ever since I seriously started thinking about thru-hiking the Appalachian Trail. All my research had indicated that too much pack weight was one of the major factors for those not completing the hike. So, of course, I double-checked the scales, maybe even triple-checked. Who was counting?

Hiker tips: My backpack was a Jansport Rainier external pack and during my shakedown hikes I really noticed a difference anytime the pack weight got over forty pounds, and it wasn't good!

I found that there were as many opinions on equipment as there were hikers, with trial and error usually proving to be the best way of finding what worked best.

As I tried different gear, I took my time and experimented. My kids came out well, being the recipients of a vast array of slightly used equipment. As Brad, the youngest, said: "Just keep buying and testing out that equipment, Dad!"

As I continued to observe other hikers, I was amazed by the weight of their packs as they wobbled up to hang their backpacks on the scales and shook their heads in nervous anticipation of carrying fifty, sixty, seventy, even ninety pounds for the 2,167 miles to Mt. Katahdin, Maine.

Leading from the backside of the visitor center was a stone walk ending with a beautiful stone arch, the beginning of the eight and a half-mile approach trail to the top of Springer Mountain, the official southern terminus of the trail. Previous thru-hikers joked that one could actually resupply with all the heavy, unwanted equipment (would you believe an L.L. Bean chair, an iron skillet and even a guitar?) strewn along the approach trail by beginning hikers who attempted to lighten their packs as they struggled toward the 3,782-foot summit. Although I was aware that the approach trail was not part of the official Appalachian Trail, I did not want to miss out on one iota of the Appalachian Trail experience and had decided to hike the blue-blazed approach trail to the top of Springer Mountain. In order to get a head start on the approach trail for the following day, I had decided to hike a section of the approach trail to the lodge, which was a little more than a mile and just off the trail. With one final look around, I headed out the door, past a shelter for thru-hikers, up the approach trail to the cutoff for the lodge and one final good night of sleep before my wife returned home to Ohio the following day.

March 29, Amicalola Falls State Park Lodge to Stover Creek Shelter (milepoint 2.5 north)

I woke up to the sound of rain and sleet hitting the lodge window; it was 4 a.m. As I struggled to take advantage of my last opportunity to sleep in a real bed, hundreds of questions concerning last-minute preparations flooded my mind. The sound of rain and sleet did not help my quest for sleep, and by 6 a.m. I had given up on sleep and rolled out of bed. While showering and preparing for breakfast, I convinced myself not to allow a little rain and sleet to stifle my enthusiasm. And wouldn't you know it, just as I was leaving my room, I got a glimpse of the sunrise from my window. The rain eased up and a beautiful rainbow appeared in the eastern sky. What a beautiful sight! "An omen of good times ahead?" I murmured hopefully.

It was 8 a.m. on a beautiful Wednesday morning as I waved goodbye to my wife and headed north on the approach trail. (In an effort to keep family and friends updated on my progress along the trail, I had made arrangements with former thru-hiker and administrator of the http://trailplace.com/ website, Dan (Wingfoot) Bruce, to keep a journal on his website. I really appreciated the fact that my family and friends could join me in my adventure). The temperature was a cool 38 degrees with overcast skies, great hiking weather! The sign at the road crossing where I was getting back on the approach trail from the lodge read "strenuous 8.8-mile hike" up to the top of Springer Mountain. My plan was to stay in a shelter on Springer Mountain in the evening and begin my journey of five million steps to Mt. Katahdin the following day. The approach trail was marked with blue blazes – two-inch wide strips of paint about six inches long. I had read that most of the side trails would be marked with a blue blaze and the A.T. (Appalachian Trail) marked with a white blaze. The ability to see one white blaze in front of me, turn around and see one behind me at all times was what I had been told to expect. But as a former thru-hiker had told me, "If you expect to rely on seeing those white blazes all the time, you may as well just turn around right now and go home!"

About a mile into my hike I was startled by the sound of rustling leaves. I quickly glanced over my shoulder and spotted a huge mixed-breed dog, and much to my delight, its master right behind. We talked briefly and when I said my destination was Mt. Katahdin, Maine, he smiled, wished me luck and said, "Damn, I really envy you." He had hiked various sections of the trail but never had the opportunity to walk the entire A.T. "My favorite sections of the trail are in Maine," he said.

"Maine," I thought to myself. "Why, that seems like a world away." But his words were a bit of encouragement nonetheless. It was turning out to be a beautiful day; the sun was peeking out through the clouds, and it appeared the rain was over for now. The trail, so far, had been relatively easy and actually reminded me of the hills in southern Ohio where I had completed some shakedown hikes in preparation for my journey.

> *Hiker tips: Along with the overnight backpacking trip with my hiking buddy, Keith, and my youngest son, Brad, in the southeastern Appalachian region of Ohio, I was able to get a final shakedown hike in the Los Padres Mountains of California with my oldest son Bruce. Combine the extremely valuable shakedown hikes with the four to five mile hikes each morning with my backpack prior to my A.T. hike, and I felt relatively comfortable with my preparation.*

After about an hour of hiking I again caught up to the hiker I had talked to earlier. He and his dog were sitting along the trail, looking out over the ridge and enjoying the gorgeous afternoon. When I asked him how far we were from the top of Springer Mountain he smiled and said, "I'd guess we're about four or five miles from the top." His parting words to me were: "Just remember, the first few weeks are the hardest." I certainly would keep that in mind.

It turned 10 a.m. and I figured it was a good time for a midmorning break and a snack of GORP. GORP stands for "Good Old Raisins and Peanuts," typically a homemade trail mix used to keep the energy level up. High in protein and nutrients to keep a hiker going during the day, it was usually a good brand of granola, assorted nuts, raisins, dried fruit, and some M&M candies. Although one could purchase a wide assortment of GORP in the various stores, my wife had put together a very tasty recipe that included jerky, one of my favorites. I hoped she would be able to send it to me from time to time in maildrops along the trail.

In the last hour, I had passed several day hikers headed back to Amicalola Falls from the Hikers Inn. The inn was located approximately five miles north on the approach trail, allowing time for a leisurely day of hiking, an overnight stay, then a hike back to Amicalola Falls the next day. According to several individuals I talked with, a number of thru-hikers had stayed at the inn with them last night. Everyone raved about the inn, apparently a very good alternative to staying in the park lodge or a shelter near the visitor center. A female hiker with one of the families I passed noticed my hiking poles and asked, "Do those skinny little things really help?" I laughed at her unusual description of my hiking poles and told her that during my shakedown hikes they seemed to have been very beneficial, especially on the down hills, and I hoped that they would help the strain on my knees. I figured time would tell.

> *Hiker tips: I began my hike using Leki telescopic hiking poles (those skinny little things). They also doubled as tent poles for my Nomad tent to save weight.*

Four Army Rangers passed me at a quick jog. When I heard them coming, I got to the side of the trail to let them pass and heard a "Thank you, Sir" as they moved on up the trail at double-time speed. I'd heard about Army Ranger activities up in the mountains and had been told to be prepared for their nighttime maneuvers.

When I passed Nimblewell Gap, I had traveled 5.2 miles in three hours. It was 2.6 miles to Springer Mountain and it looked like I would be there earlier than expected, which might mean changing plans for where to make evening camp. The excitement of the first day had overwhelmed me, and I simply could not get my legs to slow down. I was sure that would change with time.

One couple hiking down from Springer told me, "It was damn cold on that mountain last night. Our water bottles froze!" They suggested that if I tented that night, it should be on the south side of the mountain. I appreciated the advice.

I arrived at the Black Gap Shelter ahead of schedule, with Springer Mountain Shelter just two miles north. I continued to find it hard to slow down. I guess my adrenaline was still pumping with "White Blaze Fever!"

Springer Mt., first white blaze on southern terminus of A.T.

By 1 p.m. I had passed over the top of Springer Mountain. Although it was drizzling, it was too early to stop, so I took a couple of pictures of the bronze plaque identifying the southern terminus, found the first white blaze, and headed north to Maine! Checking my *Data Book*, I saw that Stover Creek Shelter appeared to be about 2.5 miles north on the trail. That would be my planned destination for the night.

I crossed Forest Service Road 42, so I had hiked about a mile on the Appalachian Trail. Many thru-hikers ride up the Forest Service Road and hike the one-mile south on the A.T. to Springer Mountain and then turned around to begin their hike, avoiding the eight and half mile approach trail. Nothing wrong with that, but as I said previously, I didn't want to miss out on any of the A.T. experience.

I stopped and talked with a nice young couple from my home state of Ohio, T.J. and Sara. Due to the weight of their packs, they were moving pretty slowly. They had stayed a day earlier at the same lodge where I had stayed. We all laughed when T.J. said, "Hell, our packs weigh sixty-five and fifty pounds apiece, and that's after we whittled them down at the lodge!" I couldn't imagine what their packs weighed before that! As I was headed north toward Stover Creek Shelter, I ran into another thru-hiker, Vince, from Wales. He had come in from USFS 42 just today, so he planned on hiking further north. A friendly fellow, he also had one hell of a big pack! About then, I remembered that I had planned to pick up a stone on Springer Mountain and carry it to Mt. Katahdin, a tradition of sorts for thru-hikers. "Nuts!" I thought, "no way I'm turning back. I guess there will be one less stone from Springer Mountain on top of Mt. Katahdin."

It started to drizzle a little harder as I passed through a combination of pine and hardwood trees, including some beautiful hemlocks. Actually the rain felt good. It was just enough to keep my "radiator" cool as I hiked up and down the mountains of the Chattahoochee National Forest.

It was mid-afternoon when I arrived at Stover Creek Shelter. I had hiked 10.5 miles, and the pain in my legs indicated that was enough! I was not sure if I would be sleeping in my tent or in the shelter. In preparation for my hike, I had read in *The Thru-Hiker's Handbook* of a resident skunk at the Stover Creek Shelter and knew a skunk was not what I had hoped for as a roommate on my first night on the trail. I decided to filter some water at a nearby stream for dinner and make a decision on sleeping location later.

At the shelter after dinner, I found a three-ring folder with a pen inside a Ziploc bag for hikers to sign in and leave messages, which made for some interesting reading! One of the entries read, "3/26 - People are betting against me. Yea, Caesar Palace has me at 2,160 to 1 odds of finishing right now. Hey, there's got to be an underdog. A long shot however, the dark horse will gallop into Maine. Hey, I thought there was a pub here. Signed, the Dark Horse."

I finished a hot meal of macaroni, cheese, and tuna. It actually tasted better than one would think, but after a long day of backpacking, I suppose a leather shoe would probably have tasted great. While I had the shelter area to myself for the night, the threat of waking up nose-to-nose with a skunk, or even worse, nose-to-tail, persuaded me to pitch my tent away from the shelter. One young hiker did stop in to rest and had a bite to eat before moving on. He said that there were a number of hikers behind me who talked of stopping at Springer Mountain Shelter. When asked where he called home, he proudly said, "Mate, I'm from the Yorkshire Dales," with quite a Yorkshire brogue.

Well, on my first day hiking I'd gone 10.5 miles, 2.5 miles on the A.T. I felt great and was looking forward to a good night's rest, hopefully without a nighttime visit from any over-friendly polecat.

March 30, Stover Creek Shelter to Justus Creek Camp (milepoint 13.6 north)

I awoke at 6:30 a.m. from a great night's sleep and felt very rested. The night before I had found an ideal campsite under a beautiful canopy of hemlock trees that were spectacular in size and beauty. *The Thru-Hiker's Handbook* also stated that the only reason the huge hemlock trees were still standing was due to the limited access for loggers in earlier times and the State of Georgia's policy of protecting the area.

A beautiful cool morning. I was pumped and looking forward to another great day of hiking. I did notice last night that the young Dalesman who stopped by the shelter to eat was not carrying a filter; rather, he was drinking his water directly out of the stream. When asked, he replied confidently, "We're high enough in the mountains not to worry about contaminated water." As for me, I heard too many horror stories about giardia, and had no interest in running from tree to tree looking for relief.

I talked with T.J. and Sara again. They had come to the obvious conclusion that they were in serious need of dropping some major pack weight and doing so quickly. "I've got to get rid of some weight," T.J. groaned as he adjusted his huge pack without much relief. "I started carrying more of Sara's gear to help her out and it's killing me."

Met up with the Englishman, Vince, at Three Forks when I stopped for a snack. We hiked together for awhile and, of course, our conversation included pack weight (his pack was more than fifty pounds), along with the other typical questions: "Where do you call home? What got you out on the trail?" and so on. Interestingly, Vince was my age – 51 – and had also just retired.

After leaving Vince, I ran into another thru-hiker from England. That made the third thru-hiker from Great Britain I had met in the first two days on the trail. Lynn was from Wales, just as was Vince, but they had not yet met; and neither was aware that a fellow countryman was on the trail. Lynn was hiking with his dog, Dillon, a very pretty and well-behaved border collie. The dog was carrying his own pack (a fairly large pack in my estimation) for food and other supplies. There were many opinions, pro and con, about having a dog on the trail. I personally had no problem with a dog as long as it obeyed and the owner used common sense when around other hikers.

I arrived at Hawk Mountain Shelter for lunch after about five miles of hiking. Lynn was leaving the shelter without his pack. He asked me: "Will you watch my pack? I'm headed back down the A.T. to find me mate. He's injured his ankle and moving kind of slow."

By the large amount of food left in the shelter I first guessed that some trail angels had been spreading some magic. On further consideration, I figured it to be food left by the many beginning thru-hikers who had lightened their packs of too much food. For the last two days, I had seen numerous items that had been left along the trail by what I could only assume were hikers reducing the weight of their enormous packs. If I had a dollar for every item discarded along the trail, I'd be a wealthy man.

Two backpackers headed to Mt. Katahdin

Headed out of Hawk Mountain Shelter after a good rest, lunch and filtering some water. I spent some time talking to Lynn after he came in with his mate's pack, shortly followed by the limping mate himself. Lynn's pal, from Virginia, had done very little practice hiking and was really hurting as he cleaned out his fifty-five pound pack, saying, "I threw out a number of items, including a pound of cheese and a goddamn potato, already today!" I also learned where everyone else was last night. Apparently they all camped on top of Springer Mountain, where there had been fifteen to twenty tents along with a number of hikers staying in the shelter. They had music and campfires going well into the night. I guess I missed a good time, but then I knew why it was so quiet at my campsite.

Coming up out of the Hightower Gap, I met a thru-hiker with the trail name of Top Dog, a nice young fellow from Tennessee. I asked him if he would take my picture with the mountains in the background, which he graciously did.

Hiker tips: I carried a small camera tripod; called an ultra pod (purchased from Campmor). It had worked great when I could not find a friendly hiker to assist me in taking my picture. With three, six-inch long fold-down legs and a Velcro strap that could be used to wrap it around a tree or hiking pole, the tripod allowed me to take a large number of pictures with me included. I also carried fold-up reading glasses by Foster Grant. In the carrying case, they folded down to 1.5 inches square and worked great on the trail.

I inquired about his trail name, and he said, "My trail name of Top Dog will probably change to Lost Dog by the end of the trail." We both laughed. He explained that his mother dropped him off at USFS 42, where he planned to hike south back to Springer Mountain to start his thru-hike. "But I was so excited when I got out of the car I went the wrong way and had to turn around after a few steps, and right in front of my mom!" he said. He added, laughing, "But what she doesn't know is that I also took a wrong turn a few hours later. I ended up walking two hours out of my way, then two hours back the same direction, for a total of four hours of hiking the wrong damn way!" I found it hard to keep a straight face.

Hiker tips: On Top Dog's behalf and as information for future thru-hikers, the Benton MacKaye trail, which he mistakenly took, is marked with white diamonds that could easily be mistaken for a white blaze on the Appalachian Trail.

To his further exasperation during his first two days on the trail, the next morning he had gone off and forgotten his hiking poles and had to walk back to camp to retrieve them. But to Top Dog's credit, he was laughing about it and moving on. A good sense of humor was a must on the trail.

I had planned to hike to Gooch Gap, a total of thirteen miles. But my legs were starting to feel the strain of the mountains, and after talking to some other hikers, I was told that there was a nice campsite about ten miles away. An added note to my encounter with Top Dog: As we were hiking along and talking, I happened to ask, "Have you seen any white blazes lately? I can't remember seeing any for awhile." His eyes got bigger than silver dollars as he said, "You're shitting me, aren't you?" To which I replied very seriously, "No, I'm not." I could see the beads of sweat forming on his forehead as he frantically began to scan the trail for a white blaze. Fortunately, we found one.

Getting over the top of Sassafras Mountain was a real butt-kicker and proof that I was no longer in Ohio! What a spectacular view – there was a little bit of a blue haze, but the view of the mountains seemed to go on forever and ever!

I headed for Justus Creek Campgrounds about 1.5 miles down the mountain as my knees really started to hurt. That gave me about eleven miles of hiking in ten hours, and my knees were telling me that eleven miles in the mountains the first few days was enough, maybe too much!

At 7 p.m., I got my tent set up alongside Justice Creek, where there were at least ten to twelve other tents. A lot of tired but contented hikers finished dinner and sat around talking equipment and pack weight. I continued to be amazed at the enormous pack weight carried by most of the hikers. One overburdened hiker laughingly joked that I could have sold my two-pound Nomad tent for "a million dollars." With most of them carrying fifty pounds or more, my thirty-six-pound pack looked better and better each day. It was not long before the talk subsided and all the exhausted hikers – including me – were sawing logs.

March 31, Justus Creek to Granny Top Mountain (milepoint 22.2 north)

I began my third day on the trail after another great night of sleep, although I did wake up around 4 a.m. to some screeching and howling that I had never heard before. I talked to a few other hikers who also heard the noise, and the only thing we could figure out was that the sound came from a pack of coyotes. I also found heavy dew on my tent in the morning and had to pack a wet tent, which meant more weight and an unhappy hiker.

I was up and out of camp early, preferring to walk for a few miles before breakfast. Physically, I felt great, with the exception of one knee which was a little sore, especially when I walked downhill. One of the other hikers, Georgia Joe (guess where he was from!), was using a brace for his knee and had me thinking about looking into wearing one if the pain increased.

As I was filtering water the night before, I had continued to notice a number of hikers not using a filter. There was a good supply of water in the area, with several springs coming right out of the mountain, but I was still not ready to take that chance, I had worked too hard in preparation for this hike to spend it sick in a shelter or worse!

I had encountered a lot of thru-hikers so far, and everyone seemed to be friendly and easygoing, albeit a little strange at times. One young man hiked into camp late last night and said he had hiked all the way from Springer Mountain. An unusual young fellow, not just in that he had hiked 13.5 miles the first day, but that as he entered camp he was limping badly. I assumed he was just sore from the miles he had put in, when he announced, "I just came from the doc's office where I got some stitches in my leg; I'll need to be more careful with that damn machete!" I watched the eyebrows rise on a number of hikers' faces as we listened to his story, and I made a mental note to myself to keep an eye on that character. I had met a number of unusual individuals on the trail so far, but the young fellow I immediately dubbed as the Machete Kid ranked right up there. That was one hell of a way to begin a thru-hike, with your knee hacked up from a machete!

Sara seemed to be getting a little frustrated last night and like a number of the other hikers in camp, she and T.J. were headed for Suches, Georgia, the first small town close to the trail, to lighten their packs. I'd felt good about my pack weight and was not interested in any side trip to town. Of course, by the time I arrived at Woody Gap (where the road to Suches crossed the A.T.) I might be singing a different tune. Having the freedom of changing my mind at any time was one of the aspects of hiking the trail that really appealed to me. On the trail this was called, "Hike your own hike," a saying I had heard more times than I could count.

Top Dog passed me. He was moving on! No way was I going to keep up with him, especially with my right knee as sore as it was.

It was 11 a.m. when Vince and I stopped for a short break and a snack. Vince had been having a lot of trouble with his fifty-pound pack and had finally concluded, "A lot of this equipment is going in the bin bag when I get to town."

"What in the hell is a bin bag?" I asked.

He laughed and said, "Why, Bloke, it's what you in the states refer to as a trash can!" At least he was following the proper etiquette of any good hiker: "Pack it in, pack it out."

I passed a day hiker headed south. At first he looked like a thru-hiker from the size of the pack he was carrying; but obviously he was going the wrong way, so I told him, "You don't smell bad enough to be a thru-hiker!" He got a good laugh out of that and responded, "Thanks, I think!" When I asked him how far to Woody Gap, he hesitantly said, "Oh, about an hour or so." I learned early on that you could not find out distance on the trail by asking other hikers. Everyone walked at a different pace and often carried lighter packs, so their hour could be two for me or vice versa. Also, miles on the trail are relative. You have to walk to everything, and the miles on side trails are usually not included as part of the total distance. A water supply could be a mile off the trail, and many of the campsites could also be a half-mile to a mile off the trail.

I left Woody Gap after a delicious lunch of cheese and pepperoni sticks. The sunny 70-degree afternoon and soft grass on the hillside made it a little difficult to get moving again. Top Dog and I went to get some water on a side trail and, wouldn't you know it, we missed the spring and walked out of the way again! When we did find the water, it was running right out the side of a mountain; so I went against my philosophy of filtering all water, didn't filter, and regretted it immediately!

As I continued north out of Woody Gap toward Jared's Gap, I realized I had my first hot spot. For non-hikers, a hot spot was usually a spot on the foot that turned red from friction and often was the first indication of a blister forming. You would never guess where my first hot spot was: on the palm of my hand! I guess my hands were not used to using hiking poles. It's important to attend to any hot spot immediately to avoid a blister, so I stuck a piece of duct tape on my palm to avoid any further irritation.

Right after that, I just managed to avoid my first major injury. When I'd stopped to use the duct tape for the hot spot on my hand, I forgot to close my micra-leatherman knife properly. After a mile or so of hiking, I looked down to see the blade of my knife sticking out of my pants pocket. Now, how would I have explained that one?

I crossed the top of Big Cedar Mountain, a good climb; my *Data Book* showed Woody Gap at 3,150 feet and the top of Big Cedar Mountain 3,737 feet, an ascent of just less than 600 feet. That had been typical of the ups and downs in the first few days, making for a real test on my knees as I moved up and down the sides of mountains.

During another break, I talked to a fellow from Massachusetts who was sucking some serious air as he told me between breaths, "Man, I'm just this far and I started last week. This A.T. is tough!" He was moving slowly with a fifty-something-pound pack that had been working him over. He'd even taken a couple of days off in Suches just to help his legs recover.

As we got over Granny Top Mountain, a number of the guys were stopping for the night and I decided to join them, needing some rest after about nine miles. Top Dog decided to go on, but we still had quite a crew camping for the night, about twelve to fifteen hikers in all. One of the new faces was Tom from South Africa, who I would guess to be in his late twenties. He said, "I've been hiking all over the world and figured when I got here in the States that hiking the Appalachian Trail would be a good way to learn about the United States!"

The Machete Kid came in as we were setting up camp, with an additional 15 pounds in his pack. He had gotten off the trail to go to Suches to get a money order and ended up buying more supplies. Most guys were getting rid of pack weight, and the Machete Kid just added weight. Unbelievable! He used the machete to slice up food and build his campfires, and we all stayed at a distance while he wielded that blade! In addition to the machete, he also had a guitar tied to his pack. I realized early on in the evening that I would be using my earplugs: the Kid played and sang well, but I needed sleep; and it was apparent that my tent wall would not be effective in muffling sound.

A number of the hikers had hung their food bags in the trees. When I asked Georgia Joe, who had been hiking in the Georgia Mountains all his life, he said with confidence, "Hell, there are no bears around here, and besides if there were any, you would never see them." I didn't know if that was good or bad but decided not to hang my food bag telling him, "If some damn bear drags me out of my tent tonight, I'll be screaming your name to my death!"

April 1, Granny Top Mountain to Neels Gap, Georgia (Walasi-Yi Center) (milepoint 30.7 north)

Called home and told my wife to come pick me up, I'd had enough! I know, that was a lame April Fool's joke. Sorry.

I was able to head out at 7:30 a.m. The birds were singing and the weather was again beautiful with a temperature of about 50-degrees. Heard quite a bit of snoring the night before. Snoring was one of the reasons I'd avoided shelters so far on the trail, not to mention the other rather offensive body noises! Put in my earplugs and that took care of the problem.

It looked as though I would really be challenged today, so the cool weather was appreciated as I crossed Blood Mountain, the highest point on the A.T. in Georgia. According to Georgia Joe, "Blood Mountain was named after a disastrous battle between the Creek and Cherokee before the coming of the white man." According to Indian lore, *The Thru-Hiker's Handbook* told it was such a furious and bloody battle that, "the hills ran red with blood." Hence the name, Blood Mountain.

Vince had his profile map out last night. "Look what's ahead, Mate," he said with a sad grin, running his finger over the drawing that outlined Blood Mountain's steep ascent. I was not carrying a profile map, as I didn't want the extra weight; and after looking at the profile of Blood Mountain, I was glad I hadn't seen it before. The prospect was totally depressing.

I passed what looked to be a homemade sign telling of water down a side trail at Wood's Hole Shelter. The A.T. had been well marked so far. I'd learned that two white blazes painted on a tree indicated a turn in the trail or another trail intersecting it. And more importantly, when coming upon two blazes painted on top of one another, a hiker had best be careful or he could end up on the wrong trail!

I arrived at the top of Blood Mountain by 11a.m. with Georgia Joe at my side. The shelter was a spacious two-room stone facility, dark and damp inside. Georgia Joe told me the Civilian Conservation Corps, one of the New Deal programs during the Great Depression, had built the shelter. "And," he added with a little shiver, "it can be one of the coldest damn places to camp on the entire A.T.!" We figured it was a good place for lunch, and before Joe and I had finished our beef stick and cheese, we welcomed Vince; Tom, the South African; a day hiker; and the Machete Kid, who was flailing away at an onion with his machete. "You sure in the hell don't want to sit too close to that boy when you eat," the startled day hiker said, shaking his head.

Joe said that Walasi-Yi Center was located at Neels Gap and the trail ran right through it. It's the only place on the entire Appalachian Trail that the A.T. actually went through a building. When I wondered out loud about the name, Walasi-Yi, Georgia Joe told me, "It's an Indian word that stands for 'the place of many frogs." I wasn't sure if he was pulling my leg or not. He also mentioned it was a good spot to resupply, and we could even arrange for a cabin to spend the night. A nice warm bed and shower sounded good!

White blaze through Walasi-Yi

Quite a large number of day hikers passed me as I headed down off Blood Mountain to Walasi-Yi. One young boy pointed in my direction and said, "Hey, Dad, I think that's one of those guys they call a thru-hiker." Thru-hikers were easily recognized (some say our smell gave us away), and there were always a lot of questions from the day hikers. I usually enjoyed the conversations; I had heard that thru-hikers were thought to be stuck-up and rude by other hikers, so I tried to be polite and answer the many questions. But soon I realized that if I stopped and talked to everyone who passed me, I would never make it down Blood Mountain, let alone to Maine! As I hiked down the mountain to the Walasi-Yi Center located on a blacktop road, the trucks and cars seemed to be flying by. Although I had only been on the trail for four days, the speed and noise of the traffic seemed to be a culture shock of sorts to my slower-paced system, and I had to be careful not to get hit.

Joe was right. The A.T. ran right through the center of the Walasi-Yi Center, and the owners, Jeff and Dorothy Hansen, were great people and very helpful to hikers. They called down to Goose Creek Cabins for a shuttle to pick up about a dozen hikers for a ride down to the cabins for the night. I decided to splurge and spend a few more dollars and get a small cabin for myself instead of sharing a cabin with other hikers. The cabins were nothing fancy, but there were a bed and shower; and after my first four days in the mountains, that was all I was looking for!

I had asked at the Center if there was any chance of my getting a ride to church and was very impressed and thankful when they called Bob and Ann Sorrelle, who immediately offered me a ride. Great people from Blairsville, they picked me up, took me to church, then to a Kentucky Fried Chicken carryout, and finally to a grocery store for supplies. Bob and Ann were avid hikers and really made me feel like one of the family as they introduced me to a number of their friends after church. Most people do not realize what a wonderful help it is to hikers to be shuttled around the different towns. It sounds like a small thing, but I could not thank Bob and Ann enough. They were the first true trail angels I had met on the trail. (trail angel is a name given by thru-hikers to anyone willing to help out a hiker.)

While there, I was able to catch a weather report on a TV down in the main lodge at Goose Creek, and it appeared that we were in for some rain the next couple of days. I also ran into Top Dog, who was staying with a number of thru-hikers in another cabin.

Just a note on the Goose Creek Cabin people: for five dollars, they do hikers' laundry. Although that sounded great, I decided to put my five dollars in the collection basket at church, figuring I was going to need God on my side a lot more than any clean pair of underwear on my trek north to Katahdin.

At Walasi-Yi Center, a number of hikers were sending home a lot of unneeded items.

> *Hiker tips: Walasi-Yi was the first place on the trail that hikers had an opportunity to mail items home and lighten their packs. The center had a very good outfitter who was quite knowledgeable on what was needed and probably more importantly, what was not needed for an A.T. thru-hike and very helpful at refitting an inexperienced hiker.*

Although I was quite happy with my pack and gear, I was able to resupply for what looked like another four days before my next town stop. My intent was to get off the trail to resupply and clean up every four or five days. Time would tell.

April 2, Neels Gap, Georgia (Walasi-Yi Center) to Low Gap Shelter (milepoint 41.3 north)

It was about 8:30 a.m. as I awoke in a dry room and toasty warm bed. It was raining hard, and the forecast called for rain all day. I felt lucky that I had been able to get out of the rain for at least one night. The owners of the cabins shuttled Top Dog, Dream Catcher, Iron Man, and me back up to Walasi-Yi Center. It was after 10:30 a.m., later than I usually headed out; but it looked like I would be walking in rain all day and possibly sleeping in the rain, so I was in no hurry to get out on the trail.

As I headed up the mountain outside of Walasi-Yi Center, it was rainy, misty and cold; and the water was running down the trail as if I were walking in a stream. I thought to myself, "The honeymoon is over."

> *Hiker tips: I had a tough time deciding on a hat for the trail and finally settled on one I had purchased in Ireland last year during a drenching rainstorm. A baseball-style hat with an oilcloth material, it worked great for shedding water.*

On top of Levelland Mountain, I found a tent that was lighter than mine: a tarp with an open umbrella at one end! According to the locals, it had rained all night, so that had to be one miserable night staying in that thing!

I stopped for a break and talked to a young man from New Hampshire with the trail name of Hedgehog; he was averaging sixteen-mile days, which I found incredible. I figured he was in really good shape, as he said that he had biked across the United States a year earlier (in just forty-four days).

After a quick lunch and a short break, the rain let up to a mist, and I felt as though I were walking in a cloud, which I probably was. Not being able to see much beyond my outstretched hand, I figured it was going to be a long day, especially since I had planned on making it to Low Gap Shelter, a good five to six miles away, and probably would not get there until about 7 p.m. The rain really slowed me up.

I met Tom and the Machete Kid back at the center before I left. They had camped out the night before instead of finding a room and were taking a shower at the center. I couldn't believe they didn't get a room, but that's what was so interesting about everyone out on the trail: they all did their own thing. I was reminded again of the phrase I heard so often here out on the trail, "Hike your own hike."

I arrived at Hogpen Gap, where a sign read, "Elevation 3,450 feet." I planned on getting to the next shelter, four miles away. That was going to put me there late, about 7 p.m., but I would rather do that than try to camp without a water source. It continued to rain on and off, but I was still finding spectacular views each time I reached the top of a mountain. I actually climbed up out of the clouds and felt as though I was looking down on the earth from the heavens. What a sight, with the upper quarter of the mountain ranges visible in all directions!

That day finally wrapped up just after 8 p.m. I had hiked eleven miles and almost crawled into Low Gap Shelter. Wet and cold, I checked out the shelter only to find it full, so I reluctantly tented again alongside Top Dog and Hedgehog. With the type of weather we'd had, hikers needed to get to shelters early to find a space. As I didn't like stopping early, it looked like I would not be staying in many shelters any time soon. The fog was as thick as smoke, and with the mist hanging in the heavy air, it looked to be the wettest and coldest night on the trail yet. Things had been going really well, so I couldn't complain about a little rain. Besides, my rain equipment had been working very well. It looked like the rain was over, but being a "flatlander from Ohio," as one of the locals called me, I found it difficult to anticipate the weather in the mountains. Also, with the change to daylight savings time, there was probably another hour of hiking; but I had come to realize I needed to listen to my body, and my knee was telling me it had done enough for the day. I also decided to hitch into Helen, Georgia, with Top Dog and Hedgehog the next day to give my knees a little rest.

At 12:55 a.m., the Georgia skies opened up! We were getting a deluge: rain, lightning, thunder, and I believe you could even throw in a little hail. My Nomad single wall tent was getting its first major test, and I was not at all sure if it could withstand the continuous pounding. The "Georgia Rain God" was certainly giving the A.T. hikers everything it had and more; I was very concerned that my tent would be ripped to shreds.

At 1:30 a.m., the rain was still beating down on my tent, so hard it was impossible to sleep. It had not let up one iota. We were tenting on a high area, so I was not worried about flooding, but I wondered about the shelter lower down on the mountain.

Another hour passed, and the Georgia Mountains continued to rock and roll with thunder and lightning! The lightning was putting on an incredible show that I could actually see through my tent. The wind had also picked up, and I was thinking about pulling my awning down to give my tent a more stream-lined effect against the wind, knowing full well I would have trouble with condensation inside my single-walled tent. It was also so loud that I needed to put my earplugs in to get any semblance of sleep.

"Ahhhhhhhhhhh!" A scream that pierced the mountaintop night jarred me to a sitting position; then there was not another sound. I was not at all sure who or what had made the blood-curdling cry, but since it had stopped, I figured the morning would be soon enough to find out what the screaming was all about.

April 3, Low Gap Shelter to Unicoi Gap (Helen, Georgia) (milepoint 50.7 north)

It was 9:30 a.m., and it felt late when I broke camp and packed a soggy and muddy tent! It truly was, as Brook Benton sang in 1970, "a rainy night in Georgia." My single-walled Nomad tent had held up, much to my great relief. The town of Helen, Georgia, was our destination for the night, a nine-mile hike with only one major mountain; so I figured I could get all my gear cleaned and dried out when we got to town.

Again I found myself sharing the trail with a torrent of running water, making it extremely difficult to see the rocks and tree roots. So with a heavy wet pack and slick, muddy trail, I figured to see nothing but my own feet for most of the day.

I passed a hiker named Jerry, who was camping in our vicinity last night. He was sitting on a stump trying to catch his breath. He said, "That storm was unbelievable last night, and I think I may have pneumonia. I've got to get to the next shelter and dry out!"

Later, I caught up with Hedgehog and Top Dog for a very windy mountaintop lunch. We compared notes about the storm, and I couldn't believe it when Top Dog said, "Storm? What storm?" He had slept through the entire storm, lightning, thunder, hail and all! Apparently, he'd been taking some strong medication and did not hear a sound the entire night. Hedgehog had a different take on the storm, having heard every crack of thunder. Like me, he hadn't gotten much sleep. With a tinge of embarrassment I said, "I know this sounds ridiculous, but I could have sworn I heard some mice running around on top of my tent last night." Hedgehog let out a laugh and said, "That was no dream! I could see through a plastic section on top of my tent during the storm and there were mice scurrying across the tent all through the night!"

"They must have been headed to higher ground," Top Dog chimed in, winking. We had a good laugh and were just glad the mice didn't try to chew their way inside!

Back on the trail, and even though it was nice and cool for hiking, I was totally socked in by fog and couldn't see more than twenty yards in front of me. I passed the Blue Mountain Shelter and it was packed with hikers already in for the night, so I was glad to be headed to a motel room in Helen.

By 3 p.m., we finally made it down to Unicoi Gap, Highway 75, to hitch a ride to town. My legs were feeling good as I read a sign on the trail showing that Low Gap (where I had camped the night before) was 9.5 miles south, so I had another good day's hike in. I had not hitchhiked since my days at Bluffton College, so I was a little apprehensive about trying to get a hitch into Helen. It was very foggy, and the cars seemed to appear out of nowhere and then disappear in the mist. We realized that getting a ride was going to be a challenge, if not impossible. "Maybe they see us and that's why they're not stopping," Top Dog said with a laugh. "Would you pick up three drowned rats like us?"

We got into town around 7 p.m. after a friendly local braved the fog to stop and give us a lift. Just after 8 p.m., as the rain poured down outside, I was sitting in our hotel room after a nice warm shower and a great sandwich. I was able to find a laundry right next to a little tavern, and I couldn't ask for much more than that: clean clothes and a brew! The weather report was calling for another bad night of storms, but the walls of the hotel were much thicker than the walls of my tent. According to the news reports, there was considerable damage in the area from the previous night's storms, which did not surprise any of us in the least. We were all glad to be spending the night in the hotel. In fact, there were a lot of hikers at the motel who had been there for a number of nights avoiding the storms.

April 4, Unicoi Gap (Helen, Georgia) to Addis Gap (milepoint 61.5 north)

Took a leisurely morning to pack up and head into the mountains from Helen, Georgia. The temperature was cool compared to those of the past week, and the forecast was for frost. I would find out that night if I had packed enough warm clothing. I talked to a maintenance man at the hotel about a lift back to Unicoi, and he said he was about to get off work and for a little gas money would give us a lift. After a forty-five-minute wait to get a ride into town the night before, I wanted to make sure we had a ride back to the trail.

I also talked to Tom, the South African, and Bob Illi; they were coming into town having spent the night at the Blue Mountain Shelter. Both were really wet from the storms. Rescuers had to go up into the mountains during the night and bring down a hiker who was experiencing hypothermia, a reminder to hikers not to underestimate the dangers of the Appalachian Mountains.

> *Hiker tips: I would suggest that thru-hikers have the financial resources to spend some time in hotels, especially when the weather becomes too dangerous to safely stay on the trail.*

We arrived at Unicoi Gap to see snow on the ground, after a very cold ride in the back of the maintenance man's pickup truck. He had agreed to give us a ride for three dollars apiece. I realized just how badly he needed gas money when we pulled up to a gas station before we left town and he asked, "You think you could give me your three dollars in advance?" He then put three dollars' worth of gas in the truck!

I topped Rocky Mountain and headed up Tray Mountain as snow flurries filled the afternoon sky and my little Campmor thermometer hanging on my zipper read 35-degrees. But at least I was not hiking in rain. I'd rather hike in cold weather than rain, even though I had to wear three layers of clothing and my gloves.

I arrived at a gap but had no idea which one, as some jackass had ripped the sign off the post. Also passed a young female hiker headed north who was really going at a snail's pace. Extremely overweight, she was really struggling with the mountains, but, to her credit, she was very positive and upbeat. It was cold and getting colder, and I couldn't see her making it to any shelter for the night. Not sure what to do, I asked, "Is there anything I can help you out with?" She gave me a valiant smile and said, "No thanks, go ahead. I'll be all right." She certainly had a courageous attitude! Not knowing what else to do, I reluctantly headed north, wondering if I had made the right decision by going on without her. That was the first time on the trail that I believed it was actually dangerous for an individual to be out on the trail alone.

By a quarter after seven that night, I reached Addis Gap, having put in about 10 miles. The hike was really good that day; I particularly liked the cool weather, and my knees were feeling better going downhill.

As the temperature continued to plummet and hikers talked about the mountain rescue the night before, I couldn't help but wonder about the young woman I had passed on the trail. Had I done the right thing by hiking on? I kept telling myself she would be okay since she appeared to have the necessary equipment to withstand the cold mountain temperatures.

> *Hiker tips: I carried a 20-degree down sleeping bag*
> *from Feathered Friends and a silk liner from Nature*
> *Co.; both helped me stay warm at night.*

Just before nine that evening, I lay in my tent and whispered into my recorder to avoid bothering anyone else. I took special care not to use my recorder around anyone, for some hikers had strong feelings about electronic devices out on the trail, and I certainly didn't want to offend anyone. But by using a tape recorder I had been able to record my thoughts almost immediately and very accurately. Then I headed to bed on a very cold night on the A.T.

April 5, Addis Gap to Dicks Creek Gap (Hiawassee, Georgia) (milepoint 66.8 north)

"What the hell is this?" I bellowed as I awoke to see a literal ice castle in my tent. Apparently the condensation inside my tent had frozen hard to the walls of the tent during the night, encasing me in a wonderland of ice! Thoughts of "Doctor Zhivago" danced in my head as I glanced from wall to wall and saw nothing but a reflection of myself in the crystal clear ice. I knew it would get cold high in the mountains, but never in my wildest dreams did I ever imagine scraping ice off the inside of my tent.

The cold of the morning made it very difficult to crawl out of the warm sleeping bag, and Top Dog was the only other hiker out of his tent as I headed north on the trail. I laughed to myself as I remembered how I had started out the night before: I had been sleeping in my shirt and pants; but before the night was over, I had added my puffball jacket, another pair of pants and a pair of socks. I was comfortable, but just barely, and would not have wanted it any colder. My twenty-degree down sleeping bag had a nice hood on it, which I had pulled up tight, leaving just a little hole from which to breathe. I also had on my silk

Balaclava (headgear), which helped a lot. Fortunately, I had remembered to drain my water hose on the dromedary bag, so my water supply was not frozen.

The day's hike looked like a short one of only six miles to Hiawassee, Georgia, where I was expecting a maildrop, something to which I had been looking forward. Notes and cards were something I'd really appreciate after a long period on the trail.

My first climb of the morning took me to the top of Kelly Knob, about 1,100 feet, and that was a good morning wake-up call. The sunrise over the mountains was beautiful, so crisp and clear in the east that it appeared to be a painted picture.

The wind continued to blow and it was still very, very cold. I got to Deep Gap and still had four more miles until I reached Dicks Creek Gap on U.S. 76. I hoped to get a ride into town from there.

> *Hiker tips: I carried Frogg Togg rain gear from Backcountry Equipment and really recommend it. It's lightweight, breathable and water-repellent. Early on in my hike, I sent the pants home, keeping the jacket for everyday wear as well as for rain.*

I caught up to Top Dog, and we walked out onto U.S. 76 looking for a ride into town. A local man, another trail angel, was dropping off a hiker and offered us a ride into town. Hiawassee was a beautiful little town with friendly people, and the owner of the hotel agreed to set us up with a shuttle back to the trail the following morning.

I also ran into Machete Kid, who had hitched from Helena to Hiawassee after going to the doctor and finding out he had bronchitis. And to add to his miseries, he said sadly, "After I hitched my ride, I forgot to check all my gear and the guy drove off with my hiking poles in his car!"

The Kid, as it happened, broke one of the thru-hiker's cardinal rules: Always check your equipment when getting a lift. I would say, "Check at least twice!" It hadn't happened to me so far, but stories were abundant on the trail about hikers who were devastated after leaving gear in cars.

At a little after two that afternoon, we checked into the Mull Motel. My plan was to get cleaned up and then hustle down to the local post office before it closed. Even though I was a day early, I hoped my mail from home would be waiting for me.

Top Dog's mother and father were coming in for the night. He invited me to dinner with them, but I declined. I was pretty hungry and was afraid I would probably embarrass myself by pigging out in front of them. His family lived nearby, so it was nice that he could visit with them.

I did meet his mother Rachel and stepfather Don and they seemed like great people. Don had hiked some of the A.T. and said he'd have loved to be hiking with us. I mentioned that Top Dog was a really strong hiker and he said, "He ought to be – he placed second in the Tennessee high school state cross-country meet." He added that Top Dog continued on to the University of Georgia, where he also ran cross-country. Now I knew why I could not keep up with him!

We also talked about trail names. I mentioned that when I first heard some of the different trail names, I found them interesting and funny but otherwise didn't give them much thought. After a few weeks on the trail, I realized how trail names simplified remembering the many different hikers met on the trail. For example, I'd met a hiker the day before who told me his given name, which I totally forgot, but I did remember his trail name: Wiley Coyote.

I did some shopping at a store right across from the motel. While I was there, a couple from Montreal, Canada, asked me if I was a thru-hiker. They were also thru-hiking the trail but had been going slowly (only four miles that day) because the wife had fallen and injured her knee. We talked about how slick the rocks were and how surprisingly rocky the trail was. After looking at her knee, I mentioned how badly swollen it looked and suggested that they might want to see a doctor in the area. The fellow laughed, saying, "I am a doctor!" Boy, did I feel like an idiot. Both retired, they had been cruising the Caribbean for the past five years, so hiking was something new for them. I enjoyed the visit and was impressed by their attitude. I don't think I would have been so positive if my knee had looked like that!

April 6, Dicks Creek Gap (Hiawassee, Georgia) to Muskrat Creek Shelter (North Carolina) (milepoint 78.4 north)

Early in the morning, I stopped at a nearby store where I purchased a nice little deli sandwich for lunch on the trail. When I pointed to the sandwich in the meat case, the clerk said, "Let me make you a fresh one. I know how you hikers appreciate a good sandwich." I continued to be impressed with the friendliness and consideration shown to hikers.

We had a shuttle to the trail planned for 10 a.m., and it looked to be a great day for hiking with the sun bright and temperature cool. I was also able to pick up an elastic knee support at the pharmacy; I wasn't sure if it would help but figured I might as well grab one while I was in town and close to a pharmacy.

By 10:30 a.m., we got a lift back to the trail at Dicks Creek Gap, and I immediately ran into two hikers from Israel whom I had met in Helen. When I asked them where they'd camped the night before, they motioned to the ground and said, "Right here." Then they laughed and said, "Yeah, we've been trying to get started for the last three hours."

It was a beautiful day to hike, but I surely could tell I had extra weight after leaving town. I enjoyed going into town but hated the heavy amount of food that came with leaving.

Earlier I had passed Gaiter, a 62-year-old thru-hiker. His age made it tough on him, but I wouldn't bet against him making it all the way to Mt. Katahdin. He told me with confidence, "I'm taking it slow but I'm going to make it to Maine. Remember the Tortoise and the Hare!"

I had been using the ace bandage purchased in Hiawassee, and it seemed to help with the strain on my knee as I hiked down hill, but I knew it was still early.

At Plumorchard Gap Shelter, a sign indicated that Muskrat Shelter, my destination for the night, was only 7.3 miles away. The temperature bordered on 60-degrees, and I changed to my shorts for the first time on the hike. Amazing that two nights ago it was in the high 20s and now it was in the 60s! The local who gave us a lift back to the trail said, "The real cold weather is unusual, but it does happen and you should expect more." It wasn't what I wanted to hear.

I spent part of the afternoon walking straight up the side of a mountain, and I mean straight up! I'm not sure what the elevation was, but the trail didn't have any switchbacks and it kicked my butt! Switchbacks, if you don't know, are trails that go up a mountain in a zigzag manner. They add distance to your hike but make it much easier going up the sides of the mountains. It seemed to me like these last sections of the A.T. in Georgia were nothing but straight up and down, although the spectacular views on every ridge made it worthwhile.

The final section of the trail in Georgia was through the Southern Nantahala Wilderness, part of the Chattahoochee National Forest. A sign indicated that foot travel was welcome; but bicycle, vehicles, horses, and pack stock were prohibited. And then I reached Bly Gap, a milestone in my hike, as I left Georgia and entered North Carolina: my first crossover into another state!

As I was headed up out of Bly Gap, there came another milestone: I was christened with a trail name. I caught up to a number of hikers sitting by the trail catching their breath. We talked for awhile, and as I got up to finish the tough climb up the mountainside, one of the hikers asked what my trail name was. I said I didn't have one, and one of the hikers, who was still in need of rest, yelled, "Why you're a damn old mountain slayer!" It wasn't long until I ran into others who had heard him, and the rest was, as they say, history. I asked them to dispel with the "damn old," but I didn't know if they would.

The shelter looked pretty crowded when I arrived, so I again decided to sleep in my tent. As I prepared dinner in the shelter, out of the wind, I was reminded why I was staying in my tent. There was a very heated argument between two hikers about the amount of smoke being put off by one of the hikers' zip stove. "Man, you're going to either have to fix that damn stove or get the hell out," bellyached a hiker already in his sleeping bag. "Oh, shut the hell up. A little smoke hasn't hurt anyone," came the reply. "Oh forget it, I'm out of here!" No sooner had the hiker with the zip stove left than a very intense conversation ensued on, of all things, the origins of the earth. I was happy to eat my dinner and retreat to my tent, where I hoped to have a good night's sleep.

April 7, Muskrat Creek Shelter to Carter Gap Shelter (milepoint 90.9 north)

I got out on the trail a little later than usual after a cool but very good night's sleep. I didn't stir until 4 a.m., which was very unusual for me. I planned for a ten-to-twelve-mile day if everything went well, and figured the big challenge for the day would be Standing Indian Mountain, the highest point on the A.T. to this point, more than five thousand feet high.

I hiked out of camp with an old fellow by the name of Sarge who had a knee that was really hurting him, so he planned to get off the trail. He was 62 and talked like he had hiked a major part of the trail previously, but he was still unhappy about having to leave the trail so early. One thing had become very apparent to me out on the trail: If a hiker had any type of injury, the trail magnified it seven-fold.

Passed a sign that read, "Chunky Gal Trail." According to *The Thru-Hiker's Handbook*, Indian lore had it that the trail was named after a very "healthy" Indian princess who, after quite a bit of teasing, took out on the trail never to be seen again.

I met up with a hiker who called himself Dead Horse. He said he was on a section hike because his work prevented him from tackling the entire trail. I also met my first southbounder, Beverly; she was doing a flip-flop. She started at Davenport Gap, Tennessee, the northern point of the Smoky Mountains; and she planned on hiking south to Springer Mountain, where she would be picked up for a ride back to Davenport for her hike north to Maine. Certainly a different way of hiking the trail, but a lot of options were available to a hiker. Interestingly, this was Beverly's second thru-hike.

Just after noon I stood on Standing Indian Mountain, six miles from my camp last night and certainly ready to take a lunch break. It had warmed up, and Julian from New Brunswick, Canada, was also ready for a break. Julian was the youngest thru-hiker I had met on the trail so far, just twenty years old. Shaker, Top Dog and Eric – all in their twenties and very good hikers – joined us for lunch. I was not about to kill myself trying to keep up with them. I did find it interesting that although I didn't hike as fast (they hiked over three miles an hour), I usually ended up meeting them in camp at night. I would much rather take my time and hike a big part of the day than hurry into camp and sit around with nothing to do.

We had our first outbreak of bugs. I called them gnats, but they were really a bit bigger than an Ohio gnat and had quite a bite! I noticed them as the weather warmed up. Luckily, I had brought a bug net for my head to use in camp, but I didn't think I would be using it so soon!

> *Hiker tips: I always tried to drink a lot of water at night in camp and would filter one and a half liters of water for my Dromedary bag, which had a hose and hung on the back of my pack. When I got up in the morning, I again tried to drink about a half-liter before starting out; that left me with enough for most of the day. I used a PUR Hiker Microfilter and a PUR Voyageur cartridge in it so that it also purified my water. The cartridge was a little more expensive, but I did like the way it worked. I also carried some Polar Pure tablets as a backup. Water had been plentiful so far on the trail, with the main sources of water identified in the A.T. Data Book. There were also other water sources not mentioned in the book, probably dependent on the amount of rain in a given year.*

I arrived at Carter Gap Shelter in the late afternoon and set up camp. I enjoyed a Lipton noodle dish – pretty good for dehydrated food and a nice change from mac and cheese. My appetite was picking up, so I would have to start carrying more food.

The bugs were a big problem in camp. They were driving everyone crazy, so I was really glad to have my bug net, and it really helped when cooking and sitting outside.

I visited the shelter and talked to a couple of thru-hikers, Smasher and her brother, Liberty Bell. Before I left, they said, "We were going to stay down where you're tented until we saw that big old skunk!" Someone added the tale of a hiker over-nighting several days back in his Bivy Sack, (a waterproof type of sleeping bag that serves as a tent and sleeping bag all in one). The hiker heard some noise outside, and when he looked out the sack's small screen window, he was nose- to-nose with a skunk! Needless to say, the rest of the camp area was soon awake as well, as the hiker cussed and scrambled, getting out of range of the smelly little creature's fragrant aim.

When I got back to camp, I immediately pulled the flap down on my tent. I didn't like to do that because of condensation, but that was better than having a skunk as a roommate. I also hung my food bag, just in case, as other hikers had told me that skunks can smell food better than any other animal out on the trail. As it turned out, I had no problems with skunks.

April 8, Carter Gap Shelter to Winding Stair Gap (Franklin, North Carolina) (milepoint 106.8 north)

I was still in my tent at 8:15 a.m., trying to pack up everything as the rain poured down. Packing gear and a tent in the pouring rain was quite a challenge, to say the least. There had been no hint of rain when I'd gone to bed the night before, so this was a surprise. I had planned to hike ten to twelve miles, but that would likely change if the weather did not clear up. I also had Albert Mountain to climb, which, I was told, was pretty much a rock climb. A new challenge every day.

> *Hiker tips: Thank God for Ziploc bags! I basically had all my different pieces of gear in individual Ziploc bags. I remembered reading somewhere that Earl Shaffer (the first A.T. thru-hiker) said that the most significant improvement in gear since his first hike in 1948 was Ziploc bags. I couldn't agree more, and in addition to the many Ziploc bags, I also had a waterproof bag for my sleeping bag, clothes, and food.*

After I was finished packing my gear in the rain, I realized there was a shelter about twenty-five yards away! It was the old Carter Gap Shelter, and it looked to be the perfect place to pack up my tent and gear in the pouring rain.

> *Hiker tips: Getting rain water off the tent really helped with the weight. I carried a chamois rag that made the task much easier and efficient.*

I finally got underway a little after 10 a.m. Once again I was the first out, this time on a drizzlingly cool morning, headed north through a tunnel of rhododendrons toward Albert Mountain.

Albert Mountain was a climb! For the first time on the trail, I had to put my poles in my pack and use my hands to climb the rock face cliff. But the Old Mountain Slayer made it up another one! Although the climb up Albert Mountain was quite a challenge, I really enjoyed the small bit of mountain climbing that was involved.

Top Dog, Eric, Shaker and I all had some lunch on top of Albert Mountain while enjoying the beautiful view. There was a large fire watchtower on top called the Coweeta Hydraulic Laboratory, which was manned only during the dry season. I decided to climb to the top of the tower and take a picture; but before I could get to the top, I heard one of the fellows yell, "Hey, Slayer, you best get down, and fast. Looks like one hell of a storm coming in!" Before I could get all the way down, a storm front came roaring in out of nowhere and almost blew me off the tower. I could not believe how fast the weather had changed! I hustled down Albert Mountain bundled up in my coat, with gloves and hat on for protection against the cold wind that blew in with the front. Ice pellets were hitting me in the face.

By mid-afternoon, it was becoming increasingly difficult to find white blazes as I hiked toward Rock Gap Shelter. The blazes were present, but they were beginning to be covered by the progressively intense snow.

It was just after 4 p.m. when I passed a couple of kids day hiking. They were the first hikers that I had seen that day other then Top Dog, Eric and Shaker. They said there was a shelter just down the hill.

Vince was at the shelter, and there was plenty of room. "All the other blokes headed for the campgrounds," Vince said with a shiver. With my thermometer reading 30-degrees and dropping, I also decided to head down to the campground, where there was supposed to be some type of lodging. It was really going to get cold, and I had no interest in sleeping in a wet tent if I didn't have to.

It was about a quarter after five when I crossed a road to the Standing Indian Campground. Although I was still following the intermittent white blazes, I did not know where I was; and it appeared that there was no type of lodging at the campground, so I decided to continue heading north on the trail to Wallace Gap. My *Data Book* indicated that the Rainbow Campground was about a half-mile north and offered lodging. Now in sleet and freezing rain, I knew I needed to get to some type of cover and figured that Wallace Gap and its campground was up over the mountain, probably only about fifteen or twenty minutes from where I was.

An hour later, as I headed to where I thought Wallace Gap would be, I thought to myself, "Damn, I should have been there by now!" The white blazes assured me I was still on the A.T., but I was totally confused and not at all sure where on the A.T. I was. The snow was really coming down, and the temperature continued to drop. Because it was getting late, I began to get very concerned and frustrated. With the extreme cold and the snow, the last thing I wanted to do was put up a wet tent. I thought to myself, "Mountain Slayer, you've got to keep walking, no matter what!" It was the first time on the trail that I really didn't know where I was. Feeling lost was not a good feeling.

About ten minutes later, I screamed out a forest-shaking, "Yes!" upon the sight of a road. But which road was it? The sign read, "Winding Stair Gap." I couldn't believe it. I had just hiked three miles farther than I had planned! Somehow I missed both Wallace Gap and the Rainbow Campground completely, but I had no idea how. But that was history, and now I had to get out of the weather by hitching a ride into Franklin, North Carolina.

A half-hour later, about 7 p.m., I checked into a motel called the Country Inn, after unsuccessfully trying to get a room at the Franklin Motel which was closer to the center of town. I was feeling much better and was glad to be safe and warm. I had received a ride to town with Ted Cook and Diana Payne, two great people. I really appreciated their help, and I certainly considered them trail angels of the highest degree! They drove me to three different hotels before I could find a place to stay.

When Ted and Diana dropped me off at the last motel, they even waited outside to make sure I could get a room. I went in and asked about a room, and the clerk said the room was thirty-four dollars. I replied, "OK," and turned to go get my gear out of Ted's car. The hotel clerk blurted out, "Thirty two dollars." I smiled, not sure why she reduced the cost, but again said, "OK" and continued to walk out to get my gear. She shouted even louder: "Thirty dollars!" I turned and said, "OK, I need to get my gear," and walked out to Ted's car, laughing. Ted asked, "What the hell was that all about?" I just laughed and said, "Hell, I don't know," and thanked him for all his help. I got to thinking about the episode later and figured the clerk thought I was leaving each time I said "OK" and headed to the car, so she kept dropping the price.

Late that evening, I watched the local weather report calling for lows in the twenties, with high winds and blowing snow up in the mountains. Although I ended up walking a total of 16 miles, more than I wanted or had ever hiked before, I was very happy to be inside. My entire room was hung with rain-soaked equipment, and I knew there was no way I wanted to be in any shelter, let alone a tent. What an adventurous day on the trail!

April 9, Franklin, North Carolina (milepoint 106.8 north)

I took my first zero-mile day, hiker lingo for taking a day off from hiking.

After checking out of the Country Inn motel, I walked uptown and checked into the Franklin Motel, which was within walking distance of stores and the self-service laundry. I had heard the motel staff would also help arrange for a shuttle back to the trail.

The cold weather brought a lot of hikers into town. The evening before, while I was looking for a room, I ran into Shaker. I asked, "I thought you guys were staying at the Rainbow Campground?" He just shook his head and said, "It's a long story, but basically the campground was full so Eric, Top Dog, and I had to pay for a goddamn taxi ride into Franklin to find a room!" They were not happy hikers.

After checking in at the Franklin Motel, I was sitting outside my room when up to the office walked the Machete Kid. He said he'd tented the night before on Standing Indian Mountain in an inch of snow. "That was the coldest I've ever been in my life," he said with a blank look on his face. The mountain was so cold, he mumbled, that he feared he was developing hypothermia; so at 4 a.m., he got up, packed his gear, and hiked out. "I actually thought I was going to die on that damn mountain," he said.

All through the morning, hikers came into town with stories about the weather the night before. One hiker pulled up in the back of a pickup and limped into the hotel office saying, "I want a room for two nights, and I don't give a damn how much it costs!"

All through lunch and laundry, I ran into hikers with stories about the cold night on the mountain. By evening, I had clean clothes, fresh supplies and a full belly; so I was ready to head out in the morning. Although I got a lot done during my zero-mile day, I was getting itchy to get back on the trail; a daylong layover was longer than I really cared for.

The Franklin Motel had a list of shuttle drivers, so I called one and he agreed to pick me up the next morning. In planning for food supplies, I looked at my *Data Book* and made plans to reach Nantahala Outdoor Center in two days. That would be twenty-six miles in two days, which might be too much. However, I hoped that with one day's rest on my legs, I would be able to make it without too much strain on my knees.

April 10, Winding Stair Gap (Franklin, North Carolina) to Cold Spring Shelter (122.6 north)

Up, packed, and ready for the trail by 8 a.m., I had a shuttle set up for 9:15 a.m.; so until then I had breakfast and visited with two other hikers, Liberty Dog and Pony. They told me about a hiker with the appropriate trail name of Monster Frog. It seemed he started out on the A.T. with a ninety-two-pound pack, and all of his gear was from his recent days in the Army. The Frog was still on the trail, they said, but his hiking partner hadn't even made it to the top of Springer Mountain – he turned back on the eight-mile approach trail. We also talked about hiking mountains. A mountain would often have two different routes: the white-blazed trail (official Appalachian Trail) that would take a hiker straight up and over the mountain, and a blue-blazed trail that would take the hiker around the mountain. Hence the term, "to blue blaze," meant to take a side trail marked with blue blazes around the mountain, usually shorter and certainly not as high. I said that I hadn't tried a blue blaze so far on my hike. Laughing, Liberty Dog told me, "Man, with a trail name like Mountain Slayer, there's no way you can ever blue blaze!" I guess that sometimes getting a trail name can get you more than just a name! We also talked about "yellow blazing," the generally derogatory term directed at hikers who hitchhiked on a road from one section of the trail to another.

My plan for the day was a sixteen-mile hike to Cold Spring Shelter, my first intentional long hike in one day, and I was really pumped to give it a try. Having given my legs a day of rest, I thought I was ready for a long haul.

So just before 10 a.m., I was heading back to the trail – and eventually, Cold Spring Shelter – with Cornell, my shuttle driver and a member of the local hiking club near Franklin. "Sounds like you have a long hike planned for such a late start," he said on the way. "But I believe you can do it." It was, he said, "a perfect day for hiking the Balds, especially Wayah Bald. That's about ten miles ahead; and if you can't go the sixteen miles, there are great camping areas along the way."

I mentioned my problem with getting lost a few days earlier, and he said I wasn't the first hiker to have trouble in that area. He said he'd tried without success to persuade the forest service to put up better signs along the trail in the Standing Indian Mountain area.

As I got to the trail, I came across Tom, the South African, packing his gear and ready to head out after what he described as a "blooming cold night!"

The birds were out and singing, sounding as though they were glad the cold night was over and the morning sun was warming everything up.

Just as I got underway, I decided I'd lost one of my handkerchiefs, probably when I was getting my pack in and out of Cornell's car. And Cornell had even mentioned to check for items, saying, "I once found a billfold a hiker left in my car. It took some doing but I was able to locate the hiker at the next shelter." There aren't a lot of people willing to do that.

The Siler Bald was just spectacular. I really didn't know what to expect, as I had never really hiked on a bald before, but the high grassy area made for a perfect view. It was definitely lunch and picture time, as off in the distance was Wayah Bald. And when I sat down for lunch, I found the lost handkerchief, stuck down in my belt. I pinned it to my pack.

Hiker tips: I carried three handkerchiefs. One was cotton and kept inside my pack for camp clean-up. Another – for colds and runny nose – I pinned in front on my shoulder strap where I could get to it without putting my pack down. The third was a Coolmax from Campmor, 100-percent polyester, which I used for perspiration. It was on my other shoulder strap where again I could get to it with out taking off my pack, and it seemed to dry rapidly as I walked along. I think the only thing made of cotton I had with me was the handkerchief I just mentioned. Cotton weighed too much and stayed wet too long, as reflected in the trail saying, "Cotton kills."

Just when I thought I was all alone on Siler Bald, up walked another hiker; his trail name was Pockets. Not a thru-hiker, he was actually a support person for his wife, Crazy Legs. She had taken a day off from her hike, so he came up to see the view from the Balds. When she was hiking, he used a truck with a camper and followed her along the trail as support. "My wife only gets in about five or six miles a day," he said, "But she is having a great time." I continued to be impressed and amazed at the different methods people used to hike the trail.

Pockets kind of raised his eyebrows when I mentioned I was headed to Cold Spring Shelter. With a grin, he pointed out Wayah Bald and said, "It sure does look a long way off, doesn't it?" I smiled and shrugged as I told him, "I have everything on my back if I don't make it."

Ran into a hiker named Oakley and was surprised when he exclaimed, "I know you!" He was keeping a journal on the Internet, and while in Helen, he stopped in the library to make an entry. While on-line, he'd read my journal entry.

As I passed a campsite, a dog came running out at me. I braced for the unexpected, but was quickly very pleased to recognize the dog as Dillon. I had met Dillon and his person, Lynn, the first day or so in my hike. It was good to see them again and catch up on how they had been doing.

When I arrived on top of Wayah Bald, at 5,000 feet, I figured I had just climbed about 1,000 feet from Siler Bald. I found a log that was begging for someone to sit for a spell. It was, I decided, a great place for a snack. I had hiked ten miles and had about six more to my planned campsite. Wayah Bald had a tower, and the perch on top provided a spectacular view of the surrounding mountains, a truly incredible sight. Cornell had been right when he said I had a perfect day for the Balds. Another hiker walked up while I was resting. From Massachusetts, she had the trail name of Bookworm, "from reading everything I could about the Appalachian Trail." We helped each other out, snapping pictures with the other's camera.

At 5:15 p.m., I was still about two miles from the shelter. Although the trail had been well marked with white blazes, I had begun to find some mountain signs were broken off when they were at gaps and near roads. It was very frustrating. Without the signs it was very difficult to figure out where I was. In bad weather, like I'd been in the other day, it could be downright dangerous.

I finally reached the shelter about 6:30 p.m. It had been a beautiful but long day, and I was hoping to stay in the shelter. The log shelter was small and very old, called Washington's Shelter for George Washington. It was one of the oldest shelters on the trail, and its age and appearance had inspired the joking idea that the shelter was so old that George Washington carved his initials in one of the logs! The small shelter was crowded, and someone had even brought a dog in, so I went looking for a campsite.

There was a nice clean water supply next to the shelter, but the dog had been running and jumping in it, a prime example of a dog owner not caring, or worse, not knowing how to control his dog. I set my campsite up on the hill above the shelter, fixed a Knorr Pasta meal, and then headed to bed. It had been a long sixteen-mile day.

April 11, Cold Spring Shelter to Nantahala Outdoor Center (milepoint 134.1 north)

The night had been cooler than I expected, and my tent site was not very level, which caused me to slide off my insulated sleeping pad and onto the cold ground throughout the night; so I didn't get the best night of sleep. The lack of insulation from my pad really made a difference.

I headed to the Nantahala Outdoor Center (NOC) about twelve miles away. Grey Bear, who tented beside me, asked if I wanted to share a room in the bunkhouse at the center, which I quickly agreed to. We had heard some negatives about the bunkhouse, especially how far it was from restroom facilities; but we were supposed to have rain coming in, so a night in any room off the trail sounded good to me.

I started the morning wearing gloves and three layers of shirts and hoped to shed some of the clothes as the morning progressed. I also noticed a slight shoulder pain when I started out and continued to use salve on my hip rash from my backpack, but, all in all, I felt good. I figured the minor aches and pains were just part of the price of hiking from Georgia to Maine.

> *Hiker tips: I found that the Dromedary bag attached to the back of my pack worked great, but I never knew exactly how much water I had. Therefore, I also carried a bottle for extra water if I ran out. Food consisted of granola bars for the morning, cheese and beef sticks for lunch and some type of pasta in the evening. I had only used two maildrops so far. I found that getting to a post office before its closing time was a real hassle, not to mention that post offices were closed on weekends. I found that the more independent I could be on the trail, the better off I was; so I would not recommend a lot of maildrops.*

I headed out of Cold Springs that morning on a downhill stretch of the trail. The sunrise was magnificent! I continued to find myself tempted to take a picture on every bald or mountain. Even as it started to cloud over, the views remained spectacular, making it tough to put the camera down. An earlier thru-hiker back in Franklin had told me that this section of the trail was one of his favorites because of the magnificent views hikers could get from the many Balds, and I certainly wouldn't disagree with him.

As I was packing up, I saw Grey Bear taking his bear bag out of a tree and asked, "Do you always hang your food?" He told me, "I learned my lesson early on when I was hiking in the Shenandoah National Park and a bear got my food."

My climb up Wesser Bald had me doing what is called heel-toe most of the way. That meant I was going straight up the side of the mountain and taking very short, tiny steps from heel to toe.

As I scrambled down some rocks on a major downhill, I saw a lake and river down off the mountains and figured that was where I was headed. The downhill portion was unyielding. My knees were screaming with pain, and the elastic bandage I'd put on that morning was of no help on such a steep and continuous downhill. The day's hike included six miles of downhill hiking, a real strain on my knees.

Gray Bear caught up with me at Rufus Morgan Shelter. He, too, was complaining about his knee as we finished the last eight miles to the NOC. He carried an altimeter as well as all the maps of the trail, which enabled him to know his elevation at all times. As I'd said to Vince in regard to his profile maps, I told Gray Bear, "Sometimes it's best not to know certain things!"

We checked into NOC, a small resort with very reasonable rates for hikers, just after 5 p.m. The rest was a godsend for my aching knees. Grey Bear and I found a bunkhouse that had a shower and restroom nearby. It was nothing elaborate, but it was clean and had a nice bed, and as Gray Bear said, "What more could two old tired-ass hikers ask for?"

I ate at the restaurant, treating myself to a big hamburger, fries, and a salad. I figured I would need all the energy I could muster as I planned to hike to Fontana Dam, about twenty-seven miles, in the next two days. Making it in two days would allow me to keep my pack weight down with less food and, I hoped, lessen the strain on my knees. All around the center, hikers talked about the six-mile hike back up to the trail. I wasn't too worried about the hike up in the morning – it was the downhill stretches that had been tearing my knees up.

> *Hiker tips: I had my water filter checked out at the NOC outfitters shop and was told three things about my water filter: First, putting coffee filters over the end of my intake tube was an excellent decision. Second, and something that really surprised me, running water will have more silt in it than standing water. And finally, I learned that Georgia water seemed to be harder on filters than the water in any other state on the A.T. because of the very fine silt.*

Grey Bear had a small palm top that weighed seven ounces, which he used for his journal. Whenever he got to a phone he was able to send his journal entries over the phone directly to the Trailplace website. It worked pretty slick, but I still preferred my tape recorder that could be used throughout the day.

I met Vince down at the store getting resupplied. "This is one of the few times I've not used my tent," he said with a grin. "Trying to save money, Mate!" It was starting to sprinkle a little, and I was glad I would be inside for the night. I just hoped the big Gray Bear didn't snore too much!

April 12, Nantahala Outdoor Center to Brown Fork Gap Shelter (150.1 north)

It was drizzling rain at 7:30 a.m. as I packed up to head north on the trail. Nantahala was a great place for hikers to stay, and I'd highly recommend the NOC to anyone hiking in the area. Gray Bear and I stayed in a bunkhouse that could accommodate four hikers, with plenty of room to air out our equipment. We were right next to a base camp area with a laundry and kitchen. I was really surprised at how few hikers were staying there, but there was a campground and shelter nearby which may have explained the small numbers.

I planned for a big sixteen-mile day, but with the drizzling rain, that would be a challenge. Before I got back on the trail, however, I had a wonderful breakfast at the NOC restaurant and talked to a number of hikers, several of them new faces. One of those new faces was Monster Frog, he of the ninety-two-pound pack. "It's good to finally meet you," I said. "I've heard a lot about you and your pack weight. You're the talk of the trail!"

He rolled his eyes and chuckled. "Actually," he said, "I'm still working on that pack weight problem. I got it down to eighty-seven pounds at the Hikers Inn. Now it's about eighty pounds." I heard my knees screaming just listening to him.

HoTye, another new face, told me something interesting. Forty percent of the northbound hikers have left the trail, he said; twenty percent leave by Neels Gap and another twenty percent leave at Fontana Dam.

Two other new faces were Walkabout and Machine, a young couple from Australia. They were on a yearlong hiking tour around the world. "We plan to hike the A.T.," Walkabout said, "then on to South Africa for more hiking."

Most of the hikers I talked to thought that my planned sixteen-mile day was way too ambitious. Most of them were only going to the next shelter. My problem with that idea was that the next shelter was only seven miles, and I was sure I wanted to go beyond that.

On the way up, I met a woman hiking down the mountain and asked if she had been to the top already. She smiled and said, "Actually, I live up there. I'm just going to work!" Now, wouldn't that be quite a commute to work and home each day?

A monument on the ridge read: "On December 7, 1968, 783 feet southwest of this point, Wade A. Sutton, a North Carolina Forest Service Ranger, gave his life suppressing a forest fire that you might more fully enjoy your hike along this trail." That inscription got me thinking of my youngest son Brad, a firefighter out West, and of the dangers of firefighting.

As noon passed, I was still climbing as I had been all morning, and I was just now reaching the top of Swim Bald. What a mountain! My sixteen-mile plan was not looking good at the moment, as the mountain took a lot out of me. I was surely glad I'd had a big breakfast!

Passed a sign that indicated the Sassafras Grass Shelter was one-tenth of a mile. I could actually see the shelter from the trail, and it was tempting; but it was only 1 p.m., and that was too early to stop. Brown Fork Shelter, my planned stop, was more than nine miles north, but with tough terrain I was beginning to understand why a number of experienced hikers thought my goal of sixteen miles was a bit much!

When I reached the top of Cheoah Bald, I was at 5,062 feet. I started out at 1,740 feet in Nantahala, and I had only hiked eight miles. What a climb! A thru-hiker by the name of Crash took my picture on the top of the Bald. I didn't know much about him except that he was a friendly young kid and one hell of a fast hiker! He did have a nice light pack, the lightest I'd seen on the trail, actually.

As I entered Locust Cove Gap with six more miles to go, I was feeling pretty good, even though my knee was hurting on the down hills. I figured that I would make the Brown Fork Shelter after all. I needed water, so I asked a group of day hikers who were making camp how far the water was down the side trail. They shook their heads in disgust, one saying, "Man, I don't know, but it's a helluva ways down and back up!" Mike, the leader of the group, offered me a quart of his fresh water. "Here," he said, "take my water. I can always go back down and get more. You look as though you've had it!" I thanked him, and mopping the sweat from my forehead, I said, "You're right, I've had a long day and still have some miles to put in. You're a true trail angel!" Mike told me that he and another experienced hiker were teaching a group of teenagers how to hike and camp on the trail. It was a diverse group of young people, mostly from the inner city, experiencing teamwork and cooperation on the trail. It was great to see young people learning about and enjoying one of our national treasures.

I stopped to take a break and eat a snack at Simp Gap and saw a beautiful farm setting down in the valley. I'd had glimpses of numerous farms off and on as I walked the ridge, and they all looked to be right out of Currier and Ives.

Vince was setting up his camp for the night in an area with no water, a place not at all ideal for a campsite. But it seemed he'd had enough for one day. "That hike was quite hard," he said in what seemed a classic understatement. Vince had the nicest stainless steel thermos bottle I had ever seen, and the second night out on the trail he'd offered me a "spot of tea." I never really liked tea but I surely did enjoy his tea that evening, and I was saddened when Vince finally gave up on carrying his thermos at Nantahala; he said the weight was just not worth the effort anymore. I know how he loved his tea, but we'd all had to make do with less when the weight of the pack started to work on us.

I got to the top of the mountain, 600 feet straight up out of Stecoah Gap. What a climb, especially as I ended a sixteen-mile day! That was really tough, without question my toughest day on the trail so far. I was tired, but otherwise OK, and was glad the day was almost over. I'd probably pushed a little too much, and it took about everything out of me. I knew one thing: I certainly had all the respect in the world for those older than I hiking this trail!

Just before 7 p.m., I arrived at Brown Fork Gap Shelter, with the last 2.4 miles being quite a climb. I found the shelter full, and it appeared to be a strange group in the shelter. So it was just as well that I preferred my tent to a shelter on such a beautiful night, even though there was not a level spot for my tent. With the day I'd had, I figured I could sleep hanging from a tree if I had to!

April 13, Brown Fork Gap Shelter To Fontana Dam, North Carolina (milepoint 161.7 north)

I awoke to a steady rain that had begun early in the morning and had not let up, so it looked like I would be packing up a wet tent again. I headed to Fontana Dam, North Carolina, about eleven miles away on a muddy and very slick trail.

Frustration was setting in early for someone. I heard an explosion of profanity from behind me: "...these goddamn poles! I hate this son-of-a-bitch of a trail!" and other words not meant for the faint of heart. When I turned around, all I could see through the morning mist was two hiking poles whirling high into the air, resembling blades on a helicopter, landing out of sight in the valley below. I didn't stop to ask any questions. If I had learned anything on the trail, it was that during difficult times it was best to keep one's thoughts and questions to one's self. This lesson had been reinforced the other evening when after a particularly difficult wet and cold day, a young hiker came into camp late, obviously having a very bad day. Without thinking, I gave him my usual greeting of "Hey, how's it going"? "It sucks. Any other questions?" was his immediate and to-the-point response. Bottom line: If the "Helicopter Hiker" happened to catch up with me, I would not ask, "How's it going?"

For some time after the "Helicopter Hiker" incident, I didn't see a soul on the trail. That wasn't surprising, as the trail became increasingly slick with thick, greasy mud – something I had not dealt with before. It made for an extremely challenging and even dangerous walk. On one occasion, I planted my right foot on a downhill stretch and immediately did a sliding and twirling 360-degree, one-footed turn before I knew what had happened. How that happened without my falling or injuring myself, only God knew!

I came down off the mountain from Walker Gap and the grandeur of the Fontana Dam seemed to jump out at me. "Good God, look at the sight of that dam!" was my immediate overwhelming impression.

When I arrived on Highway 28, a sign indicated that I was just 1.4 miles from the Fontana Dam Visitor Center; and to my amazement, there was a phone right off the side of the road to call for a shuttle to town!

I ran into Crash, the young thru-hiker I'd met earlier, and he filled me in on the plight of Helicopter Hiker. He shook his head as he said, "The damn fool is hiking in sandals!" Apparently Helicopter Hiker twisted his knee badly in the mud and was really upset, hence the cursing and throwing of hiking poles.

I passed a shelter near the dam for thru-hikers only. Nicknamed the "Fontana Hilton" because of its close proximity to the Fontana Dam Visitor Center and an opportunity for hikers to take a shower. Nice, but still a shelter. I was headed for a clean bed and good meal in the little town of Fontana Dam. In addition, I was looking for a maildrop in which my wife was to include some fuel tabs for my cooking stove along with the usual cards and notes that I always enjoyed.

Hiker tips: I used an Esbit stove that was very small and lightweight and heated water in a small .85 liter Titanium Kettle to cook my dehydrated meals. I usually used one fuel tab per meal. The tabs were very light but difficult to find on the trail, hence the use of maildrops. Knorr, Lipton or mac and cheese were my standard dinners.

April 14, Fontana Dam, North Carolina to Russell Field Shelter (milepoint 176.4 north)

I learned some interesting things about Fontana Dam. It started as the town of Fontana back in the 1800's. The logging industry was in the area, and it's believed that the name Fontana was chosen to honor a company owner's wife. The biggest thing to happen to the town was the dam, built before World War II by the Tennessee Valley Authority to provide electrical power to the region. Fontana became a boomtown for a short time, but most of the people left after the dam was built; and it was now a little resort town, a very nice place to stay for hikers.

After finishing a nice buffet breakfast, I was joined by two female thru-hikers, Dream Catcher and another hiker whose name I did not catch. We had an enjoyable breakfast as we reviewed the past few days and discussed what the Great Smoky Mountains National Park had in store for us. Dream Catcher was a good strong hiker whom I first met at Goose Creek Cabins, but her friend was not quite as strong and was having some problems. She was very frustrated, going much slower than she had anticipated – about five or six miles a day – and to top it off, she'd left her hiking poles in a car after someone gave her a lift. The hiker's nightmare! Both women were concerned about the Smokies and the rule there of camping only at the shelters, an obvious problem for any hiker who was having a difficult time and might not be able to hike the distance between shelters. To compound these concerns, they both added pack weight due to the fact there were no resupply points within the national park. Many hikers were hiking out of Fontana Dam with heavy packs containing food supplies for seven or eight days. I wasn't going to do that. I was carrying three days' supply of food, figuring that I could make it to a highway where I would hitchhike into Gatlinburg, Tennessee, for a bed and resupply. I saw no reason to carry all that food through the Smokies, but some hikers coveted the solitude and therefore did not want any part of Gatlinburg. As they say, "Hike your own hike!"

I was ready to get back on the trail and was waiting for the shuttle. My plan was to hike thirteen miles to Russell Field Shelter, but if that was too far, I would stop at the ten-mile shelter. We were expecting rain over the next few days, which could make finding space in the shelters a real challenge. For the sake of my knees, I had decided to try hiking twelve or thirteen miles a day, along with keeping my pack weight down. I was determined to cut down on those big mile days because even though I felt rested, I knew my body was beginning to wear down some.

We had a full van as we drove to the drop-off point at Fontana Dam. Among the hikers were Bob Illi, whom I had not seen for a number of days, and Buffalo Soldier, a very fitting name for the first African-American thru-hiker I had met on the trail. Bob expressed some disappointment that he was planning to leave the trail in Gatlinburg, but he was expected home for Easter.

It was a clear cool morning as I headed across the dam and up into the Smokies. A hiker went past me, headed back to the dam carrying two water bottles and no pack. He had a look of major disappointment on his face and grumbled, "I can't believe I forgot my damn water!"

As we were crossing the dam, I mentioned to a couple of hikers my plans to hitchhike into Gatlinburg when I got to the road. "I'm not sure you are allowed to hitchhike within the park," one of them said. That threw a curve into my plans to carry only a couple days' worth of food. But I'd come to accept the many uncertainties of thru-hiking, never knowing what obstacles lay ahead. I figured I would work something out.

Before we could hike the Great Smoky Mountains, we had to fill out a registration card. We got information on rules and regulations from an amiable park ranger sitting on a rock next to the trail. In the national park, thru-hikers could stay at any shelter. All other hikers were required to have a reservation to stay at a shelter, but were also given priority. I continued my climb up to the ridge top, said to be the hardest part of the Smokies because of the several miles of uphill climbing. Once on the ridge, I'd have much less up-and-down climbing than I'd had so far on the trail. As I went up, a hiker called Guinness caught up to me. He said he got his trail name from his favorite beverage!

Unfortunately, I "got" to climb up to the ridge top twice, and I could have kicked myself! I had to walk down to Birch Spring Shelter to refill my water supply, and as I was headed back up to the ridge, I felt water on the backs of my legs. I hadn't secured the cap and had lost half of my water supply, which meant I had to go back down and refill – not one of my smarter moves! But I finally reached the top of Shuckstack Mountain on a beautiful sunny day with just a few scattered clouds and the famous blue haze that gave these mountains their name.

I passed another hiker, one with the unusual trail name of Just Mary. She asked me how my day was going. "Not good," I said quickly, and then told her of my water misfortunes. It gave her a laugh, maybe too big a laugh. It's always nice to bring a smile to others! Anyway, it was a beautiful day, and I was not sitting in an office!

Caught myself thinking about what I was going to have for dinner, and I could not believe I was dreaming of macaroni and cheese, a clear sign that my appetite was kicking in!

Hiker tips: At every town stop, I tried to eat as much fruit and vegetables as possible due to the lack of fresh fruit on the trail. I also took a One-a-Day multivitamin to compensate for the lack of vitamins in my diet.

Another benefit of thru-hiking that I had not expected or thought about was the ability to eat whatever fatty foods I wanted. Normally, at a buffet I would try to limit my fat intake, but with the physical activity of a thru-hike, that obviously was not a concern on the trail!

I arrived at Russell Field Shelter by 5 p.m., and the shelter was almost full, creating a dilemma; for in the Smokies, hikers were not supposed to tent (due to bears) unless the shelter was full. But a policy that required thru-hikers to move out of the shelter if hikers with reservations showed up, put the thru-hiker between a rock and a hard place. A couple of day hikers with reservations said they'd tried to get more reservations but were told that all the reservations for the Russell Field Shelter were taken. So I decided to put up my tent, just in case some late hikers came in with reservations. With rain in the forecast, I hated the idea of needlessly getting my tent wet.

When it got to 7 p.m. and no other hikers had showed up I took my tent down, gambling that no one with a reservation would be coming in late and mumbling to myself, "Someone will have a tough time pulling me out of my sleeping bag this time of night!" I understood the need for the reservation system, but it seemed to me there should be a time limit for using the reservation.

The stone shelter, typical of the shelters in the Smoky Mountain Park, held fourteen people, had a chain link fence across the front to keep out bears, and a fireplace inside the shelter. This would be my first night in a shelter since I had been on the trail.

I spent some time in the evening talking with Vince about my limited hiking in England. He shared his experience of hiking coast-to-coast there, from the Irish Sea to the North Sea. "The nice thing about hiking in England," he said, with an obvious twinkle in his eye, "is that you get to stay in a pub every night!" Before we turned in, Vince also provided me with a good chuckle. He'd decided to stay outside in his tent, and just before he went to bed, he whispered, "Mate, are you going to lock the chain link fence door when you go to sleep?" With a puzzled look, I said, "I hadn't really given it any thought. Why? What do you care?" He whispered seriously, "Bears! If one shows up, I want to make sure I can get inside the shelter!" That had me chuckling as I went to sleep. Oh, what I would have given to see Vince high-tailing it to the shelter with a bear on his heels!

April 15, Russell Field Shelter to Double Spring Gap Shelter (milepoint 192.4 north)

I headed out from the shelter on a beautiful morning. It had rained during the night, so I was very happy I'd been in the shelter. Fortunately, the other hikers who had reservations were no-shows.

My first shelter experience was good, even though I slept on a wooden platform that I found harder than anticipated. I'd heard a lot of negative stories about shelters before I started on the A.T., and I was not sure what to expect; but we had about twelve people in the shelter including five day-hikers, and it was fine. I asked the local day-hikers about my plan of hitching a ride out of Newfound Gap into Gatlinburg. Apparently, they had tried it once and had to wait a very long time for a ride, as they just said, "Good luck!" They suggested I might want to consider the possibility of a cab if I could not hitch a ride. It was good to know, even though I hoped I didn't have to resort to an expensive fifteen-mile cab ride into Gatlinburg. Everyone was ready for sleep by 10 p.m., and it stayed quiet all night. We did see mice scurrying around the shelter as it began to get dark, especially as hikers prepared their food.

> *Hiker tips: Due to the large number of mice in the shelters, I hung my food bag on strings with small tuna type cans (found in almost every shelter) tied on to prevent the mice from crawling down the string to my food bag. I also would unzip all the pockets on my pack, so that if a mouse wanted to get into my pack, it would not chew its way in. Don't forget to put toothpaste, and any other tasty little treat that mice would like, in your food bag.*

Was starting to feel a few more aches and pains, and along with the sore knees and hip, I noticed that the muscles in my back were sore from what I was sure was the constant pull of my pack. I really noticed it when I was rolling up my sleeping pad and a very sharp pain shot between my shoulder blades. Although it was uncomfortable, the pain was not intolerable, and I figured it was part of hiking every day with a heavy pack.

I headed out, taking only a few steps before realizing that something was wrong: I had forgotten my hiking poles. I noticed it right away because I'd become accustomed to them; they'd become something like extra arms and legs, and I couldn't get very far without them.

My next destination was Clingmans Dome, the highest point on the entire Appalachian Trail, and I was hoping it would be a somewhat gradual ascent. It was another mountain, however, that was dominating my brain. The night before, I'd read in my *Data Book* that I would be crossing Rocky Top Mountain, the inspiration for the song. And now I couldn't get that damned song out of my mind!

During a short break, I ate the Payday candy bar my wife sent as a surprise in my last maildrop. Although Snickers candy bars seemed to be the candy bar of choice on the trail, due to having nuts for protein and a high number of calories, a little variety was always nice.

> *Hiker tips: I usually would stick a couple of candy bars in my pockets each morning, along with a bag of GORP, to nibble on in the morning before lunch and in the afternoon before dinner. I found that the snacks seemed to help keep my energy level up throughout the day.*

Another milestone: I met the famous Grandma Sole, one of the legendary thru-hikers on the A.T. A lovely lady seventy-five years old, she appeared to be extremely fit and was thru-hiking the trail for the second time. "This is my last fling!" she told me with a sparkle in her eyes. Although she had a support team that provided her with a lot of assistance, she said with pride, "I still carry my own pack and follow the white blazes."

I stopped at Derrick Knob Shelter for another quick break and talked with a number of hikers who were already in for the night. I had a good laugh before I left the shelter, seeing a guitar and a number of folding chairs there. It was truly amazing what people would bring out on the trail, then leave when it got too heavy!

As I hiked on up the trail, it seemed like everyone was in a hurry, probably due to the fact that there were so many people out on the trail there might not be enough room for everyone who wanted to stay in shelters. The weekend brought out a lot of people for day or weekend hikes, and this was probably the most people I had seen on the trail so far.

Siler Bald Shelter was kind of dumpy and packed with a lot of people, so I decided to gamble and go a little further to the next shelter, less than two miles north. While I was at Siler Bald Shelter, Bob Illi did me a favor. I asked him how far it was to the water, and he said it was a pretty good hike on a blue blaze. Then he offered me his water, saying, "I'm done for the day and can always get water later." What a kind gesture! That certainly saved me some time and energy and proved that a fellow hiker could also be a trail angel.

I arrived at Double Spring Gap Shelter at quarter to five. There was bunk space, so I planned to stay in the shelter; but I contemplated setting up my tent outside just in case I got bumped sometime during the night. A really nice shelter with a spring right next to it, Double Spring Gap was actually much better than Siler Bald, so I was glad I'd walked the extra couple of miles. I'd walked sixteen miles for the day, which was more than I intended; but I felt good, and all I needed was dinner and my sleeping bag!

Before I retired to my sleeping bag, I was reminded again by the talk in the shelter how one needed to be careful when hiking. A hiker told the story about a young woman hiking up on Albert Mountain, looking out over the mountain as she walked. Her distraction led to a slip off the edge of the mountain, where she luckily caught a bush. There she hung until a couple of hikers heard her call for help and pulled her to safety.

April 16, Double Spring Gap Shelter to Newfound Gap (Gatlinburg, Tennessee) (milepoint 203.2 north)

Up and out on the trail not long after 7 a.m., and I could see my breath. I'd gone to bed early, so I was awake and up early even though it was really cold outside my sleeping bag. With the chill, the fire in the shelter made for an excellent night's sleep. My twenty-degree, down hooded sleeping bag added warmth, and I was very glad to have it, although I could not say the same about my three-quarter length Therm-A-Rest sleeping pad. I chose the three-quarter length to save weight, and was using four sections of a Z-Rest pad to sit on around camp and place at the foot of my sleeping pad at night. That worked fine until I moved around during the night and the Z-Rest pad slipped out from underneath my feet, making for some cold toes! I did take advantage of the fire and hung my socks close in an effort to dry them, which made for a nice treat of warm socks in the morning. One drawback to being near the fire was that the smoke hung around the area, and everything picked up the smell of burnt wood.

My first goal for the day was Clingmans Dome, a 2.2-mile hike, and then it would be on to Newfound Gap, where I planned to take a shuttle into Gatlinburg for the evening. I had my clean pair of pants and shirt on that I normally only wore for bed and hoped that clean clothes would help me get a ride into Gatlinburg.

Hiker tips: I always kept a dry, clean pair of pants and shirt in my pack that I only wore in camp and into

town. Although some hikers considered that a luxury, I
felt it important to always have dry clothes to sleep in,
and the benefit of relatively clean clothes to wear while
hitchhiking into town should not be underestimated.

Obviously, I could not do much about my smelly body after three days of sweating and sleeping in smoke-filled shelters, but I hoped the clothes would help. I was looking forward to a shower and planned to resupply at The Happy Hiker store in Gatlinburg as well as have my pack checked for adjustment. I'd mentioned in the shelter the night before that I had a very sore rash on my hip from my pack and was met with a chorus of, "Join the club!" There's no sympathy from thru-hikers. One of them told me that the rash is part of "the price one pays for the opportunity of a lifetime."

Dying trees were very noticeable as I got closer to the Clingmans Dome area. The Fraser Firs were dying! It was very sad to see.

Finally, I saw my first wildlife on the trail. It wasn't the fearsome bear or the elusive deer I had hoped to see. No such luck; it was just a skinny little rabbit!

I got my first glimpse of Clingmans Dome from the trail, and I could see people walking up the ramp to the top. Clingmans Dome, said to be the highest point on the A.T., has a handicapped-accessible observation tower just a half-mile from the day-hiker parking lot. It was kind of an eerie feeling to see the dome at a distance, with the tower rising up out of the forest in the shape of a space ship and people going up and down the ramp like aliens shuttling back and forth to the ship. To be honest, I didn't find it a pretty sight after having walked for weeks, and seeing only the natural forms of mountains and forest.

When I passed a sign that read, "Clingmans Dome, .3 mile," there sitting on top of the sign was a can of Sprite with a note that read, "For Grandma Sole." Evidently a trail angel had been up early! I was tempted to take a drink, but didn't. Still, I thought, those trail angels shouldn't tease me like that. As I headed toward Clingmans Dome, I went through and over a number of blow-downs right on the trail, which puzzled me. Then, with an "Ah!" I suddenly realized why the trail was a mess: I'd gotten off the A.T. and onto a side trail to the parking lot. Backtracking to the A.T., I realized I would put an extra mile on my day because I wasn't paying attention to the white blazes.

When I got back to the A.T., I noticed the soda for Grandma Sole was still there. She was lucky it wasn't a Guinness, considering the mood I was in after hiking a mile off the trail. On I went, and as I passed under the Clingmans Dome tower, I reached another milestone: an elevation of 6,642 feet, the highest point on the trail.

When I stopped for lunch, I checked the sore on my hip, and it looked worse than before. I had used some duct tape to keep the Band-Aid from rubbing off, which worked, but what I didn't expect was that the duct tape would cause more sores. Live and learn, I guess. I would be glad to get into town and get the sores cleaned up.

I had some fun with a couple of boys who came hiking along, obviously very tired. When they asked how far it was to Clingmans Dome, I answered with a straight face, "Oh, about ten miles." Their chins dropped to the trail before I told them I was just kidding. As they hiked on, I heard one of them mutter something like, "...damn old crazy hiker." Obviously, they did not appreciate my attempt at some trail humor.

It turned out to be easy to get to Gatlinburg. A fellow by the name of Leon was hanging around the parking lot at Newfound Gap. "Five bucks will get you to Gatlinburg," he sang out with a local southern drawl, music to my ears. But Leon wouldn't start his car until he got paid. "I was ripped off once when I took a hiker to town," he said. "I didn't collect the money until we got to town, and wouldn't you know it, the SOB said he didn't have any money! Now I collect before we leave the Gap!" He took me and a couple other hikers to the Grand Prix hotel – which had special rates for hikers – and agreed to pick me up in the morning for a shuttle back to Newfound Gap.

After checking in and cleaning up, I walked to the nearby Happy Hiker camp store and had my picture taken as a thru-hiker for the year 2000. I wondered if this was the same camp store where Bill Bryson, in his book, *A Walk In The Woods*, stopped and decided to get off the trail after looking at a wall map of the entire Appalachian Trail. I saw a map hanging on the wall and asked the owner, who proudly told me the story was true, adding, "That is the exact map he was looking at when he realized he had only come two inches!" I had to admit, when looking at the entire distance of the trail on the wall map, the two hundred miles I had walked so far did seem quite insignificant.

I met up with Bob Illi and we went to O'Charley's for dinner, where Bob told me about an emergency he'd been involved with in the Georgia mountains. Bob was one of the thru-hikers who came across a hiker in his tent, suffering from hypothermia. Bob hiked on to the Blue Mountain shelter for help and luckily met a hiker with a cell phone who was able to call in an emergency crew to remove the young hiker from his tent. "I don't know if he would have survived if he hadn't been rescued," Bob shared in a very serious tone.

After dinner came laundry, and it took a long time. The lines in the laundry area could get long when hikers came in off the mountain, and with the talk of rain, a lot of hikers were coming in for the night.

Had the opportunity to also make final arrangements to meet my wife in Hot Springs for our first visit since I had been on the trail. Her Easter weekend break from teaching had come at a perfect time to allow a brief visit and an opportunity for me to take a day off from the trail.

April 17, Newfound Gap (Gatlinburg, Tennessee) to Tri-Corner Knob Shelter (milepoint 218.2 north)

Got out onto the trail about 10 a.m., which was later than I had planned. When Leon picked me up, I talked him into taking me to the post office before heading up to the trail. He reluctantly agreed but said he would need to stop for fuel first. When Leon went in to pay for the gas, I reached into the special zipper pouch inside my pack where I kept the traveler's check. As a matter of caution, I'd wait until no one was around before getting my money out of my pack. But this time I was still in the process when Leon came back, which caused me to rush, and I ended up misplacing the check! I looked all over the interior of the car before I got out, but I couldn't find it. At least it was a traveler's check.

I had a big day planned, hoping to get to Tri-Corner Knob Shelter about fifteen miles away, which meant I would be hiking most of the day. It was cool and misty, and this made the Smokies look very smoky, as if they were on fire! My pack felt a lot better, thanks to some assistance from staff members at The Happy Hiker camp store. It seems I had been carrying my pack too low on my hips, hence the severe abrasion.

I talked to a section-hiker and asked him about Mountain Momma's, a restaurant and lodging facility famous among thru-hikers just off the trail in Tennessee near Davenport Gap. He said that he had eaten there last year (had the famous big hamburger) and thought it was still open. I had not been able to get any firm information as to whether Mountain Momma's was still open or what the hours were. I'd bought some extra food in Gatlinburg just in case it was closed, so I wouldn't be stranded without food.

I walked along a cliff called Charlie's Bunion which, according to the *Appalachian Trail Thru-Hikers' Companion*, was created by a landslide after a disastrous rain in 1929. The cliff got its name when it was discovered by two hikers named Horace and Charlie, who, as the story goes, thought it looked like the bunion on Charlie's foot. The

National Park Service blasted the trail out so hikers could safely cross. This section of the trail was actually what I envisioned the A.T. to be like, as I was up on the ridgeline, eye-level with the surrounding peaks.

It started to rain again, making me glad I'd left my pack cover on. The rain reminded me of a story Bob Illi told. He and Tom, the South African, had been trying to set their tents up in a hard cold rain and were having a great deal of trouble. The water was running off the mountain so hard that everything was awash, and Bob couldn't find a level place to stake down his tent. He resorted to digging a trench around his tent and was busy working on his plan when he heard Tom shouting. "Illi! Illi! Illi! I'm floating away! I'm floating away!" When he reached Tom, it took all the strength they had to pull Tom's tent back up out of the water. As he told me the story, Bob could hardly hold back the tears of laughter at the thought of Tom believing he was about to float away.

When I arrived at the shelter, soaked to the skin in the numbing, frigid rain, I asked, "Any room in the shelter for one more?" and was greeted with silence and blank stares. The entire scene brought to mind a picture I had seen of prehistoric cave dwellers. The wet, shivering, mud-stained hikers huddled together in the cave-like stone shelter resembled – at least a little – prehistoric cave dwellers, with a small wood fire emitting a cloud of smoke that hung throughout their damp, dark shelter.

I set my tent up in a cold, cold rain that evening. With the combination of rain and my perspiration from the rigorous hike, I was soaked both inside and out. So as soon as I got my tent up and filtered some water, I changed out of wet clothes – drying off the best I could – and climbed into my sleeping bag. Was I glad to have a set of dry clothes! I don't believe there was any way I would have survived the night without them. It was raining so hard and was so cold that I broke all the rules about not cooking in my tent, especially in the Smokies. I lay wrapped in my sleeping bag and cooked my meal in the tent vestibule. Not only that, but I didn't hang up my pack or food bag, just praying that I wouldn't attract every damn bear and varmint in the Smokies. Regardless, the warm beef and noodles – a dehydrated meal I'd purchased back at Newfound Gap – really hit the spot after a freezing, wet, fifteen-mile hike. It wouldn't be a pleasant night, but at least I figured to be dry and warm. With the rain pouring down and the temperature plummeting, I was not going anywhere but to sleep, and I could tell this was going to be one of the nights on the Appalachian Trail that would truly test my mettle!

April 18, Tri-Corner Knob Shelter to Davenport Gap (Mountain Mama's) (milepoint 234.5 north)

I got up just before 8 a.m. after one cold, wet, miserable night --- without question the worst night on the trail yet. I'd had to add layers of clothing during the night. Thank God for my puffball jacket, which allowed me to get through the night! By the time I got up, I had a very wet tent, and all my clothing was wet as well. I was extremely glad my down sleeping bag had a special coating on the outside to keep it dry.

As if being soaked weren't bad enough, one of the shelter occupants approached me as I packed up my rain-soaked tent and gear. He had the audacity to ask, with a very obnoxious grin on his face, "Did you survive the night?" I was tempted to bust him in the mouth but resisted the urge and simply gave him a look that it seemed he instantly deciphered. He wisely moved on. I found it interesting that he'd not been at all concerned about my welfare the night before, and I wondered if I was correct in assuming that the morning's inquiry was simply an attempt on his part to get me talking about how miserable I'd been. I tended to think so! As I'd heard early on in my hike, the nice thing about the Appalachian Trail is that when you meet a jackass of that caliber, you just hike on! Enough said!

> *Hiker tips: A word of caution to potential thru-hikers in regards to the supposed unwritten rule, "There is always room in a shelter for a hiker on a dangerously cold wet night." Do not count on that. If you are planning to hike without a tent, do not do it.*

It looked like it was going to be a long day, with sixteen miles on the trail and a one-mile road walk down to Mountain Momma's. But after the ordeal of the night before, I didn't think a five-hundred pound bear sitting in the middle of the trail would stop me from getting a roof over my head! I just prayed that Mountain Momma's was open and that there was room in one of the cabins. I needed to dry out!

The water rushed down the trail as if I were walking upstream on a cold, windy and rainy day in the Smokies, but at least the water wasn't muddy, and by 8:30 a.m., I already had four miles in. The day before, I hadn't gotten onto the trail until ten o'clock, a major negative of hitchhiking into town.

I hiked toward Mountain Momma's with Gecko Goat, a former thru-hiker who appeared to be quite knowledgeable of the trail. When I asked how he knew so much about the trail, he roared, "Hell, I tried thru-hiking four different times before I finally made it!" He had decided to try it one more time for the year 2000. "God knows why," he said. He sheepishly mentioned he had been in the shelter last night when I asked for space, and he tried to justify not responding to my question by saying there had been twenty-five people in the shelter, but I could tell he was embarrassed at not making room for a fellow thru-hiker. He did tell me that Mountain Momma's closed at 5 p.m., so I needed to be there before that in order to eat or get lodging. He added that he'd heard that Mountain Momma's might not have bunks anymore at all. Not what I wanted to hear!

When I passed by the relatively new Davenport Shelter, at first I thought it was someone's home, the smoke rising from what looked like a quaint little forest cabin. Although tempted, I decided to take a chance and hike on to Mountain Momma's. The pull of her legendary hamburger overpowered any thoughts I had of stopping at the shelter.

I hiked up to a road and found a sign that read, "Mountain Momma's Kuntry Store, bottom of the hill turn left, open seven days a week 8 to 8, 1 1/4 miles." Just what I had been looking for! Besides yearning for a tummy-busting hamburger, I really needed to set my tent up and let it dry out. But there would be no hitchhiking. From the look of the small gravel road, it seemed unlikely I would be seeing any type of motorized vehicle. Another sign down the road read, "Mountain Momma's Kuntry Store, Your almost Thar." There was no question of what part of the country I was in!

A little after 10 that night, I prepared for bed in the small bunkhouse next to Mountain Momma's. A number of hikers were staying the night. Most were staying in the little bunkhouses that reminded me of small tool sheds you might find in backyards. Just a roof, rafters and siding, but that was all I needed to keep me out of the rain. Besides, what could you expect for ten bucks? And I was able to take a warm shower, enjoy a good hot meal, and talk with other hikers until Mountain Momma's closed up at 8 o'clock.

> *Hiker tips: Mountain Momma has a nice little country store where she serves a great hamburger and hikers can relax in a booth or at a table. The food and lodging made for a great layover just outside the Smokies, and I certainly would recommend it. A caution, however: Have cash, as Mountain Momma doesn't accept checks or credit cards!*

As I drifted off, I realized that I was officially out of the Smokies: seventy miles in five days! Although it had been an enjoyable hike, the rain and hassles involved with the shelters made me glad I was through the Smokies.

April 19, Davenport Gap (Mountain Momma's) to Max Patch Summit (milepoint 250.5 north)

After a relaxing night's stay in the Mountain Momma's Hilton bunkhouse, we were treated to a most unusual and enjoyable shuttle back to the trail: a flatbed wagon pulled by an old 1951 John Deere A tractor. The familiar "putt, putt" had the thru-hiking city boys wondering, "What the hell is that noise?" as Mountain Momma's husband fired up his old Johnny popper in the barn for the ride back up the mountain to the trail.

A section-hiker with the trail name of Dead Horse, who had been hiking with Bob Illi, asked if I minded company. I told him that would be O.K., but reminded him that I would be hiking my own hike and assumed he would be doing the same. Having seen him on the trail, I knew he had a faster pace than I did. At times his erratic pace had actually reminded me of a wild horse, so I told him I didn't want him walking all over me. He smiled. "I know what you mean," he said, "and I actually want to slow down a bit anyway."

I crossed a creek with a six-pack of Old Milwaukee's best lying in it, along with a note from Lone Wolf saying, "Have a great day!" I'd met Lone Wolf earlier in the hike. He knew a lot about the trail, and I think he had hiked the section a number of times and now had turned trail angel. It was a little early for me to be drinking a beer, though.

The trail was very slick, and a moss-covered log Dead Horse stepped on was particularly slippery. He went down like he'd been shot with a rifle! I asked him if he was hurt. "Nothing hurt but my pride," he said with an embarrassed grin. Once I knew he wasn't hurt, I could not hold back my laughter: as he lay on the trail, splattered in mud, with his glasses sitting cock-eyed on his head.

Seconds later, I sat in mud up to my waist. "Damn, would you believe it? As soon as I laugh at old Dead Horse, down I go. That should teach me." Luckily, I had landed on my butt, unlike Dead Horse, who took a real header into the mud. I could tell that my tumble made Dead Horse feel a little better, although he would not admit it.

As we were walking along, I glanced over at Dead Horse and noticed that one of the lenses from his glasses was missing. I again had a good laugh at how comical he looked with his mud-spattered face and one of the lenses missing. I asked him about it and he had no idea what I was talking about. "Heck!" he said. "I didn't even realize it was missing. That fall back there really shook me up."

We passed a sign that read, "Watch your step, beware of woodchucks." That was a first for that type of sign on the A.T. I wasn't sure what it meant, perhaps only that someone had an interesting sense of humor. As we continued up Snowbird Mountain, we hiked with one foot in North Carolina and the other foot in Tennessee.

We reached Max Patch Bald about half past six that evening. What a beautiful sight! As I lay in my tent on top of Max Patch and watched the most magnificent sunset I had ever seen, I couldn't help but think, "This is definitely the best spot that I have camped." The view certainly explained the large number of people who had driven up on a nearby road.

A local couple told me that Max Patch was originally forested but that early settlers cleared the mountaintop to graze sheep and cattle. The Patch was so large that at one time it was used as a landing strip for small airplanes. The U.S. Forest Service now used mowing and controlled burns to maintain the panoramic views of the Smokies to the south and Mount Mitchell to the east.

A few other hikers were also camped at Max Patch for the night. One in particular, whom I named Solitary, was – to put it gently – a strange young fellow. As I was setting up my tent, I gave him a friendly "Hello!"

He said very sternly, "I'm up here for solitude."

I thought to myself, "Well, excuse me," and went about my business of setting up my tent and visiting with a couple of locals from Tennessee who had come up to view the sunset. We were taking pictures and discussing the area when Solitary meandered up and asked, "Would you take my picture?" So much for solitude. But he was young, and I should give him the benefit of youth and just assume he was still trying to find himself.

Enjoyed a gorgeous evening and sunset, and then watched the lights of the towns and cities appear off in the distant mountains and valleys. I bedded down in God's lap for a good night's sleep!

April 20, Max Patch Summit to Hot Springs, North Carolina (milepoint 270.5 north)

I awoke to a beautiful sunrise on the summit of Max Patch. It had been twenty-three days since I started my hike, and I still marveled at the magnificent views – pictures simply could not do them justice. And Max Patch was no exception.

Once on the trail, we soon arrived at Walnut Mountain Shelter, the shelter that would have been our stop for tonight if we hadn't pushed further than expected the day before. It was not a very nice shelter and I was glad we weren't staying for the night. But then, compared to Max Patch, none of the shelters could measure up. We were making good time and began to talk about going all the way into Hot Springs, but that would be twenty miles which I had never done in one day.

By a little bit after noon, Dead Horse and I felt dead after climbing Bluff Mountain, which has an elevation of 4,686 feet. It was break time and I got out my GORP! It was a beautiful day for hiking, but eleven more miles to Hot Springs seemed like a lot to my already tired body.

Two very tired hikers, we made it to the shelter by 4 p.m.; and the urge to get into the town of Hot Springs pushed us north. I wasn't sure what pushed Dead Horse; but for me, the motivation was a scheduled reunion with my wife, who would be arriving in Hot Springs the next day. Even so, a little more than an hour later the hike into town had turned us into zombies. It had been a long day and too long a hike! Far too long! Exhausted physically and mentally, we had pushed ourselves too far.

But we finally made it to Hot Springs, the Old Mountain Slayer reaching the city limits with Dead Horse right behind. "Old," this time, was appropriate, for my rubbery legs made me feel like I would expect to feel when I'm 90. We'd hiked 19.8 miles, and that was too many.

There was a nice plaque at the city limits welcoming A.T. hikers into the town. The trail travels right down the center of town, past diners and hotels, and we hoped to find a nice place to stay and enjoy a good meal after ten hours of hiking. My body was screaming for rest and food!

April 21, Hot Springs, North Carolina (milepoint 270.5 north)

Although the nearly twenty miles we had hiked the day before was too much, it certainly was nice waking up in a nice warm bed at the Alpine Motor Lodge, especially after hearing the rain on the roof throughout the night.

I was looking forward to a relaxing day in town and to seeing my wife for the first time since starting the trail. After experiencing the terrific night on Max Patch, I hoped to drive Connie up to the mountain so she could actually get a feel for the views I had been raving about almost daily.

Dead Horse and I ate dinner with a young man whose trail name was HaHa, the youngest thru-hiker I had met on the trail. He'd just graduated from high school the year before. We found out that he was the hiker who had left the guitar in one of the shelters in the Smokies. "Man," he said, "it just got too heavy!" I asked HaHa how his parents felt about his hiking the trail at such a young age. "They're very supportive," he said. "As a matter of fact, my dad hiked for the first two weeks, and he was having such a great time he actually thought about quitting his job and hiking the entire trail!" HaHa told us, dejectedly, "I had planned on quitting the trail here in Hot Springs. I was just getting too depressed and lonely." But several friends had talked to him about the idea, he said. "So I thought I would continue for awhile and see what happens."

Connie arrived about 3 p.m., and we toured the booming metropolis of Hot Springs to see the sights. Not a real challenge: Hot Springs was a very small town, about 650 people, with most of its businesses right along Main Street. More importantly, though, it was a trail-friendly town. We had dinner at the Smoky Mountain Diner just up the street from our hotel. We had made reservations for the hotel about two weeks earlier, and it was a good thing because there were no more rooms available.

Although I was not able to actually meet with Dan Bruce (Wingfoot), who lived in Hot Springs, I was able to have a nice talk with him over the phone. His web page (http://trailplace.com/) had made it possible for me and other thru-hikers to post journals for friends and family to read.

With my wife's assistance, I washed and dried my filthy sleeping bag, tossing a tennis shoe into the dryer with it to help it fluff up. We both enjoyed the message posted in the laundry room:

"Do not sit on the Dryers or Washers and PLEASE remain CLOTHED at all times while in the laundry room-Thank you." A message not without merit!

We visited the Bluff Mountain Outfitters store, and I found I had lost more than fifteen pounds since starting my thru-hike. My weight loss was very noticeable when I put my blue jeans on: I took my belt in a couple of notches. A sure-fire method of weight loss: put on a forty-pound pack and start hiking north from Springer Mountain.

> *Hiker tips: The Bluff Mountain Outfitters, located right on Main Street, was very hiker-friendly and even helped arrange to shuttle hikers to nearby towns for rooms. It was a seventy-mile hike to the next town on the A.T. after Hot Springs, so hikers needed to resupply before heading out. There was also a hiker hostel in town.*

April 22, Hot Springs, North Carolina (2nd day) (milepoint 270.5 north)

My second zero-day, and we finally made it to Max Patch where I had spent a beautiful evening a few days earlier. I had been looking forward to sharing the magnificent view with my wife and could not believe what we encountered on top of Max Patch: fog, sleet, and snow! The ground was covered with snow, the trees were coated with ice, and I could literally not see across the parking lot because of the fog. It was thirty-three-degrees, tremendously different from the beautiful evening I had spent there earlier in the week. How quickly and dramatically weather could change in the mountains!

On our way back down the mountain we picked up two hikers trying to get to Hot Springs. It was my first chance to help out a couple of fellow hikers, and it was interesting comparing notes. It appeared the two were actually doing what is called yellow blazing, a term thru-hikers use to describe hikers who hitchhike sections of the trail.

Back in Hot Springs, we checked on church for the evening and found a small Jesuit Mission Church with a 7 p.m. Mass. The small A-frame chapel had windows high above the altar that gave us a wonderful view of the mountains as evening settled on the quaint little village. Only 18 worshippers attended, which made the service unique. After Mass, we went to dinner at the Creekside Inn, where I pampered myself with a dinner of baked cod in crabmeat sauce, knowing it would probably be awhile until I got another opportunity to have as nice a meal.

I was not particularly happy about the cold and rainy forecast, so I put an extra coating of "snow-seal" on my shoes as I prepared to head out the following morning toward Erwin, Tennessee, which would be a good four-or-five-day hike.

April 23, Hot Springs, North Carolina to Little Laurel Shelter (milepoint 291.3 north)

On a sunny Easter morning, I crossed the French Broad River and headed north out of Hot Springs. Although it was sunny, as I looked up into the mountains, I could see a lot of clouds reinforcing the rainy forecast for the next few days. The two-day layover and visit with my wife had been a perfect time to rest my legs and take a break from the trail, as the weather had been terrible for hiking. Taking two days off also gave me the opportunity to clean all of my equipment and restock my supplies.

One of the major decisions I'd had to make during my two-day layover concerned my Nomad tent. Although the tent had served me well, I was a little concerned about the moisture build-up on the inside of the single wall tent. Given the particularly wet and cold weather I'd encountered during the last week of hiking, I'd asked Connie to bring my other tent, which had a rain fly, just in case I wanted to change. After lots of wavering, I decided to stay with my Nomad. It had worked well except for the moisture build-up, and, ultimately, its light weight persuaded me to stay with it. Besides, I planned on staying in shelters more as the thru-hiker population diminished the further north I hiked.

Just a mile or so out of town, I passed another trail ornament, a little-used camp chair.

> *Hiker tips: The unneeded equipment always looked so good on the store shelf, but after a few miles on a hiker's back, especially hiking uphill, it didn't look nearly as good!*

I passed through a small grove of honeysuckle in full bloom. The aroma was wonderful, but a closer sniff told me they were covered with bees, a good reason to head north a little faster!

As I crossed Rich Mountain, I met my first hiker of the day. His trail name was Molasses. While we visited over lunch, Molasses said, "I'm taking the un-polluted way home to Long Island, New York!" I asked how he got the trail name Molasses, and he said with a wink, "Guess I'm just going as slow as molasses."

Near Hurricane Gap, I passed a tombstone by the trail that read "In memory of Briggs R. Rufford, 1922-1983." Then, a short distance up the trail was another tombstone: "Jackie May Kelly Morris 1940-1990." I couldn't imagine a more beautiful location for a final resting-place.

As I arrived at Spring Mountain Shelter, I had traveled eleven miles, and the next shelter was eight miles away. Reading the register inside the shelter provided some laughs:

> *"April 22-Cold, Cold, Cold, I wish I was told. No, I have no fear, but I could still be drinking Beer! - Silver Tongued Rebel"*
> *"April 21- Guy at the outfitters said it would clear up today! Bastard got my hopes up! - Forest Outer"*

As I hiked on, I passed my first thru-hiker impersonator and had been told by other thru-hikers about people out on the trail impersonating thru-hikers. After weeks on the trail it was relatively easy to spot other thru-hikers, taking into account pack size, skin tone, cleanliness, what they knew, what they said, and, yes, their smell. What really puzzled me was why a hiker would try to pass as a thru-hiker when it was very obvious he or she wasn't.

Arrived at the Cherokee Forest, and I was looking at putting in another twenty-mile day. I didn't know what had gotten into me. I'd told myself that I would ease up on the big-mile days, and here I was doing another big day. I hadn't intended to hike so far, but, on the other hand, I couldn't see wasting time in a shelter on such a beautiful day. According to my *Data Book*, I had five miles to go to my planned stop at Little Laurel, and it looked like an elevation gain of a thousand feet.

It was quarter after six when I arrived at the Little Laurel Shelter. Although still nice out, I planned to stay in the shelter. There was a lot of talk around the shelter about rain coming in.

There were seven or eight of us in the shelter. Two of particular note were a young woman with the trail name of Miss America, who had a smile and body measurements to match, and Xena, a nice young lady who happened to be a former Marine with the looks of Xena, the television warrior princess. Xena mentioned that she'd had her dog with her on the trail for awhile and was going to be getting it back in the next few days. She really missed her dog, but having it with her, she said, "caused a lot of bad feelings on the trail. Other hikers really got upset when my dog was drinking out of a water supply close to camp."

During the evening, another of the hikers told me that a train from New York City (Train 22) went right over the A.T. near Bear Mountain. I filed that away mentally to share with my daughter, who lives in New York City. She was planning to hike with me for a few days.

Late in the evening, Xena went to the latrine; and when she came back, she was stuttering and stammering and her eyes were the size of a silver dollar. When we asked her what was wrong, she said, "I heard something moving around outside the latrine while I was on the head." She smiled hesitantly, then added, "It certainly was *not* a bunny!" Her tale sparked a lot of speculation about bears, and I said jokingly, "What the heck, as long as we have Xena the Warrior, we have nothing to fear, right?" There was no reply, just a feeble hint of a smile. I could tell it would be a quiet crowd in the shelter, and I thought, "Pity the poor S.O.B. who comes into this shelter late tonight!" Fortunately, for all concerned, it was an uneventful evening.

April 24, Little Laurel Shelter to Flint Mountain Shelter (milepoint 302.5 north)

I got up and packed on a drizzling morning. It had rained throughout the night, so it was nice to wake up in a dry shelter and not have to pack up a wet tent. I felt good, even after the twenty-mile hike the day before. With one big mountain planned for the day, I hoped my legs would not tire out.

Finally made it to the ridgeline after a climb of 1,200 feet straight up, no switchbacks! I was learning that when I looked up the mountain, and the trail had logs every four or five feet to prevent erosion, I would be in for a steep climb.

> *Hiker tips: To save weight, I had cut the pages out of my Data Book and my handbooks, then put several week's worth of pages from each book in a Ziploc bag. My wife would send new pages periodically in a maildrop. That meant they were much lighter to carry, stayed dry and I could also read the pages through the bag, rearranging the pages at night in the shelter or tent.*

Saw another new face on the trail, Wild Rover. Since I had been putting in some big mile days, I was meeting a lot of new hikers, an unexpected treat of hiking bigger miles.

I reached Jerry Cabin Shelter in the rain, and a huge piece of plastic was hung across the opening of the shelter. It must have been cold the night before. It looked like I would be tenting in the rain tonight, as there were six more miles to go until the next shelter.

As I climbed up Big Butt Mountain (Don't you just love the mountain names?), there was a pair of pants and a shirt lying along the trail, and I remembered noticing a pair of hiking shoes in a corner back at Jerry Cabin Shelter. I just hoped I wouldn't find a body lying along the trail!

Another memorial along the trail read, "Howard E. Bassett of Connecticut. Died Nov. 9, 1987, hiked A.T. in 1968, ashes on this spot, 1988." There was a small cairn of stones with some flowers around it.

I arrived at the top of Big Butt Mountain to find great views and automobile-sized boulders. There were several memorials and tombstones as well. One of particular interest was that of William and David Shelton, uncle and nephew. They were Union sympathizers who enlisted in a U.S. regiment during the Civil War. While headed home for a family gathering, they were ambushed and killed near that spot by a Confederate force.

It was just after four o'clock when I hiked up to the Flint Mountain Shelter. I had walked more than twelve miles, so I was pleased with my progress in spite of the fact that I was stopping earlier than planned. A fellow named Dave was already bundled up in his sleeping bag. From the warmth of his sleeping bag, he mumbled, "A hell of a big group of hikers just left and planned on staying at the next shelter." Given that, I figured it was best to stay at Flint Mountain for the night to ensure a dry place to sleep. It looked like another cold and rainy evening in North Carolina.

I cooked a hot dinner, which tasted very good on a cold, wet night and then headed straight for my sleeping bag.

April 25, Flint Mountain Shelter to Bald Mountain Shelter (milepoint 321.3 north)

By 7:30, I was up on a cold – but for the moment, rainless – morning, headed to a shelter about eighteen miles up the trail.

The shelter had been crowded last night, and some hikers slept in their tents. Not everybody was happy. As I headed north on the trail, I passed Dave, who growled, "I'm glad to be out of that damn shelter!" He was particularly irritated with a young woman who hiked in, and even though other hikers were tenting or moving on because of the crowded shelter, she pleaded, "Oh, please make some room for me." She eventually squeezed in, much to the dismay of others who had no room to spare.

It had also been noisy in the shelter. Some people just liked to talk more than others, so sharing space with strangers could make for some interesting group dynamics. But I thought that the benefits of dry gear and a quick start in the morning outweighed the value of sleeping in a tent when the weather was poor. I tried to be very quiet when I got up, but very soon most were getting up. Still, I continued to be surprised at how noisy and inconsiderate some of the hikers were in the morning. One fellow got his stove out and lit it up right in the middle of the shelter, and I swear it sounded like an F-14 Tomcat taking off! He was obviously not the most popular person in the shelter; but when you stay in the shelter; you need to be prepared for an assortment of people.

Dave admitted he was emotionally down and thinking about getting off the trail, so it didn't take much to ruffle his feathers. His wife had been hiking with him but she'd had enough by the time they reached Hot Springs and had left there. With that and with his feet really hurting, he said it wouldn't take much more for him to call it quits.

I told him, "The nice thing about the trail is that if you don't like the people in the shelter you can just hike on."

"Not really," he groused. "It seems that the people who are really getting on my nerves happen to be walking at the same pace as I do, so I've been with them every goddamn night!"

Met a nice young couple in the shelter last night. The woman was from New York and her fiancé was from Georgia, two obviously different backgrounds. She said that her father was helping finance their hike, saying, "If you two can walk from Georgia to Maine and stay engaged, then you have a good chance for a successful marriage and my blessings!"

I passed the most bizarre trail ornament I had seen abandoned along the trail to date: a sleeping bag left open by the side of the trail! I could see getting rid of gear to reduce weight, but your sleeping bag? Some things are just baffling.

It started raining hard enough that I had to put on my rain gear. I took shelter in a tobacco barn by the side of the trail to put my pack cover on. Just off Boone Cove, the barn was neatly kept, and I could tell that hikers had been using it for a shelter because of the strings with the tuna cans tied to them to keep the mice from getting to their food bags.

I slid coming down off Frozen Knob mountain on a very foggy, wet day, which turned the hard-packed trail to grease, giving me the sense of skating on ice. I fell hard several times. The trail was very slick and extremely difficult to hike, but luckily, I didn't break or pull anything.

Even though it was still raining and the hiking was very difficult when I arrived at Hogback Ridge Shelter, it was too early to stop and I hoped to make it to the next shelter ten miles away.

Not long after that, I found myself totally fogged in. I had no idea where I was except that I was hiking up a mountain, and thank God for the white blazes! Sloshing along in mud and rain, I decided to take a picture of the only things I had seen all day: my feet. It was bitterly cold, and according to my *Data Book*, I had about four more miles to the shelter. I prayed there would be room for me. I didn't even want to think about trying to dry out, eat dinner and sleep in my tent!

I was at the top of some bald but had no idea which one, still following the white blazes, the only thing I could see in the thick fog. With no signs visible, I assumed I was getting closer to the shelter as I took the last bite of the Snickers bar I had kept stashed in my pocket. It tasted as if I had just taken it out of the freezer. The weather stayed windy and rainy – just plain miserable – and even though I was tired, there was no way I could possibly have stayed on the mountaintop. I would have frozen to death.

"Thank God!" I found my first sign in hours. It read, "Big Bald, Elevation 5,568 feet." I had to be getting close to the shelter now and was just praying for room at the inn.

Just then, I felt a burning sensation in my shin as I went slipping and sliding down the mountainside as though I were on snow skis.

These were, without a doubt, the most treacherous conditions I had experienced so far on the trail. I could only hope that I would arrive at the shelter instead of ending up comatose on the side of the mountain.

I finally staggered into the shelter about 6:15 p.m., and even though there was a large number of people in the shelter, they immediately made room for me. I really needed to rest my legs after the nearly nineteen-mile hike, which felt more like twenty-five in the mud and fog. I was never so happy to be anywhere in all my life than in the shelter. If there hadn't been so many people there, I believe I would have kissed the damn thing!

April 26, Bald Mountain Shelter to Erwin, Tennessee (milepoint 338.1 north)

As I prepared to head out of the shelter, I certainly had a number of individuals to thank. When I struggled into the shelter the night before, a Boy Scout Troop from Mentor, Ohio, not only made room for me but also shared some very warm and greatly appreciated bean soup. Not only that, but before the night was over, three hikers – Dandelion, Siler and Summertime – and a ranger squeezed in as the weather turned very cold with pounding rain and sleet: a night that demanded a shelter. When Siler came in showing all the symptoms of extreme hypothermia, again the Boy Scouts and their leader jumped into action, getting him into dry clothes and giving him some warm food. "I wasn't sure if I was going to make it," Siler mumbled. It was a dangerously cold night in the mountains.

So I was headed to Erwin, Tennessee, wearing my only dry clothes; I just could not bring myself to put on wet, cold clothes. I figured I would definitely find some place in Erwin to sleep, then clean and dry everything out.

> *Hiker tips: Not only is it nice and comfortable, but it can be vital to your survival to not only have a set of dry clothes and sleeping bag, but to keep those items in a waterproof bag!*

"The sun, the sun!" I yelled, as – for the first time in two days – the sun peeked out from wherever it had been hiding. The trail was still in miserable condition, however, and I slid with every step, especially on the downhill, sending a blast of pain up my right shinbone as if someone was kicking me in the shin with boots on.

At Spivey Gap, I decided to try out the PurLife water bottle I'd had Connie bring to Hot Springs. It worked just fine.

> *Hiker tips: I began using the PurLife water filter, a squeeze bottle that held about a liter of water and had*

*a filter on top of the bottle. All I had to do was fill it up
and the water was filtered as I drank. That eliminated
the need to carry large volumes of water (pack weight)
or spend time during the day getting my other filter out
and filtering water.*

I could see Erwin off in the distance and hoped to be there in a couple of hours. My leg seemed to improve with the condition of the trail. Oh, what a difference the weather can make in the outlook and mental state of a hiker!

By half-past-four that afternoon, I came down out of the mountain and found Johnny's Hostel right off the trail on the edge of Erwin, Tennessee. Johnny didn't have any private rooms for the night, which I really wanted. He said there were some rooms in town and offered to let me use his phone. About that time, I met a super trail angel named Jack, who was at the hostel helping out any thru-hiker he could, greeting us with a six-pack of beer! He also had his truck parked at the hostel and shuttled another hiker and me to the post office, the grocery store, and a coin laundry before finally taking me to the Holiday Inn.

I planned to treat myself to a very pleasant evening at the Holiday Inn after the last few nights in such adverse conditions on the trail. Besides, I wanted to make some calls and found it much easier to call from a phone in my room than one on a corner somewhere.

During the evening, I saw a few hikers I hadn't seen in the past few days, including Crash, who was staying at the Holiday Inn. "I hiked north ten miles out of town and blew out a shoe and had to come back for new shoes," he told me. His easygoing demeanor was certainly impressive.

April 27, Erwin, Tennessee to Cherry Gap Shelter (milepoint 354.5 north)

I doctored myself a little in the morning before heading out on the trail. The abrasion on my hip was inflamed and needed constant cleaning and care. One of my legs was stiff and sore, but I figured it would be all right; and while I knew my body needed another day's rest and I thought about staying, the weather was just too nice to spend indoors. I had food supplies for three days but hoped to reach Elk Park, North Carolina, before I ate all of the food, and I figured the planned fifteen-mile days would be a good test for my leg.

Someone had a shuttle lined up at the hotel, but I had eaten my breakfast and wanted to get on the trail early, so I walked out of the hotel and hitched a ride to the trail with a lady taking her kids to school.

It was still very cold. I had noticed the night before on the news that frost warnings had been issued for the area. I bet it was cold in a tent or shelter overnight in the mountains, I was wearing gloves and several layers just to start out the day. Some of the locals had commented on how late the frost was this spring, very unusual for Erwin, they said.

It was a beautiful morning! I continued to marvel at the extremes in weather: one day was just beautiful and the next might be miserable. I had come to learn to enjoy the beautiful days, to not take them for granted, and to accept and tolerate as much as possible the miserable days.

> *Hiker tips: With regards to carrying a cell phone on the trail, interestingly enough, up to Erwin, I hadn't heard one conversation on the topic. If hikers were carrying cell phones, I had not seen or heard them, so evidently hikers had been discreet in their use and therefore not been a concern one way or another. I did not carry a cell phone and saw no need to, but as long as the user is courteous and discreet, there should be no problem.*
>
> *A former thru-hiker said it best when he alluded that a cell phone should be used discreetly and in private, "as if it were toilet paper!"*

Around noon I stopped at Curley Maple Gap Shelter to eat a sandwich that I had carried from town, and I could tell my leg was not doing well. There was sharp pain with each step, and I realized I should have given it another day. I needed to reconsider my options, fearing I could be making it worse by hiking on it. According to my *Data Book*, there was a road ahead from which I could probably hitchhike back into Erwin. I really didn't want to do any back tracking, and if I were not making my leg worse, I figured I could handle the pain and hike out of it. Amazingly, as I was considering my options, I met another hiker who mentioned that there was a doctor with the trail name of Blaze hiking right behind me!

I talked to Blaze. He indeed was a doctor, and he graciously examined my leg. "I don't think you're making it much worse, but you're surely not helping your knee recover, and it does need some relief time to heal," he told me, advising rest and ice. He also suggested that I take Ibuprofen every two to three hours to help reduce the inflammation. How lucky could I be, running into a doctor on the trail when I needed one? Blaze was fifty and was hiking the trail for the second time. He'd been on the trail since March 22nd, and I was surprised I had not heard of or met him before.

I decided to stay on the trail and limp to the next shelter; and just underway again, I entered the Beauty Spot, a place that definitely deserved its name. I met two more trail angels up on Beauty Spot. A man and his wife were out for the day, and I asked them where I could find the closest water. They told me, but then kindly said "Better yet, you hike down the A.T. to the road and relax for a minute, and we'll bring you water." I hiked down to the road, and sure enough, up they drove in their pickup truck with a big cool jug of water. Blaze was there and they gave him some water, as they did for Lethal Weapon, a thru-hiker who hiked up just after they had arrived with their water.

I finally made it to Cherry Gap Shelter about 7:40 that evening. A number of hikers were staying in the shelter, including another group of Boy Scouts who flaunted the fact that it got down to 20-degrees last night at the Roan High Knob Shelter. That wasn't surprising, for I had heard that Roan High Knob was the highest shelter on the entire A.T. and was usually extremely cold. It was a beautiful evening, and I was very tempted to stay in my tent; but being too lazy to do so, I staked out some territory in the shelter. I still couldn't believe it could be so nice one moment and so wet and cold the next.

Some of the evening's camp stories were interesting. One hiker, whom I have yet to meet, has received the trail name of JERK. Apparently, he walks into shelters at the end of the day and immediately begins to order people around. If it happens to be a rainy day and the shelter is full, he simply informs everyone, "I do not have a tent, so someone is going to have to move over or get out!" Not a way to make friends on the trail!

Also in the shelter last night was the thru-hiker who came up while the trail angels were sharing water, a young woman – I would guess she's in her mid-twenties – with the trail name of Lethal Weapon. When asked how she got such a unique trail name, she said with a laugh, "When I decided to hike the trail, my father was so concerned for my safety he gave me a can of mace, a stun gun, a billy club and several other self-protection devices!" She said her father also walked with her the first day and realized that, if she wished, she could be in the company of other hikers the majority of the time. That, she said, seemed to ease his concerns at least a little.

April 28, Cherry Gap Shelter to Roan High Knob Shelter (milepoint 369.6 north)

Headed north on the trail at 7:30 a.m., and — what a surprise! — it was raining. The rain had started during the night, and for once it paid off to be lazy: by staying in the shelter I was headed out of camp with a dry tent and gear. The evening started out so beautifully, with not a cloud in the sky. Who would have ever thought the rain would have started so early last night?

I was a little stiff, and my right shinbone was still hurting; I hoped a couple Ibuprofen every three or four hours would help with the pain.

A thru-hiker named Woodchip, sixty-four years old and one tough lady, wasn't letting a little rain get her down. She tented the night before and got wet, but she had a smile on her face even as she packed up her tent in the rain.

As Woodchip and I hiked together for a few miles, I learned that we had a little in common. She, too, was a retired educator, in her case a one-time elementary physical education teacher. A member of a hiking club in New Hampshire who had hiked all over the world, she was an extremely articulate and interesting lady to chat with. Not only a strong hiker but also a very smart one, she kept a very even pace, which included frequent rest stops to replenish her energy level. As I said earlier, she was also very tough and determined: If anyone out on the trail were going to make it to Mt. Katahdin, it would be Woodchip!

I had been walking in the rain for most of the morning, so I decided to stop at Clyde Smith Shelter for a quick lunch and some water. I could tell I was getting higher up in the mountains, as it was very foggy and cool. I continued to remind myself that I needed to accept the bad days and remember they were part of the hike just as were the good days, but that acceptance is sometimes easier said than done.

At Hughes Gap, I topped the 4,000-foot elevation and headed to Roan High Knob, which is at 6,285 feet. I was definitely headed up. My leg was hurting badly, but I decided to walk through the pain. To be honest, I didn't have many alternatives.

I was still climbing when I met a couple of section-hikers headed south, down off the mountain, and they said I had a couple more miles — straight up! Oh, how those day hikers seemed to find real pleasure in making thru-hikers cuss.

Still hiking up at about 3:40 p.m., I couldn't believe my eyes. Snow? It was going to be one cold night on Roan Mountain!

Hiker tips: The saying, "You can send your warm clothing home after the Smokies" is not correct. The conditions on Roan Mountain, as well as at other locations, require that a hiker not send winter gear

*home until after Damascus. If I had not had my winter
gear for Roan Mountain, I would not have survived! I
was especially glad I had a set of warm dry clothes. I
would hate to think of trying to get through that night
on the mountain in wet clothes.*

Just took a picture of myself standing in snow six inches deep on
April 28! I figured I was on top of the mountain, but the fog was so
dense I could only see a couple of feet in any direction. Finding the
shelter was going to be tough in the fog.

It took me until 7:30 p.m. to locate the Roan High Knob Shelter.
What an ordeal! I missed the shelter sign and had to backtrack at least a
mile on the trail to find it. A very small wood sign up in a tree
identified the turn-off to the shelter. It was almost impossible to see,
especially in the thick fog. Lethal Weapon showed up a little later.
"You believe that damn dinky shelter sign?" she exclaimed. "I can't
believe I saw it!" We were really concerned about Woodchip; she had
told me she planned to stay at the shelter. With the fog and snow, we
knew how difficult it was just to follow the trail, let alone find the
shelter, and we certainly hated the thought of Woodchip tenting
overnight on the cold mountain. I even set my tent up inside the shelter
for extra warmth, while Lethal Weapon told me confidently, "I'll be in
good shape – I have a minus-20-degrees bag!"

After my arrival, I did go back to where the side trail to the shelter
met the Appalachian Trail. "Woodchip, hey Woodchip, you out there?"
I called, but there was no answer. I tried to make a crude arrow
pointing in the direction of the shelter, but I feared she had already
passed by.

While we ate dinner and before we hustled into our sleeping bags,
Lethal Weapon told me she was from New Jersey. She said she had
recently received her master's degree in sociology, but was no longer
sure that was what she wanted. Along with hiking the A.T., she had
also hiked in Ireland and Scotland in hopes of sorting things out. "My
parents are hoping I will find out what I want to do for a living, and
soon," she said with a hopeful smile.

Oh, was it cold, especially on the floor of the cabin! Looking at
the positive side, though, I had plenty of snow to ice down my leg.

*Hiker tips: Along with putting up my tent inside the
shelter, I boiled a liter of water in my Nalgene water
bottle and put it between my legs. I had read
somewhere that if you keep the main arteries in your
legs warm, the rest of your body would be warm and it
seemed to work!*

Compared to most, the Roan Mountain Shelter was actually very nice. Once a fire warden's cabin, it at least had four walls and a door.

According to the *Appalachian Trail Thru-Hikers' Companion* Roan Mountain was the coldest spot, year-round, on the southern A.T., and I didn't question that one bit. It was once the site of Cloudland Resort during the late 1800s and early 1900s, with the North Carolina-Tennessee state line running right through the Cloudland Hotel Ballroom, which was demolished in 1915. Roan Mountain was now famous for its rhododendron gardens, which usually bloomed in June.

"Bam, bam!" A pounding on the door and an explosion of activity came as three young hikers came bursting into the shelter! They looked to be almost frozen, decorated with icicles formed from the sweat of climbing the mountain. They were panting and laughing at the same time, as if they were overwhelmed with relief at finding the shelter. And I was utterly amazed that they were able to find the shelter in darkness after all the trouble I had in daylight! Maybe they had spotted my sad excuse for an arrow pointing toward the side trail? I did notice one of the hikers was a hiker I'd met before named Granite, but I was too cold to stick anything out of my sleeping bag and tent besides a nose and eyeballs. I figured morning would be soon enough to hear their stories, so I went back to sleep with the warm water in my water bottle tucked between my legs, still keeping my body comfortable.

April 29, Roan High Knob Shelter to U.S. 19E (Elk Park, North Carolina) (milepoint 384.3 north)

I left the coldest damn shelter I had ever stayed in, or hoped to stay in, at about 7:45 a.m., and headed back to the trail. Granite, one of the hikers to come in late, said that trail angel Jack was going to be down at the road at 4:30 p.m. and would take any of us into town who wanted to go. That sounded great, but my biggest goal at the moment was just to make it to the road. My leg was hurting already, and I had only walked across the shelter floor. The trail looked familiar as I headed north on a section of trail I had backtracked while looking for the shelter the night before. No one said that thru-hiking the A.T. was going to be easy!

Hard to believe, but the sun was popping out. What a beautiful sight! It looked like it was going to be a great day, an amazing contrast to the day before.

The views off the mountain were spectacular, and it was actually great to have any view at all, after seeing nothing but fog for the past few days. Up on Round Bald I had Roan Mountain behind me and to the north, the trail was laid out for as far as I could see!

When I arrived at the Stan Murray Shelter, I was damn glad I had not tried to reach it the night before. It would have taken me about three hours to hike down the mountain, and there was only enough room for ten people. Several tents were still up around the shelter, so there was no way I would have found room.

I passed a couple of "good old boys" digging what they call "Rams," or wild onions. "We fry them up with taters and eggs," they said. "Boy, are they good, but you really have to work for them."

"Stop with all that talk of taters and eggs," I begged. "You're killing this hiker!" One of them laughed, saying, "Sorry about that. We didn't know you Yankees liked taters and eggs!" "Now, how did you know I was a Yankee?" I joked with a smile.

Much to my surprise, I caught up with Woodchip on top of a bald about half past noon. She had, in fact, missed the shelter last night. "I had to keep going for fear if I stopped I would freeze to death!" she said. She told me how she walked down off the mountain in the fog. When she saw a road and parking lot, she decided to pitch her tent even though it was still wet from the previous night. "Then I saw an old pickup truck with a camper," she said. "I walked up and grabbed the handle on the camper door, and to my great relief it was unlocked, so I crawled inside with my pack and went right to sleep. It was great," she said with a tough, determined grin.

I thought to myself, "Now, that's one tough lady!"

Ate lunch on top of Hump Mountain, elevation 5,587 feet, with a beautiful 360-degree view of the quaint and peaceful towns and valleys. I had been hearing talk of cattle grazing up on the highlands, and as I dodged the cow patty evidence on the trail, it wasn't long until I came upon a herd of long-horned cattle that would seem at home in Texas.

I had not heard much about the Roan Highlands beforehand, but they really had some great vistas of all the little towns and farms tucked neatly into the valleys. Framed in the background of that picture were the beautiful mountains that seemed to go on and on, mountain upon mountain, in all directions. I could see it all from the highlands.

On passing Apple House Shelter, a 2000-mile hiker was setting up camp, a patch on his pack indicating he had already hiked the trail once. "Where did you stay last night?" he asked with a grin, knowing full well.

"The highest, coldest damn shelter on the trail," I responded without hesitation.

"You were on top of Roan Mountain last night, right?" he asked, answering his own question.

Gray Jane walked up and told me, "A trail angel by the name of Jack is waiting for you and your friends down at the road with a cold beer!" I turned and headed to the road, warning the others; "Anyone in my way will be run over!"

After a few minor detours, by 9 p.m. I was finally in a hotel room. The only hotel in Elk Park offered me a thirty-dollar room that was not clean. I was not happy; and Jack, the local trail angel, told me to jump back in the truck. He drove me to Johnson City, where he lived and I could get a room. Before that, he had told several of us hikers that we could not hike through this area without stopping at Shirley's Restaurant in Hampton for the best food for miles around. He said it was family style and all you could eat, a thru-hiker's panacea! He was right!

April 30, U.S. 19E (Elk Park, North Carolina) (milepoint 384.3 north)

My third zero-day on the trail was spent in Johnson City. I was really dirty when I came in; so cleaning up, getting a great night of rest, and icing my leg down really perked me up. When Jack dropped me off at the Holiday Inn, he and his wife invited me for dinner and really surprised me by offering to take my dirty clothes home and wash them. Only a former thru-hiker who really knew how to help a hiker would do something like that!

I called the local Catholic church in the morning for a schedule of services, then called a cab for a ride to the church. I was missing a beautiful day on the trail, but my leg really needed the rest; and the opportunity to go to church helped ease my desire to get back on the trail. Anyway, I had a maildrop to pick up in Elk Park.

> *Hiker tips: Elk Park has a post office, but due to logistics and office hours, it is not a very good place for a maildrop, especially on a weekend. A much more convenient maildrop would be in Damascus, Virginia, where the trail literally travels right through the heart of town.*

At St. Mary's Church in Johnson City, the priest was greeting people as they entered church. I asked him if he knew of anyone who would give me a ride back to the hotel. "Not to worry," he assured me. "That can be arranged. Just see me after Mass." After the service, he invited me to join the parishioners and have some juice and doughnuts. He said he would drop me off at the hotel himself. Father Gahagan introduced me to the congregation at the end of Mass and had me talk about home and my thru-hike on the A.T., so I had numerous people to talk with while I waited. I enjoyed my visit. I found that visiting churches along the trail was a bonus to the hike that I had not considered.

After a nice visit with Jack and his wife and some great strawberry shortcake I arrived back at my hotel room. My plan for the rest of the evening was to ice my leg. Jack's wife, a physical therapist, thought I had tendinitis and shin splints. Jack was good enough to take me to a Wal-Mart where I got an elastic wrap, which his wife thought might help along with some much needed rest and ice.

May 1, U.S. 19E (Elk Park, North Carolina) to Moreland Gap Shelter (milepoint 397.9 north)

I felt rested and clean. The layover had been wonderful and had really rejuvenated me, and I was more than ready to get back into the woods. I headed to Moreland Gap Shelter, about fifteen miles north, with perfect weather and birds singing again. It was certainly much more pleasant hiking in dry weather.

As I headed north on the A.T., the first creature I shared the trail with – to my great surprise and amusement – was a steer! The contrary bovine ambled up to within inches of my nose and would not budge. He looked me straight in the eyes as if to say, "Out of the way, hiker. This is my territory." After a couple of minutes in a stand-off, the steer snorted, shook his huge wooly head in one final demonstration of defiance, and reluctantly stepped off the trail and let me pass. Could it be my hiker smell finally paid off?

I had heard that the section I was hiking through was at one time a very hotly contested acquisition for the A.T. Apparently the A.T. had used a number of country roads and crossed private land in the area for many years without any trouble. But as the government decided to acquire the land to ensure access and get the A.T. off the roads, eminent domain was employed to obtain the land, and that created some understandable hard feelings among a number of the locals. The rumors concerning retaliation with the use of fishhooks hung from trees and placed in fence posts along the trail were doubtlessly tall tales, but they were disconcerting to thru-hikers just the same.

As I passed numerous hikers, I noticed they were all cheerful, with wide smiles. Good weather always raises the spirit of hikers.

I had talked with my daughter the evening before about the logistics for her joining me on the trail, and as we finished, she'd asked for my opinion on a matter she was dealing with at work. I probably hadn't been very helpful – I'd had trouble getting back to reality after being on the trail the past month.

> *Hiker tips: Many hikers found that after an extended time on the trail of dealing with nothing but the basics of life – food, water, and shelter – real-world affairs seemed mind-boggling. In many cases, hikers talked about their trail lives and their lives before the trail as separate worlds.*

The white blazes escorted me through a Christmas tree farm, with the aroma of spruce and pine absolutely invigorating. It was hard to believe that the same trail had been horrendous just a couple of days ago: wet, muddy and slick. Oh, what a difference the two days of dry weather had made.

While I ate lunch, I soaked my leg in a cold, cold mountain stream for about ten minutes, but that was about as long as I could take the bone-freezing water. Not long after I got underway again, I walked upon a snake, surprising myself and – I think – the snake. Even though it wasn't very big, I gave the reptile a wide berth. I'd been willing to take on a cantankerous steer, but there was no way I was going to challenge a snake.

I arrived at the Moreland Gap Shelter just before 5 p.m. after a fourteen-mile day and decided to find a spot in the shelter, as it looked like rain again. Cincinnatus and Brandon, two of a trio of young thru-hikers from Montana, were starting a campfire and planned on making bread, which was an interesting idea.

HaHa came into the shelter, and it was apparent he was still struggling with the decision of whether to stay on the trail. His recent challenges in getting to a maildrop in Elk Park, North Carolina, had not helped the situation. He grumbled, "I had a maildrop in Elk Park, and do you think I could get a lift? Hell, no! I had to hike two miles just to get back to the trail."

The smoke from the Montanans' campfire drifted into the shelter, so they courageously moved the fire without putting it out – not an easy task. And the homemade bread they made was a celebrated success, which had everyone salivating. As we ate, there was a lot of talk about the trail town of Damascus not far north. It was a stop we'd all heard so much about, said to be the friendliest town on the trail.

To my relief and delight, it turned out to be the first night I'd spent in a shelter that I didn't have to use earplugs. No one was snoring, an unexpected and appreciated treat.

May 2, Moreland Gap Shelter to U.S. 321 (Hampton, Tennessee) (Braemar Castle Hostel) (milepoint 412.6 north)

I left the shelter on a beautiful morning. I thought maybe I would have two days in a row without rain. It was turning into such a pleasant day that I actually stopped and zipped the legs off my pants to cool down. With all the cold weather, I had not seen my knobby knees in quite awhile.

> *Hiker tips: I hiked exclusively in Ex Officio hiking pants. The many pockets worked well for my different snacks and supplies, the pant leg zips were ideal for the continuous weather changes, and being 100 percent nylon, they were very tough and fast drying. The ability to use them as long pants or shorts enabled me to carry an extra pair, which I only used in camp and town. Although they were a bit expensive, I felt the convenience and durability were well worth the cost.*

I took the opportunity to take another break and soak my leg in the Laurel Falls Creek, as it was running full and again provided me with ice-cold water. While at the creek, I met three slackpackers – Straight Jacket, Candy Lady and Yaffa – all headed south to the Kincora Hiking Hostel in Hampton, Tennessee, an apparent haven for slackpackers. The term "slackpacking" describes the practice of hiking a section of the trail without a pack; a slackpacker gets a lift up the trail without a pack and then hikes back.

When I arrived at the Braemar Castle Hostel in the small town of Hampton, I was surprised there was only one other hiker staying. Apparently the two hostels that were right on the trail were getting most of the thru-hikers. The Braemar had nice clean rooms, a laundry, and a large kitchen that hikers were welcome to use; and the owner, Sutton Brown, even agreed to give me a ride back to the trail in the morning.

May 3, U.S. 321 (Hampton, Tennessee) (Braemar Castle Hostel) to Double Springs Shelter (milepoint 436 north)

As I waited for Sutton to give me a ride back to the trail, I read some old newspaper clippings about the hostel that were taped on the wall. "The Castle was originally constructed by the Pittsburgh Lumber Company to serve the Company workers staying in the Laurel Gorge area from 1909 until 1925." Sutton – whose grandfather had once owned the Braemar Castle – and his wife Beverly now offered hikers space, kitchen, and showers for ten dollars a night. "The original wood frame building contains fifty rooms," he said, "and the river rock from the area was added as a face to give jobs in the 1930s, and that gives it the look of a castle."

Also at the hostel the evening before had been a thru-hiker by the name of Turtle and his father. Turtle's father offered a little trail magic by taking some items to the post office for me so I could get an early start. The hostel was a fine place to stay. Beverly actually washed, dried, and delivered my clothes to my room while I was out, which I truly appreciated.

As I got going, I hiked past the Montana boys, who'd camped near the lake. They were up and had a fire going. They told me, with the clichéd bravado of youth, "We took a short swim in the lake last night. It was a bit refreshing!" The fine weather continued to put smiles on all the hikers' faces.

During the morning, I crossed the dam to Watauga Lake, where a sign indicated that the dam is 318 feet tall and 900 feet long. It was built by the Tennessee Valley Authority from 1942 to 1949, and, according to the sign, is "the only electricity-producing dam made of earth in the world." When it was built, it displaced about 700 people living along the riverbanks.

Right after noon I stopped at Vandeventer Shelter to have lunch with TC, whom I had not seen since Hot Springs. His trail name stood for his hometown of Travis City, Michigan. Quite a generous fellow, he gave me a small amount of water, all that he could spare. I was completely out of water, but the spring at the shelter was a half-mile off the trail, and there was no way I was going to walk a mile out of my way for water unless I was spitting cotton.

Later on I still had no water when I ran into Walkabout and Machine, the young couple from Australia hiking around the world. Good kids, they too were out of water. I told them, "You go ahead and smell the water out for me." With all the confidence in the world, Walkabout replied, "Will do, Mate."

It was 5 p.m. when I finally found water, and by that time, I was spitting cotton. And I wasn't at all surprised when I heard other hikers at the shelter also complaining about the distance between water and the apparent misinformation in the *Data Book*. Although the shelter where I got water was reasonably nice, with such a pleasant day, I decided to pass up the shelter to see what I could find up the trail.

I passed the Nick Grindstaff Monument, which was just an old chimney. According to *The Thru-Hiker's Handbook*, Grindstaff, known in the area as "Uncle Nick," was said to be one of the South's most famous hermits, having spent forty-six years living in the mountains as a recluse with a rattlesnake for his only friend!

Just after 7 p.m., I hiked up near Tennessee Highway 91. According to my *Appalachian Trail Data Book 2000*, there was a shelter about two and a half miles north. But it was late, so I picked out a site and started setting up my tent. With the high volume of traffic, I really didn't feel comfortable tenting right next to the road, so following my gut instinct, I packed up and headed north to the shelter.

I arrived at Double Springs Shelter in the dark. I had hiked twenty-three miles, from 7:30 a.m. to 8:40 p.m., and my body screamed that thirteen hours of hiking in one day was too much. But there was room in the shelter, and I felt much safer there than right next to a highway.

At the shelter I met a new hiker by the name of Giggle Girl, and believe me the name fit perfectly. Enough said. I also heard a lot of mice scurrying around the shelter, and when I mentioned it, one hiker concurred, "Had a mouse trot right up and over my sleeping bag."

May 4, Double Springs Shelter (Tennessee) to Damascus, Virginia (The Place) (milepoint 454.3 north)

I felt good in the morning, considering the previous day's high mile count and my late arrival at the shelter. Surprisingly, I hadn't been the last hiker in. Granite, a night owl, came in even later.

It was eighteen miles to Damascus. I planned on checking out the hostel there, but I was a little leery about staying in hostels after hearing Beta's tale. I'd met Beta – another thru-hiker – about one week earlier at Shirley's Restaurant near Elk Park, North Carolina. He'd had some gross-looking black matter attached to his ear, and when I asked about it, he shook his head in disgust and groaned, "It's a fungus I picked up from a hostel I stayed at and can't get rid of!" Not all hostels were dirty. The Braemar Castle Hostel was a good example of a very clean hostel, and I could only trust that there were no more hostels like the one Beta had unhappily found.

It was another beautiful day for hiking, and I kicked up a little dust on the trail and thought to myself, "Dust! Dust on the trail! This is the first time I've seen anything that resembles dust on the trail for God knows how long!" It would be my last day in Tennessee. I had been told that Virginia would level off for awhile, but I'd believe that when I saw it, for I'd heard that kind of bullfeathers many times on the trail.

Wolfman caught and passed me as I was talking into my tape recorder. "Man," he said, "am I glad to see you're talking into that recorder. At first I thought you had lost your mind and was talking to yourself!"

I took a quick break at Abingdon Gap Shelter before pushing on to Damascus, and by the entries in the register I wasn't the first hiker to come through the shelter looking forward to Damascus. One entry read,

"Damascus fever has taken over my mind, twenty three miles today, beer and burgers on the brain!"

It had been a lovely day, but about a mile from the Tennessee/Virginia state line, I found myself walking in rain again. I suppose it was a fitting end to my hike through Tennessee, and it would not have surprised me if I'd had a little hail and snow to go along with the rain. As I crossed into Virginia, the rain stopped long enough for a picture, and I muttered to myself, "Only three and a half more miles to hike for the day. Let it rain."

If I ever say, "Let it rain" again, I hope someone is around to smack me. No sooner had I uttered those words than the Virginia skies opened up, and pouring rain continued the entire three and a half miles to Damascus.

I lay in my bunk just after 5 p.m. at The Place hostel, feeling lucky to get one of the last bunks in a hostel that offered a relatively clean shower and bunk for $3. Then I headed out for dinner and a good cold beer at a local bar called Dots Inn.

Chapter 2
Damascus To Skyland

May 5, Damascus, Virginia (The Place) (milepoint 454.3 north)

I was up at eight the next morning. Even though I was taking the day off from hiking, I couldn't sleep in. Maybe it had something to do with the hard bunk.

I met TC at breakfast. He'd spent the previous night in the mountains and was more than ready to take a couple of days off. We were comparing the various trials and tribulations of trail life, and he told me about some of his tough times on the trail. He said that back in Tennessee and North Carolina he had been so cold a few nights that it worried him. "I was actually concerned for my life," he said. "I didn't know if I was going to make it through the night!"

Fatigue was a problem too, he said; "Why there were days I was so exhausted from not getting any sleep in the shelters that I actually fell asleep on the trail while hiking!" Although TC may have been stretching the truth a little on that one, I laughed so hard I thought I had ripped a muscle in my belly.

TC was staying at the Appalachian Trail Inn and gave me an invitation to an evening cook-out, which I readily accepted.

At the self-service laundry not far away, I ran into Badger, the thru-hiker from Wisconsin I had first met at the Nantahala Outdoor Center. At that time he'd been hiking with a friend who since had to leave the trail because of a stress fracture. There seemed to be a lot of hikers in Damascus trying to recover from injuries before they headed back out on the trail, and there were others simply talking about hanging up their hiking boots all together. While my clothes were in the washer, I walked over to a store to get some ice for my leg. When I asked how much the ice cost, the clerk gave a nod toward my leg and asked, "You're a hiker, right? Just take it!" A trail-friendly town indeed!

According to information I found in the hostel, The Place was run by the First United Methodist Church and had been in operation for twenty-four years, serving Appalachian Trail hikers as well as bikers on the National Transcontinental bike trail. The Place had served more than two thousand visitors a year for the last few years and thirty thousand to forty thousand from all over the world during its existence. Operating on an honor system, the hostel asked for a three-dollar-a-night donation. When I was there, the church was renovating the structure so that it could stay in operation. I certainly recommend the hostel to any thru-hiker.

May 6, Damascus, Virginia (The Place) to Lost Mountain Shelter (milepoint 470.1 north)

Badger and I headed out early. There had been a rowdy bunch in the hostel the evening before. Perhaps they were celebrating crossing into Virginia. Who knows? Regardless, Badger had been in a room where they were really loud, and he was not a happy hiker. But the cookout at TC's had proven to be a thru-hiker's feast: corn on the cob, salad, and chicken. TC surely knew how to throw together one very nice feed.

I headed north up the trail on a gentle grade while swapping trail stories with Badger. We both had a good laugh as he recalled one night in a shelter when everyone was settled in for the night, and the camp area had gotten quiet as hikers drifted off to sleep. Suddenly, there came a blood-chilling howl: "Ahhhhhhhhhhh! It's got me! It's got me!" Apparently a mouse had dropped from the ceiling down onto a hiker's neck, and the hiker instantly began screaming as he squirmed to get the mouse off his neck.

Wolfman passed us at almost a run. He was really moving, and although I couldn't say for sure, I thought he turned on the wrong trail. By the time we got to the turnoff, however, he was long gone. Maybe he knew something we didn't.

We had hiked five miles and for a short distance crossed onto the Virginia Creeper trail, which, I had been told, began as a Native American footpath. Pioneers, including Daniel Boone, later used it, and then in the early 1900s a railroad was constructed along the route. The Creeper Trail stretches thirty-three miles along the old railroad bed from Abingdon, Virginia, to the Virginia/North Carolina state line. We stopped for a break, and I sat down in what I thought was a perfect spot to rest. It wasn't. I scrambled to my feet, howling and slapping my ass and every other part of my anatomy with the speed of a casino dealer. I'd sat smack dab on top of a very active red anthill! I eventually clambered into the woods to rip off my clothing and remove the little creatures more efficiently.

Wolfman passed us, again. I had guessed right. "I just flat missed the white blaze," he complained as he went by.

I mentioned to Badger that we had not seen any young thru-hikers on the trail, which wasn't surprising, considering the three dollars a night lodging and the party atmosphere in Damascus. Hikers could really get sucked in, especially young hikers who liked to party.

About a mile from the Lost Mountain Shelter, we had to stop and put on rain gear, which definitely reaffirmed where I would be sleeping for the night. Lost Mountain was a nice, new, and very clean shelter;

and its condition certainly eliminated any question about hiking on. Will Do, Can Do came in later along with several new faces, so we had a full shelter, but at least everyone was dry.

The evening was spent sharing some tall tales. Will Do, Can Do, an experienced thru-hiker, had the best story of the evening when he told us about Baltimore Jack – a thru-hiker and trail legend – finding a dead body at the infamous Doyle Hotel in Duncannon, Pennsylvania, during one of his many thru-hikes.

May 7, Lost Mountain Shelter to Wise Shelter (Grayson Highlands Park) (milepoint 487.5 north)

The sun was rising earlier each morning, and I found myself doing the same. It was 6:30 a.m. The singing of birds filled the morning air, and the sun peeked up over the mountains. You couldn't find a better day to hike.

There was a lot of talk in the shelter about the rowdy party in Damascus. It seemed that many people were upset at the behavior of a few hikers. Someone said that the police were even called to The Place because of the disturbance, and we all hoped that the behavior of a few would not ruin the opportunity for other hikers to use the facility.

It was already humid as we entered a pasture with beef cattle. "Oh no," Badger groaned as we exited through a narrow gap in the wooden fence that allows hikers – but not cattle – to depart. He, with his huge backpack, was stuck like a cork in a bottle. And we both laughed as I reminded him, "I told you your pack was as big as a damn cow!"

Badger, with his pack and large hiking staff, got me thinking of another story a former thru-hiker had told me about his walk into New York City a few years back. When the thru-hiker was on the A.T. near the Hudson River – you can actually see the city skyline from the trail on a clear day – he decided to visit New York City. He'd never been to the Big Apple and figured, "What the hell – I may never be this close again." He got on a train and into the city he went in his full hiking regalia: hiking staff, pack, and all. Almost immediately, he encountered several young men who encircled him and taunted, "Hey, Moses! Hey, Moses! Where you going, Moses?" which quickly escalated to, "Hey, Moses! You got any money on you, Moses?" Becoming bolder by the minute and moving in closer like a pack of jackals, they started pulling at his pack. Knowing he had to do something, he yelled out a feeble, "Leave me alone! Just back off and leave me alone." They laughed, pulled out their knives and waved them, threatening, "Moses, we're gonna stick you." With all the fortitude he could muster, he said in his slow Tennessee drawl, "Boys, you may stick me, but I'm not sure it is going to hurt me half as bad as when I stick you all with this hiking pole where the sun don't shine!" They took another step. The hiker lifted his pole and prepared for an attack, and one of the pack declared, "I believe old Moses is serious," then turned and walked away. The Tennessee hiker was so rattled and shook up that he went to an all-night theater to collect himself, and he fell asleep until morning. When he awoke, he was on the first train he could find that was headed out of the city. "I had seen enough of New York City to last me a lifetime," he told me.

As we hiked, Badger and I met a ridge runner called Tamerac, who had been hired to hike the A.T., helping people out and reminding them to "leave no trace." She told us "The pay isn't much, but you can't beat the work environment!"

As we entered Mount Rogers Park and hiked along the Grayson Highlands, anxious to see a group of wild ponies we had heard so much about, Badger and I soon realized that we could smell them well before we could see them. I laughed and asked Badger, "You think day-hikers and others smell us before they see us, like we do these ponies?"

We hiked up to the Thomas Knob Shelter for lunch after passing a unique privy. Exiting the privy was thru-hiker Ace, who said, "Mountain Slayer, you've got to go in there!" Now, I'd been told to do a number of things on the trail, but never had I been told when to use an outhouse. It turned out that Ace was referring to the cleanliness of the privy and how it lacked the typically pungent smell of the typical outhouse. This was the first privy we'd encountered on the trail that used a rooftop solar panel to operate an exhaust fan. It also had a great view, said by many to be the best view from an outhouse on the entire trail.

At the Wise Shelter, we met Pancake, a section-hiker who was also staying at the shelter. He hiked a couple of weeks in the spring and fall each year, usually getting in about 300 miles of the A.T. a year, and hoped to complete the entire trail in about six years.

At dusk I watched a number of deer mill around the shelter area and was surprised how close they came to the tents and shelter. I had already eaten and noticed that my appetite had really picked up. That would mean a change in my meal plans to include more food.

May 8, Wise Shelter (Grayson Highlands Park) to Raccoon Branch Shelter (milepoint 505.1 north)

We were up and ready to go at 7 a.m., and although full, the Wise Shelter was a very nice new log structure, not cramped like many of the older shelters. That didn't solve the problem of snoring hikers, however. "Damn near blew the roof off the shelter," Badger said with a shake of his head.

Hiker tips: Be sure and invest in a good pair of
earplugs. You won't regret it.

Not long after we got underway, we walked right by a double white blaze painted on a rock instead of a tree. We had not noticed it. "Damn, what a way to start the morning!" I moaned to Badger after we realized we had gone the wrong way. And then, I reached into my pouch and realized I no longer had my *Data Book*. It must have fallen out somewhere back on the trail, but there was no turning back, even though I would really miss the crucial information.

We topped Iron Mountain and were two miles from Virginia Highway 16, where we were considering going into Troutdale to get something to eat if we could get a ride into the town. We got lucky. We got to the highway just as a trail angel by the name of Dave was dropping two hikers off. So we had a great lunch at a little country store called the Trading Post; and after a quick hitch, we were back on the trail. I told Badger, "I may not smell any better but I sure feel better!"

Raccoon Branch Shelter was our stop for the night, and when we arrived, there was an inviting campfire blazing. Everyone was talking about the next shelter, Partnership Shelter, supposedly one of the best, if not the best, shelter on the trail because there was a shower plus a phone only a few hundred yards away at a Ranger Station. With a phone so near, we could almost smell the pizza and taste the beer.

One of the other hikers in the shelter was really bitching: "I waited by the goddamn side of the road for an hour and a half to get into town then just gave up." On the other hand, Badger and I got a quick ride to town and were back to the trail in minutes. It had to be luck. I knew very well it was not our looks or smell.

May 9, Raccoon Branch Shelter to Partnership Shelter (milepoint 518.1 north)

I headed north out of Raccoon Shelter trying out the donut padding I had carved out of a section of my Z-Rest for the abrasion on my hip. It looked as though Badger and I would have a nice morning for hiking.

The thru-hiker appetite had hit me full bore. I couldn't get enough to eat. I'd eaten like the proverbial horse the day before and had still gone to bed hungry. Now I was already snacking on candy bars after finishing off breakfast.

It seemed like every tree I passed lately had poison ivy growing up its side! Poison ivy was popping out everywhere, and the sight reminded me of the female hiker I had overheard on the phone at The Place in Damascus trying to find a medical clinic. The one-sided conversation went something like this: "I need to see a doctor as soon as possible." A pause. "Not until next week? That won't work!" Another pause. "But you don't understand, I've got to get in to see a doctor right away. I've got poison ivy." Pause. "What? Well if you have to know, I was taking a pee on the trail and sat in some poison ivy, and I am now in a great deal of misery! Are you laughing? Well I hope not, it's not very damn funny!" Final pause. "Thanks, I'll be right over."

> *Hiker tips: I picked up this tip from another thru-hiker. Instead of leaning my pack up against a tree when I took a break, he suggested that I use my hiking poles to prop my pack up. "Too easy to get poison ivy on your pack when you lean it up against a tree," the thru-hiker suggested, then continued, "I learned that the hard way and had poison ivy on my back so bad I couldn't carry my pack for a week." A month and a half on the trail and I was still learning!*

I made it to the Partnership Shelter around 1 p.m., and it definitely lived up to expectations. It was the nicest shelter on the trail so far, especially so with a hot water shower attached. There was also a ranger station about 200 yards from the shelter with a phone, and Pizza Hut delivered! A thru-hiker's girl friend drove up to pick him up and brought some beer, treating anyone who cared to indulge. I heard a thru-hiker exclaim, "Pinch me! A hot shower, pizza, and beer! I think I'm in thru-hiker heaven!"

We had hiked thirteen miles over some pretty level terrain, which seemed like a really short hike. I was feeling a little guilty (not really!), as Virginia was treating us nicely.

The shelter was not very full, as a number of hikers – due to the beautiful weather – tented. During the evening, Old Dave, a 72-year-old professor turned hiker, entertained us. He said that one of the counties we would be passing through was, "at one time, one of the biggest marijuana-producing areas east of the Mississippi." He asked one of the young hikers what his trail name was. "Cheyenne," replied the hiker, "but don't ask me how to spell it." Old Dave laughed and said with a wink to the other hikers, "You've got to know how to spell your trail name or you won't be able to sign the trail registers." Old Dave then proceeded to spell, "C-h-e-y-e-n-n-e," while the young hiker took his pen out and scribbled the letters on his arm. We all laughed.

There were a lot of new faces in the shelter, and I couldn't help but notice the large number of hikers smoking. One lady was burning the tar and nicotine from the time she arrived at the shelter until she woke up early the next morning with a cigarette hanging from her lips. The smoke was not a problem, as there are only the three sides to a shelter; but it surprised me that so many hikers would be smokers. It seemed to be a contradiction, hiking and smoking.

May 10, Partnership Shelter to Atkins, Virginia (milepoint 529.6 north)

Pancake had joined Badger and me on our hike even though he was not thru-hiking. We all were about the same age and hiked at about the same pace. Pancake was leaving the trail at Brand, Virginia, and had offered to give my son Brad and me a ride back to Brad's car in Atkins, Virginia, on Saturday. That would help, as my plan was to meet Brad (beginning his summer break from college) at Atkins and spend a few days with him, hiking from Atkins to Brand.

I walked into a pine forest again, and the combination of the aroma from the pine and hiking on the soft and cushioning needle-covered ground continued to be a favorite of mine. But I was quickly jarred back to civilization as I walked under a power line that was making such loud snapping and crackling noises that I was almost afraid to walk under it. I hiked up to the restored Lindamood Schoolhouse, originally built in 1894. Cheyenne had already been to the school, and I laughed to myself as I observed his name written in the register. It was spelled correctly.

It was noon as I hiked down to the Village Motel in Atkins. On my way into town I could see the trail wind down to the small town from the top of the hill as a couple of young hikers caught up with us. For some reason, I decided I was not going to let them beat me to town, and as Pancake and Badger said later, "The old Mountain Slayer took off like a horse headed home to the barn." I was practically at a full gallop to keep in front of the two young hikers and really cruised into town. I'm not sure why, but I couldn't slow the old legs down. I was probably just anxious to see Brad and looking forward to hiking with him for awhile. After checking into the hotel, I headed out to get something to eat with Pancake and Badger, where they were razzing me about the speed of my hike into Atkins.

May 11, Atkins, Virginia to Lynn Camp Mountain (milepoint 544.3 north)

Ducking under roaring traffic on an Interstate-81 underpass, Brad and I headed out on the trail early after having a quick breakfast and picking up a couple of deli sandwiches for lunch. My new hiking partner had already been blessed with a trail name by his grandfather and would be hiking with me for a few days before heading to Utah and a summer of fighting forest fires – hence, the trail name Smoke. So it was Smoke and the Old Mountain Slayer as we headed out on the A.T. on a cool, clear day.

We finally escaped the traffic and found the solitude of the woods refreshing. Speaking of noise, our motel the previous night had to be one of the noisiest I had ever slept in. If I hadn't known better, I would have sworn we were sleeping in the median of I-81.

The geese were calling as we hiked north past the headwaters of the Middle Fork Hullas River and stopped for a little snack and a break at the Davis Path Shelter. It was a beautiful day for hiking, and it was very special to be able to share the trail with my son Smoke.

We started the morning with a 1,000-foot climb up Gullion (Little Brushy) Mountain. It was a good climb, and from the top we could see the city of Atkins, Virginia, and what I believed was Mount Rogers. I had tried to describe the numerous breathtaking views in my journal entries that Smoke had read on-line, but it was extra special being able to show them off.

As Smoke and I headed up the mountain, we saw two, size thirteen boots sticking up out of the bushes, and I shouted, "Hey, Cheyenne!"

Cheyenne jumped up with a start. "How did you know it was me?"

I laughed and told him, "I'd recognize those big dogs anywhere!"

Cheyenne was a big fellow and had just quit his truck-driving job to come out and hike part of the A.T. As we continued north on the trail, Brad chuckled and whispered to me, "Dad, did you check out that road atlas he was carrying for his trail maps?"

"Yeah," I said. "I guess you can take the hiker out of the truck, but you can't take the truck driver out of the hiker!"

By noon, we had hiked ten miles already, so we stopped on top of a hill in a pasture for lunch. It was a gorgeous day, and the views from the top of the hill as we looked back on the mountains to the south were spectacular, although I believed Smoke enjoyed the deli sandwiches more than the mountain views.

We arrived at Virginia Highway 42 and celebrated the twenty-five percent milestone in a little shelter off the side of the trail. I had walked 540 miles, one-fourth of the trail, and celebrated with a Snickers bar, the thru-hiker's candy bar of choice.

It was 4:30 p.m. when we walked into Lynn Camp Stream. We'd done about sixteen miles, probably way too much for Smoke's first day, but he wasn't complaining. We'd planned on stopping at Knot Maul Shelter, but there was no water supply and we were out of water. Interestingly, according to *The Thru-Hiker's Handbook,* the Knot Maul Shelter got its name from the knot wood taken from the area to make wooden mauls.

Machine and Walkabout came by, planning to hike a little farther. When we warned about the high mountain just ahead, they headed out, one of them saying, "Well, Mate, guess we will give this little old hill a go." I love that Aussie brogue!

As we sat around a little campfire and settled in for the night, Smoke and Pancake laughed at the way I hung our food bags. "A bear would have to be totally disabled not to be able to get those food bags," said Smoke. I had to admit I really botched the job, but I tried to save face with a feeble excuse: "I'm really only trying to keep the food away from the skunks and mice!"

May 12, Lynn Camp Mountain to Jenkins Shelter (milepoint 562.7 north)

Smoke and I had both slept well, and from what I had been told about our seven-mile uphill hike out of our camp, we needed the rest. We planned on hiking seventeen miles, and having done sixteen miles the day before, we were probably hiking too many miles for someone beginning his hike.

I asked Brad how he felt. He rubbed his shoulder. "A little stiff," he said. I had forgotten about the stiffness at the start of my hike, and reminded myself to watch our mileage.

As we set off, I removed another stone from my shoe. I had been wearing long pants up to the last few days, and they had prevented stones from getting into my shoes. I was thinking about getting a short pair of gaiters to wear with my shorts.

> *Hiker tips: A few hikers on the trail wore gaiters over their boots, but the majority did not. The common complaint was how warm they made your feet. Obviously, it's a matter of individual choice.*

I also noticed my hand swelling a little and was at a loss as to why until I realized it was the hand that was now without a hiking pole. I had loaned one of my poles to Smoke, and the swelling was most probably from my hand hanging by my side.

Smoke and I headed up a four-mile climb of 2,000 feet to the top of Chestnut Knob Mountain, and I told him with a laugh, "We had to have at least one mountain for you to climb, otherwise you would think I was pulling your leg about all the mountains I've been hiking over."

We met up with Julian, the young fellow I hiked with back in Georgia. He had hitched ahead to Bastian, Virginia, and was hiking his way back south to Trail Days in Damascus, Virginia. It wasn't a bad idea for those who wanted to do a little partying at Trail Days. And there were other attractions too, Julian said. "It's kind of neat hiking south for awhile and catching up on all the news from the hikers I've overtaken on the trail."

Brad and I found a tremendous view from the mountaintop at Chestnut Knob Shelter, and we got a good look at an unusual geological feature: a crater-shaped depression surrounded on all sides by a high ridge, aptly nicknamed "God's Thumbprint." I had read in the *Appalachian Trail Thru-Hikers' Companion* that the region was Cornelius Vanderbilt's first choice for the Biltmore estate, which he eventually located in Asheville, North Carolina.

We headed down the mountain with about ten more miles to the next shelter. Smoke was holding up well and wasn't complaining, but I knew it had to be tough for him – not the best way to break in a new hiker to the trail. A number of hikers came in during lunch and made me feel guilty as they asked Smoke how his second day was going and he told them the number of miles we were doing. "What you trying to do, Mountain Slayer? Kill him off?" they asked. I had to admit it was too many miles, especially with our earlier 2,000-foot climb.

Our water supply was low, with no source of water in sight. Up on the ridge, it was as dry as a bone; and as we arrived at Virginia Highway 623, where there was supposed to be water, we could not find a single drop.

We still had found no water at 4:45 p.m., and we were almost out on a very hot afternoon. We sat down to squeeze out every drop of water in our bags when Smoke realized his bag had a kink in the hose. He had about a liter of water left. Thank God we had that much, but that only amounted to a half-liter of water each; and according to my *Data Book* we had three and a half miles to go.

We talked to a day hiker headed south who had a global positioning unit. He made matters worse by announcing, "Sorry, fella, but my global positioning unit reads you have four and a half miles to go." Not what we wanted to hear.

At 6:30 p.m. we still had no water and no shelter in sight. I slipped my pack off and bushwhacked down the side of the mountain, following an old sign pointing to water, but I didn't find any. Not only were we out of water, but the hill kicked my butt as I climbed back up.

We staggered into Jenkins Shelter right after 7 p.m. We were whipped. We had hiked from 7 a.m. to 7 p.m., and that made for a long day. Without a word, Smoke headed down to the creek to take off his shoes and cool off his aching dogs – the twenty-mile day had them barking.

May 13, Jenkins Shelter to U.S. 21/52 (Bland, Virginia) (milepoint 574.7 north)

We did not sleep well in the shelter. It was noisy, and the bugs were out in full force; so Smoke and I were up and heading out early. During the night I'd thought I heard something outside the shelter. I sat up, flashed my penlight out into the woods, and saw a large herd of deer. There was something eerie in the way the deer meandered around the shelter and the tents in the moonlight, smelling and licking as if they were pet dogs.

All the hikers were complaining about the lack of water and how much more difficult that made the hike. Smoke said he felt OK; but he looked a little tired, and I had to believe the previous day took a lot out of him. We had thirteen miles to Bland, Virginia, and that would probably seem like a breeze to him after the past two days. Before leaving camp, Brad and I filled all of our water bottles. That meant extra weight, but we were not about to go through another day like the day before.

An hour and a half out of camp, we arrived at Wolf Creek. "Here we are loaded up with water, and this creek has all the water anyone would need," Smoke complained. It had been a relatively easy hike so far and such an enjoyable morning that Smoke boasted, "I believe I'm ready to hike right on by Bland!" I figured I would talk to him at the end of the day and see if he still felt that way.

We found a good place for a snack at Laurel Creek and, having plenty of time, decided to take a snack break. I didn't sit very close to Smoke for fear he would take a bite out of me, as he was eating everything in sight. He laughed as he pointed out a very unusual trail ornament hanging in a tree: a pair of fire boots, "Now, who would ever leave their fire boots out in the middle of the woods?" the veteran firefighter wondered as he scratched his head.

Just after noon we started getting glimpses of Bland; and by the way Smoke stayed out in front, I could tell he definitely had a bad case of town fever. Smoke and I reached Highway 52 and found a nice shade tree to rest under until Pancake, who had planned to connect with his daughter, caught up. Pancake showed up a little later, and seeing only Smoke and me, laughingly said, "Where is all the trail magic when you need it?"

Brad with a pair of trail ornaments

No sooner were the words out of his mouth than a thru-hiker and his visiting sister drove up with cold soft drinks and snacks! We couldn't believe it. The thru-hiker Mr. Bunker and his sister planned on hiking from Bland to Atkins, Virginia, and decided to provide some trail magic of their own.

Pancake's daughter showed up shortly after he met us by the highway, and she took us back to Atkins to pick up Smoke's car. Smoke and I drove back to Bland and checked into the Big Walker Motel. We showered, had a bite to eat, then followed that with a trip to a grocery to resupply. It was a nice end to a very enjoyable visit with my son Brad, but he wasn't saying a word about hiking on.

May 14, U.S. 21/52 (Bland, Virginia) to Wapiti Shelter (milepoint 600.4 north)

Smoke dropped me off on the A.T. and headed for home, hoping to get there in time to take his mother out for a Mother's Day dinner. It was difficult to see him leave, just as it was when Connie had left after visiting me in Hot Springs: a little homesickness that I was sure would be cured by hiking. It felt strange hiking alone. I had not been alone on the trail since I had met Badger in Damascus. I headed north, hiking the homesick blues away.

Hiker tips: There are those who suggest not having friends and family hike with thru-hikers on the trail. They believe it disrupts the hike. Personally, I believe that's nonsense. Quite to the contrary, those visits just added to the enjoyment of thru-hiking the A.T. There is something special about having the opportunity to share the hike with loved ones.

It was pretty cold up in the mountains, and I had sent some of my winter clothes home with Smoke, not at all sure now that was very smart. I had a gorgeous view from up on the ridge line, where the tree tops on the surrounding mountains reminded me of a fluffy green carpet stretched out for miles in all directions. I figured I would soon be doing a lot more hiking in the "green tunnels" of Virginia that I'd been told to expect.

I hiked with a section-hiker for about a mile up the side of the mountain as he told me he'd been hiking with his son for the past few weeks. They had been section hiking together for the past sixteen years.

Team Cleveland, two fun loving young fellows from Cleveland, Ohio, who were good company on the trail, passed me. They'd been at the last shelter I had passed and had quite a hike planned for the day, all the way to Wapiti Shelter. That would be twenty-six miles for me, and I didn't think that would happen.

By the time I left Jenny Knob Shelter, I had hiked twelve miles and wasn't sure of my destination for the evening, only that I felt great and the weather was perfect, which made it a good time to hike on. Badger had signed the shelter ledger, so it looked like he was twelve miles ahead of me.

I crossed an impressive wooden suspension bridge that spanned the Kimberling Creek. Then I ran into Team Cleveland again. They were hiding their packs in some bushes along the trail so they could hike down to a convenience store for some cold drinks. They offered to pick something up for me, too. I thanked them for the offer but didn't want to wait around. I figured that I had already hiked nineteen miles and only needed seven more to reach the Wapiti Shelter. It was a perfect day for me -- cool and overcast -- and it definitely began to look like my first "Marathon Day," hiker lingo for twenty-six miles.

Twelve hours of hiking and I never felt better. If anyone had told me a few weeks earlier that I would be hiking twenty-six miles in one day, I would have said, "No way!" But there I was contemplating exactly that – a twenty-six mile day.

I burst out of a wooded section of the trail and startled a woman in the act of pulling up her pants! "Whoa, sorry about that," I said with a sheepish grin. She didn't respond, and hustled on up the trail. A short while later, I ran into her and her husband. "Guess you caught me with my pants down, didn't you?" she said with an embarrassed smile. "What can I say?" I said, shrugging my shoulders for the lack of a better response in front of an unusually big and burly husband.

It was after 7 p.m. as I hiked up to the Wapiti Shelter and peeked in. "Mountain Slayer, how the hell did you get here?" Badger shouted, grinning in disbelief. "Simple!" I boasted. "I just pulled off my first Marathon Day!"

Team Cleveland arrived at the shelter in the early evening, and threw me a can of soda, saying, "Here you go, Mountain Slayer! Enjoy!" Knowing that I would really enjoy a soda but did not have the time to wait around, they bought one for me on their excursion to the store.

May 15, Wapiti Shelter to Pearisburg, Virginia (milepoint 617.1 north)

As we left Wapiti Shelter on another cool morning, I kicked myself for sending my gloves home and was damn glad I hadn't sent my warm sleeping bag too. A number of the thru-hikers complained about being too cold to get a good night's sleep.

I heard an interesting Damascus story in the shelter about a male hiker who was wearing a skirt when he stopped in one of the local bars. He was getting a lot of stares from the locals but little else until he got up to leave and one of his hiking buddies yelled, "Show us your ass!" He promptly leaned over and shot the moon to the entire bar! Needless to say, a number of the local patrons took exception to the display of his anatomy, and a verbal battle between some of the hikers and the locals almost turned into a good old down-home brawl. The argument ended with the local law being summoned, and some of the hikers thought the locals were overreacting and didn't really like hikers. I didn't agree with the assessment and said that I'd been in the same bar for lunch in Damascus and the locals were very friendly – a couple of fellows even bought me a beer as we shared hometown stories. Although Damascus is a trail-friendly town, I figured some of the locals were getting fed up with the poor behavior of a few hikers. Sadly, there was talk that – due to the excessive drinking and rowdy behavior of some hikers – the town of Damascus was considering putting an end to its annual Trail Days celebration.

As we left Doc's Knob Shelter after a quick lunch, the aroma from the azaleas – in full bloom – nearly knocked me over. I loved the smell and the spectacular colors.

I passed Chuck Perry, a member of the Roanoke Appalachian Trail Club, out working on the trail. The entire A.T. is maintained by dedicated people like Chuck, who come out on their own time to volunteer hours and hours for the simple love of the trail.

We arrived in the town of Pearisburg, and even though the Rendezvous Motel was right off the trail, Badger and I decided to get a lift to the Holy Family Church Hostel, a place we'd heard a lot about. I should say we got a lift toward the hostel. The friendly local who gave us a lift warned, "I can take you across town but can't take you up to the hostel." When we inquired why not, he articulated in his slow southern drawl, "Well, Boys, that thar hostel sits on a high hill and I'm afraid of hills, seeing that I don't have no brakes!" Of course, he divulged that information to us after we were in his car headed toward the hostel. Badger and I looked at each other with wide eyes and said, "That's OK, just across town will be fine." But luck was with us, for as soon as he dropped us off at the bottom of the hill, another local in a pickup truck gave us a lift the rest of the way up the hill.

Did I say luck was with us? When we got to the hostel, there was only one bed left and the only shower wasn't working. Neither one of us wanted the other to sleep on the floor, so Badger and I bummed a ride back down to the Rendezvous Hotel. It was a hassle; but the price was right at the hotel, it was close to the trail, and the owner was good enough to shuttle us uptown for a bite to eat. So we came out okay.

May 16, Pearisburg, Virginia to Pine Swamp Branch Shelter (milepoint 636.1 north)

Before we left the motel in the morning, I ran into the lady whom I'd caught in the compromising position of hitching up her shorts the day before. With a mischievous grin, I asked if she remembered me. "I sure do!" she said with what seemed to be lingering embarrassment. "Certain people and occasions you don't soon forget!"

Badger and I were back on the trail at 8 a.m., loaded down with food for about four days, again leaving a town with too heavy a pack load. The shelter we'd set our sights on was nineteen miles away; and with the late departure, we knew that would be a challenge.

We crossed the New River, said to be the second oldest river in the world. It flows north to the Ohio River, whereas all the rest of the rivers we would be crossing flowed east to the Atlantic Ocean. A fellow in a pickup passed as we crossed the bridge and gave us a roaring, "Go for it, all the way to Maine!" Obviously, some folks in town were familiar with the ultimate dream of all thru-hikers.

As we headed on, a big old snake slithered across my foot, acting as a wake-up call to get the old blood stirring. I headed north with a bit more spring in my step.

At noon, as Badger and I stretched out on the side of a sun-soaked mountain for lunch, we heard, "O what a beautiful morning, O what a beautiful day . . ." being belted out by a passing hiker, and I mean belted out! As we watched and listened, a slackpacker went whizzing by, high speed matching his high volume. I believe I would've had to run just to keep up with him as he continued to sing at the top of his lungs. I could still hear him even after he was well out of sight.

More hikers passed, this time a couple of slack-packing male thru-hikers headed north, one wearing a skirt. He was the third male thru-hiker I'd seen wearing a skirt. "I've been told that skirts were cooler in hot weather," I casually mentioned to Badger. "What do you think?"

"What do I think?" Badger said with raised eyebrows and his Wisconsin grin. "I think it would have to get damn hot out here for me to start wearing a skirt!" I smiled to myself at the thought of Badger in a skirt.

It was after 7 p.m. when we arrived to a full house at the Pine Swamp Branch Shelter. We were glad to be able to squeeze in as it began to rain. It was also good to see Woodchip. Her husband and their dog had come out to hike with her for a few days.

There were also a couple of new hikers in the shelter: Melt Down and Tree Bumper. They had the typically interesting stories associated with their trail names. "While cooking dinner inside my nylon tent," Melt Down confessed, "I got careless and – swoosh! – it went up in flames!" Melt Down had hiked part of the trail a few years ago, but she'd been injured and was now trying to finish up sections she had skipped. "Don't go skipping different sections of the trail if your intent is to hike the entire trail," she advised us with a frown. "It's a real hassle trying to come back and hike the missed sections."

When we asked the other new hiker how she got the name of Tree Bumper, she just laughed as her face turned red and moaned, "Don't even ask!"

May 17, Pine Swamp Branch Shelter to Laurel Creek Shelter (milepoint 654.4 north)

We left the full but pleasant stone shelter with its comfortable fireplace after a rainy evening, thankful we'd been in the shelter during the night. It's almost impossible to express how great it feels to be lying in a warm shelter as the rain pours down outside, knowing that you and your gear will not be soaked in the morning. It's a feeling one needs to experience to appreciate.

Badger and I reached 4,100 feet after starting the morning at 2,400 feet, so we had finished some major climbing and stopped for lunch. My menu was a bagel with peanut butter and a stick of beef and cheese, topped off with GORP, definitely the most I'd eaten for lunch along the trail. My appetite continued to explode.

We hiked through a tunnel of azaleas in full bloom – the fragrance was superb! – as we headed out of War Spur Shelter with our destination for the evening five more miles of hiking ahead. While resting in the shelter, we met a hiker by the name of Relic who was calling it quits for the day after twelve miles. He'd done nineteen miles the day before, and being 65 – hence the trail name Relic – he rubbed his shoulders and groaned, "My old body told me twelve miles is enough for today." We also met the lightest traveling hiker we'd seen on the trail to date, a slackpacker carrying nothing but a tin cup!

It took an hour and a half hike straight up to reach the top of a mountain that afternoon. It was the toughest climb I'd had for awhile. At the top, my stomach heaved in and out as I caught my breath. Badger joined me, sucking in air. "Oxygen," he said with a pained smile. "I need some oxygen."

We made it to the Laurel Creek Shelter about 5:45 p.m. Can-Do, Will-Do was there, as was Fig. Woodchip, the 64-year-old thru-hiker, came in a few minutes later; she'd been doing very well on the trail. It was just the four of us old-timers in the shelter. Evidently, a lot of the younger hikers left the trail to go to Trail Days in Damascus. The trail talk centered around wildlife on the trail. "I saw a rattler," said Can-Do, Will-Do, who added that he'd heard some hikers talking about seeing a couple of bear cubs and had even seen a picture of a mountain lion taken on the trail. Badger chimed in that he'd seen a bobcat. And there I was with my death-defying encounters with a snarling bunny rabbit and a headstrong cow!

May 18, Laurel Creek Shelter to Trout Creek, Virginia (milepoint 675.6 north)

Badger and I left Laurel Creek Shelter around 7 a.m. unsure of our exact destination. The first shelter was just twelve miles north and the next one was twenty-two miles. One seemed too close, the other rather far. We figured we'd just start out and see where we ended up and how our legs felt. We'd had a fairly good night's sleep, considering the presence of a couple of heavy-duty snorers in the shelter. I was glad I'd located my earplugs.

Although Granite had come into the shelter late, he and Can-Do, Will-Do, were out before daylight with hitchhiking signs, hoping to get a ride back to Damascus and Trail Days. All the young hikers seemed to be attracted to Trail Days. Most were hitching or hiking south, and some were even teaming up and renting cars to get back to Damascus. We were expecting some great stories when they all got back to the trail.

Fig passed us, heading north. As he did, I inquired how he got his trail name. He chuckled and said, "My last name is Newton – take it from there!"

We left the woods and moved into a pasture area. We'd been in the woods for the majority of time the last three days and it was nice to be able to see the distant mountains for a change. A tattered wanted poster hung from a fence post as we left the woods: "Wanted by the FBI, Eric Robert Rudolph," it read in bold print, giving a description of the man thought to be responsible for the bombing attack at the 1996 Olympic Games in Atlanta. At one time, it was believed that Eric Rudolph was traveling the A.T.

Badger and I stopped at a farmhouse just off the trail where there were cold drinks and fresh fruit for sale. Maps of the United States and the world hung on the front porch for hikers to place pushpins marking their hometowns. I was amazed that hikers had come from all over the world to hike the A.T. As the lady of the house told us how they used the extra income from hikers to purchase school supplies, her little boy came running up to the house breathless, yelling, "Mister, mister! Come quick! The mule's eating your pack!" Badger and I exploded off of the porch swing and bolted to where we had leaned our packs up against the fence, waving our arms and shouting, "Get out! Get out of there, you damn mules!" Fortunately, the boy had noticed the mules nibbling on our packs before any real damage was done, and I laughed as we swung on our packs. "You run pretty fast for an old man," I said to Badger. "Only when I have to," he replied, panting but obviously relieved.

We stopped and I took a picture of the Keffer Oak. According to *The Thru-Hiker's Handbook*, it's eighteen feet around and more than 300 years old. It's the largest tree on the A.T. in the south, as the Dover Oak in New York was reported to be slightly larger. Either way, the old-growth trees on the A.T. were pretty rare and a treat to behold.

We then hiked past the Sarver Cabin, a rundown old homestead dating to the 1800s, and referred to in the *Appalachian Trail Thru-*

Hikers' Companion as home for "George," a resident ghost that has supposedly shown up on some hikers' photos.

"Look out, Badger! Here comes one!" I screamed as a big hairy goat came barreling down the side of the mountain, seemingly bent on knocking us right over the narrow cliff we were hiking. But to my amazement, and – I must say – delight, the goat came to a screeching halt just short of us and began to aggressively lick our arms, legs and any other exposed flesh. It seems that the herd of goats on that mountainside learned early on that smelly, sweating hikers were walking salt blocks. It was difficult to get past

Badger, is finger-licking good!

them. We laughed, and I told Badger, "At least it's nice to be wanted, even if just for our sweat." Up ahead, Woodchip was also surrounded by a pack of the sweat-seeking creatures. With a grin, she said, "Not a good place to stop for lunch."

We had hiked by a lot of azaleas in full bloom on the mountainside, and I knew I would never smell another azalea without fond memories of the A.T. They certainly had a delightful fragrance. Of course, any sweet fragrance was a delight after being around smelly thru-hikers all day. As we passed Niday Shelter, there was so much mountain laurel blooming that the woods looked like they were covered in snow – a beautiful sight!

Badger and I arrived at the Audie Murphy Monument, erected by the local A.T. club for Audie Murphy, the most decorated American soldier of World War II, who single-handedly captured a large number of German soldiers and became a legend. The monument seemed out of place on the isolated section of the A.T., but apparently Murphy had died in a 1971 plane crash nearby.

We were still hiking at 6:30 p.m., unable to find a decent area to camp, so we planned to bust on through to a creek and campgrounds further north on the trail. We weren't really happy about continuing to hike; it was going to be a bigger day than we had planned. We'd heard that there were some great camping areas at Audie Murphy Monument, but we surely couldn't find any.

We passed a hiker named Brother Jules, who said he got his trail name from a character in the movie *Jeremiah Johnson*. Brother Jules was a big man who carried a good part of his body weight around his waist. He confided that after being on the trail for just a short time, "I thought I was going to die and went back home for a rest." Back on the trail after getting a hitch north, he was breathing deeply as he slumped on a rock near the trail and looked as though he would not be going much further.

We arrived at Trout Creek, Virginia, near Highway 620 around 7 p.m. to find a nice camping area with a creek close by. A fellow who lived down the road stopped by and offered us some water and told us that liquid refreshment was often placed under the bridge in the cool Trout Creek for thru-hikers. I hustled down and checked it out. Sure enough, there were a number of cans floating in a makeshift cooler of rocks in the creek. At first I thought it might have been beer and was looking forward to a cool brew, but the cans turned out to be grape soda.

While at the creek, I decided to wash up; but before I could take my first piece of clothing off I slipped and fell in. As I scurried to get out of the muddy water, I banged my head on the bridge. Not the end to the day's hike I had hoped for.

May 19, Trout Creek, Virginia to Catawba Mountain Shelter (milepoint 690.5 north)

Even though we were camped along the road, I slept well after the twenty-one mile day.

From reading the *Data Book*, it appeared the day would hold one very big climb to the top of Dragons Tooth on Cove Mountain, and we hoped to stop in Catawba to get a bite to eat and resupply before going to the next shelter.

Although I no longer had wraps on my knee or ankle, I still had a problem with my hip and a painful bruise and/or blister under a heavy callus on my foot. But I'd get no sympathy from fellow thru-hikers. All of them were also dealing with the many nagging injuries associated with thru-hiking the trail.

As we entered another pasture, there was an inviting B&B just off the trail. It was too early to stop, though, so we continued north among a herd of cattle that had little or no interest in us. Virginia certainly had a variety of hiking terrain: from woods to rocks to pastures, there had been some interesting hiking.

We sat down at a table in the Homeplace, right outside Catawba, Virginia. A popular place for locals and hikers alike, the all-you-can-eat fare of roast beef and chicken was a real draw. We'd been fortunate to meet a trail angel by the name of Horace Green who picked us up where the A.T. crossed the road, dropped us off in town for an hour to have dinner, then returned to take us back to the trail. Horace was checking out the trail for his planned section hike in June, and he could not have picked a better time to visit the trail as far as we were concerned. We couldn't thank him enough for the ride or the Snickers and the granola bars he gave us as we headed back to the trail.

"Oh, nuts!" Badger said as Horace drove away. "I left my hiking stick at the Homeplace." That was too bad. Badger had grown attached to the hiking stick and had carved the initials of each state carefully into the staff as we hiked across each state line.

A storm was forecast for the evening, and I could hear thunder off in the distance as we headed to the next shelter at a hurried pace. I had to laugh as we passed two hikers and their dachshund dogs. The hounds' bellies were hitting every rock on the path as they scooted down the trail to beat the rain.

As we arrived at another full shelter at 7 p.m., the rain let loose with a vengeance. It was great to be in the shelter during the storm, especially with a full belly.

May 20, Catawba Mountain Shelter to Cloverdale, Virginia (milepoint 708.1 north)

As Badger and I left the Catawba Mountain Shelter, I was looking forward to getting into town for a shower and clean clothes. It was getting to be a real drag putting on wet, stinking clothes each morning.

We headed up to McAfee Knob, considered by many to have the best view of Virginia in the state. The *Appalachian Trail Thru-Hikers' Companion* said that McAfee Knob was a tempting campsite for watching the sunset or the sunrise but noted that camping was not allowed in the area. "What a view! What a view!" was all I could think, as I reached a rock ledge and watched the breathtaking sunrise.

The view was beyond description, just spectacular.

Morning sunrise on McAfee Knob

"Geez!" Badger shouted as a large black snake slithered across the trail. I believe he jumped five feet in the air.

I could hear and see the Cloverdale/Troutville area from on top of the ridge although it appeared we still had at least a four-mile hike into town. It was 4 p.m. as we exited the trail onto Highway 220, and I was sucking air. The day had made for the best views in Virginia, no question, but the hiking was tough. Right off the trail, we had an Econo-Lodge or Best Western to choose from, as well as a Pizza Hut and several other restaurants right next door – a hiker's fantasy.

Showered and feeling much better, I went down to get a soft drink and found a hiker's map, some money, a credit card and some traveler's checks lying near the soda machine. I picked the stuff up and notified the front office. The management was able to contact the person, and his son sheepishly came up to our room to claim the lost money and cards. Later, his father came up and wanted to thank me personally, saying, "My son left my wallet by the soda machine while he was getting a soda. I could have killed him." Needless to say, the father was very grateful and insisted on giving me ten dollars. I repeatedly told him a reward was not necessary, but he insisted, saying, "Please take the ten dollars – it's the least I can give you. I don't know what we would have done if I hadn't gotten my money back." They were apparently southbound hikers, and I could certainly understand the dilemma they would have been in.

I called home and found out that a friend from home, Jim Poeppelman (Pep), was headed out on his motorcycle to hike with me a few days. It should be interesting trying to connect with him.

May 21, Cloverdale, Virginia to Fullhardt Knob Shelter (milepoint 713.1 north)

It was 7:30 a.m., I couldn't believe I was up so early. You would think that I would sleep in when I had the opportunity, but I couldn't. But it had felt sooooooo good to sleep in a clean bed and put on clean clothes.

> *Hiker tips: A word on shelters: Some are OK but most are filthy. Badger was in the laundry, and a hiker washing his sleeping bag told him, "I don't like washing my sleeping bag, but I picked up fleas in the last shelter."*
>
> *Badger and I had never thought about the possibility of getting fleas, but we had noticed a lot of little biting insects at some of the shelters. Hence, town stops were not just nice but were a must in order to maintain some semblance of healthy hygiene.*

We hit the grocery store to restock, and once again, I picked up too many things.

> *Hiker tips: When hiking, never use a grocery cart while shopping for food. Always use a basket that requires you to carry items, so you know how much weight you're adding to your pack.*

A local fellow outside the store stopped us and asked about our hike. I could see the envy in his eyes as he learned we were thru-hiking. "Good for you, Guys," he said. "Go all the way." If there was one negative about hiking the trail, it would be that the trail remained mainly up in the mountains, and thru-hikers did not often get to meet the residents of the towns along the way. I had heard that Earl Shaffer, the first to thru-hike the A.T. back in 1948, hiked the trail again in 1998, at age 79, and mentioned that he didn't like the modern trail as well, saying he spent a lot more time in the mountains.

I talked with the fastest hiker I'd met so far on the trail. He left Springer Mountain, Georgia, on April 16 and planned to complete the trail to Mount Katahdin in three and a half months, averaging more than twenty miles a day. Of course, he was young and in very good physical condition.

By 1 p.m., when we had yet to cross I-81, we realized we had gone the wrong damn way going out of town. Not very well marked, the

A.T. divided as it left town. With no white blazes in sight, we took the fork that appeared to be the most traveled, but after about a mile the trail just disappeared. As I told Badger, "It probably looked the most traveled due to the fact that everyone walked it *twice*, just like we did."

We passed a section-hiker headed south who told us, "I attempted a thru-hike in 1994 but quit after a few weeks." I could hear in his voice that he wished he'd completed the hike. Potential thru-hikers leave the trail for all kinds of reasons, some very understandable. Nevertheless, deep down inside, I think they all have that nagging feeling about not completing the trail.

We arrived at the unique Fullhardt Knob Shelter early in the afternoon after a short day. The shelter had a cistern for water that was collected from the roof runoff, and even had a faucet. I also met my first thru-hiker who had returned from Trail Days. Fix-it said he had a great time. There was a big crowd, but it was well-behaved due to the large number of police present for crowd control.

It really felt unusual to be at the shelter so early, but it did give us a chance to dry out our clothes, which were wringing wet from the sweat of a very warm afternoon hike. I enjoyed my powered fruit juice mix that we picked up in town, my attempt to liven up the increasingly boring taste of water.

It started to rain hard as we finished eating dinner; again, it was great to be inside a dry shelter watching the rain. Two hikers came into camp and put their tents up in the rain. I laughingly whispered to Badger, "What the hell is that all about? We have plenty of room here in the shelter, and besides, we just took a shower!"

As I talked with Fix-It, he told me he got his trail name by helping people out with their equipment when he first started the trail. As we talked, he mentioned the heaviest pack he'd seen, a 105-pound pack carried by a fellow with the trail name of House.

May 22, Fullhardt Knob Shelter to Cove Mountain Shelter (milepoint 730.5 north)

We left Fullhardt Knob Shelter on a cool and overcast morning. It had rained through the night, but the rain had stopped and I figured I had nothing to complain about.

I decided to have my wife send my puffball jacket back, as there had been a number of times that I could have used a warm jacket in the evening. Besides, I used the puffball as a pillow and didn't realize how much I would miss having it.

I met a southbound couple, a husband and wife team called Dynamite and TNT, who had a unique plan of thru-hiking the A.T.

They were flip-flopping the trail by starting at Harpers Ferry, West Virginia, and walking south to Springer Mountain, Georgia. Then they planned to get a ride to Mount Katahdin, Maine, and hike south back to Harpers Ferry. It was a good plan for slow hikers or those starting later in the season. It was clear they could handle adversity, as the two of them laughed when Dynamite said "We tented in a low spot last night, and the water created a small lake inside the tent. What a mess!"

We arrived at the Wilson Creek Shelter and another milestone, one-third of the way to Mount Katahdin, Maine. We celebrated with GORP and a Snickers bar.

At milepost 97, we crossed the Blue Ridge Parkway for the first time. According to my *Data Book*, we would be crisscrossing the Parkway and Skyline Drive for the next 200 miles.

We arrived in the town of Buchanan, Virginia, and I was quickly told by a friendly local it was pronounced, "Buck Canon." When I checked *The Thru-Hiker's Handbook* concerning Buchanan, it read, "hard hitch, not recommended as maildrop location," due to the difficulty of getting a ride into town. But Badger had a scheduled maildrop, and although the highway into Buchanan looked deserted, we attempted to hitch a ride. Just when we began to wonder about ever seeing a vehicle, up pulled a truck. Badger and I were quickly dropped off at the local post office and soon found that a truck would be in order for all the supplies he had received in his maildrop. Man, did he have the supplies! He promptly sorted items to mail ahead to his next maildrop so he would not have to carry so much. I told Badger, "You may have to change your trail name to Packhorse or Mule."

> *Hiker tips: Probably the biggest problem with maildrops was getting too many supplies. I found it worked better for me to buy the supplies I needed and use the maildrops for only those supplies I couldn't get along the trail, which, I found, was not much.*

Badger and I lucked out and got a quick hitch back to the trail with a former thru-hiker by the trailname of Zip Drive.

> *Hiker tips: I usually shaved every few days. Besides just the feeling of being cleaner, I found it much easier to get a ride when I was clean-shaven. I used a great little travel razor that was extremely light and had shaving cream right in the handle.*

Zip-Drive told us that he'd heard that a person was killed by a bear attack in the Smoky Mountains the day before. Although the information was sketchy, he was told the female hiker was just out in the woods with her husband who was fishing. Badger chimed in that a local in town told him that there was a bear in the Cove Mountain Shelter area that tore into some hikers' gear. We would be hanging our food high in the trees. I personally looked forward to seeing a bear, so I had my camera ready.

We only had three more miles until we reached the Cove Mountain Shelter and it was still early. With eighteen miles in, as well as the maildrop pickup, we were really feeling good about our hike; and unless we fell off the side of the mountain, it was going to be a great day of hiking.

Got to the shelter at 6:30 p.m. after hiking nineteen miles for the day, and everyone was talking about the bear attack.

We also heard about more trail magic, as Fix-it had crossed the Parkway and met a fellow with a cooler of beer. He offered Fix-It a beer and said, "Take a few for your friends." So there I sat in the shelter with a beer from a trail angel and a sandwich from town. I was in hiker heaven.

I also heard another trail story in camp. A hiker found a rattlesnake on the trail and wanted to show it to the other hikers, so he caught it and carried it the ten miles into camp. Apparently, there was a great deal of skepticism as he told his story about the snake, at least until he reached into his pack and pulled the snake out, rattler and all, for a show and tell! The other hikers became true believers as they scattered throughout the camp!

May 23, Cove Mountain Shelter to Thunder Hill Shelter (milepoint 749.5 north)

It was 6:30 a.m. as we left the Cove Mountain Shelter and, for the first time in a long while, was the second hiker out. Sea Otter, the first out, was planning to put in some big days in order to complete the trail in three and a half months. He said something about a girlfriend, and I guess a guy would do anything to get back to his girlfriend. No bears yet, so it looked like we would save the first bear sighting for Pep, my friend from home.

A young hiker passed Badger and me as we made our way down the mountainside. He was really picking them up and laying them down. As he passed at super-sonic speed, I yelled, "Hey, what the hell's the hurry?" to which he replied, "I'm letting the gravity flow!" I told Badger, "If we let the gravity flow like that, we would find ourselves lying in a crumpled heap at the bottom of the mountain."

We stopped briefly at Bryant Ridge Shelter, one of the finest shelters I had seen on the trail. It was too bad it was so early because it would have been a great shelter for the evening. Completed in 1992, the tri-level timber-frame shelter was one of the largest on the A.T. A couple of the old-timers I had talked to in Buchanan bragged, "Son, you need to stop by the new Bryant Ridge Shelter and take a gander." They were really proud of it.

There appeared to be a lot of section-hikers on the trail. We could always tell the difference between the section-hikers and the thru-hikers. Most thru-hikers on the trail after a couple of months were "lean and mean" as Badger would say. I would also conclude that thru-hikers smelled a little lean, too!

Badger and I got to Cornelius Creek Shelter, and that was a good place for lunch with Thunder Hill Shelter, our destination for the night, only five more miles ahead. A number of hikers ate lunch with us. Most were headed to Thunder Hill Shelter, making for what I was afraid would be a very crowded shelter. I could see one hell of a mountain off to our north, and I guessed it to be Apple Ridge Mountain, over 4,200 feet.

We entered the Thunder Ridge Wilderness and passed under the "Guillotine," a giant boulder that was stuck between two rock formations over the trail. According to *The Thru-Hiker's Handbook,* it's one of only three places on the entire A.T. where thru-hikers walk under a rock.

In the midst of a forest of azaleas, we hiked up to the Thunder Hill Shelter, a lovely place to spend the evening. I figured I would begin leaving messages for Pep in the possibility that he would stop at one of the shelters. It surely was going to be tough meeting up with him. We had a few rude hikers come into the shelter late who decided to cook right in the shelter while people were trying to sleep. Thank God for those trusty earplugs.

I woke up during the night to find a mouse in my pack and could not help but notice how bright and beautiful the moon was. I didn't think I had ever seen it so bright and actually believed that I could have been hiking by the light of the moon.

Another hiker in the shelter, Sicily, was also planning on meeting someone, and we agreed that it was difficult trying to make connections. Sicily had lost twenty-five pounds and was anxious to meet up with her husband and son and see their reactions to her weight loss. Weight loss was definitely a positive side effect of thru-hiking, as long as a hiker did not lose too much weight.

May 24, Thunder Hill Shelter to Johns Hollow Shelter (milepoint 766.8 north)

Badger and I were up early and headed north through another

beautiful stand of azaleas. The aroma was particularly pleasant considering that no one in my immediate vicinity had showered for a number of days.

I believed I had found the perfect trail to hike on: hard packed dirt and pine needles, with trees all around offering shade but open enough so I could see the azaleas in full bloom. Top that off with a cool breeze and sunshine, and you had the perfect trail.

The young fellow who passed us the other day saying he was letting the gravity flow caught up to us again. When we saw him at the next shelter, I asked him what his trail name was. "You know," he said, "I don't have one."

I winked at Badger and told the young hiker, "You do now, Gravity Flow."

At Mats Creek Shelter, I wrote a quick message to Pep in the register and talked with six high school boys from Pennsylvania, who told me they were hiking the A.T. as a special project for the last month of school. I wasn't sure about the benefits of hiking the A.T. as an educational experience. Being a former high school principal, I figured it was just a ploy to get the hell-raising seniors out of the building during the last month of school. But as I left, they were in an intense debate about where to spend the night, and I could tell they were learning cooperation, teamwork, problem-solving, and compromising.

While I was trying to get some water at the creek, I stepped on a moss-covered rock and went down like a shot. I broke my water filter top. I was lucky I didn't break my neck

We hiked into Johns Hollow Shelter about mid-afternoon and I took a quick bath down in the creek before other hikers arrived on the hot and sweaty day. The six senior boys arrived and planned on camping in their tents, which made me one very happy hiker. In no way did I want to deal with six high school boys in the small shelter. Besides, given the large number of mosquitoes buzzing the shelter, sleeping in tents was probably not a bad idea.

> *Hiker tips: I would highly recommend carrying a mosquito head net on the trail. The buzzing of mosquitoes in my face or ears had been practically eliminated with the bug net*

Around 9 p.m., just as I was ready to retire, in came Apollo, a thru-hiker I had met earlier in my hike. He was celebrating becoming an uncle with a six-pack of beer and kindly offered me one, which I gladly accepted.

Apollo filled me in on how several hikers whom I had met earlier in my hike were doing. He also mentioned Plumber, who was said to leave a lasting impression on anyone he met on the trail due to the seven-foot copper pipe he carried as a hiking stick. "You can hear that damn plumber coming five miles down the trail," Apollo said, exaggerating at least a little.

May 25, Johns Hollow Shelter to U.S. 60 (Buena Vista, Virginia) (milepoint 786.2 north)

Apollo, Badger, and I headed out on the trail after a rather restless night's sleep, due to the warm weather and mosquitoes. We hiked up Big Rocky Row, a 1,000-foot climb and quite a wake-up call, but at least it was much cooler up on the mountain.

A small box turtle crossed the trail in front of us. I told Apollo, "I'm so damned hungry, I could eat that turtle." The scary part is that I was halfway serious! Talking to Apollo at lunch, I found out that he got his trail name at the exact same spot I got mine, at Bly Gap, when some hikers said he looked like a rocket as he climbed the mountain. Thus, the trail name Apollo.

As Badger and I stopped at a creek to filter some water, a local was dipping his plastic jugs in the water and filling them up directly out of the creek. Although he didn't say a word, I could feel he was looking at me as if to say, "What the hell, you too good to drink out of the stream?" So I casually said, "I try and filter all my water, just to be on the safe side."

In a somewhat irritated voice, he replied, "This here water is safer than that damn city water you fellows drink!" Although I was not a city fellow, and with the movie *Deliverance* still vivid in my mind, I figured it best to keep my mouth shut. So with an agreeable nod, I headed north up the trail.

As we hiked into Brown Mountain Creek Shelter, there was no sign of my friend Pep. The town of Buena Vista, Virginia, was only two miles away; and since I was out of food and had not showered for five days, I decided to hike out to the road and get a hitch into Buena Vista. Due to his last gigantic maildrop, Badger had more food than he knew what to do with and elected to stay on the trail. He would tell Pep where I was if he showed up.

When I reached U.S. Route 60 where the A.T. crossed, I put my thumb out for a ride as I walked toward Buena Vista. There was supposed to be a little general store about a mile away that had a phone, and I figured I would get a lift or at least have access to a phone.

A half-hour later I still had no ride and the general store was out of business, so no phone. But luck was again on my side when a taxicab, returning from the trail after dropping off another hiker, stopped and offered me a ride to town for five bucks.

I checked into a little motel across from a Burger King and a convenience store. I talked to Connie on the phone and found out that Pep was in the area. The clerk at the motel also mentioned that he thought a fellow on a motorcycle had been there looking for a hiker. So I headed to do my laundry and hoped to hear from Pep. I was also able to call my oldest son Bruce, and he was teasing me about reading an article in *Backpacker* that talked about the traditional A.T. nude hiking day in June. I told him I had heard there was a fellow out on the trail hiking nude, but I had not met him yet.

May 26, U.S. 60 (Buena Vista, Virginia) to Fish Hatchery Road (Montebello, Virginia) (milepoint 802.5 north)

It was 8 a.m. as I sat in my hotel room. Not having heard anything from Pep I had arranged a ride back to the trail. Just as I was about to set out, up rode Pep on his motorcycle. When we checked on each other's whereabouts the previous night, we couldn't believe that we had stayed in separate hotels in the same town! I had even checked the hotel he stayed at, but evidently he hadn't yet checked in when I called. Regardless, he and I were headed for the A.T. and planned to hike together for awhile before he hiked back to his motorcycle and then rode ahead to meet us near Montebello, Virginia, further north on the trail. It was really nice to hike with a friend and catch up on the news back home.

After about two hours of hiking and talking, Pep turned around and hiked back to his cycle as I headed north to catch up with Badger. I picked up a submarine sandwich to share with Badger for lunch. I figured he was about an hour ahead of me, so I had to hustle to catch him by lunchtime.

Passing Cow Camp Gap Shelter, I met some people looking for Team Wisconsin. They told me they talked to a fellow from Wisconsin a short time earlier. That had to be Badger, so I was closing in on him.

I caught up to Badger at noon. He was talking with a trail angel by the name of Piney, who was handing out cold soft drinks. They went well with the sub sandwich I had packed. Piney told us with a grin, "I used to have beer, but a young hiker drank one too many. She got so drunk I was afraid she was going to walk right off the side of the mountain when she left here, staggering down the trail!"

The conversation got around to nude hiking day. "I remember when the nude hiking day started back in the 1980s," Piney said with a smile. "A few young people did it for a lark, and it's been a tradition ever since."

We met Crash again and heard his wild story about a rat-infested shelter he had stayed in. Not having a tent, Crash always slept in the shelters, and said with horror, "I woke up in the middle of the night and realized there was no one left in the shelter except me and a rat the size of an opossum!" He continued with wild eyes: "As I scrambled to get out of the shelter, the rat actually hung on to the sleeping cloth I took with me and I had to shake it loose!"

Unexpectedly, I met Pep coming up the trail and his first comment was, "Guess who's cooking dinner?" It turned out to be the Montebello Fire Department! Plans had been to meet Pep in the little town of Montebello and ride on his cycle for food and lodging. But there was no lodging in town, evidently because of Memorial Day, so Pep figured we would have to stay in a shelter on the trail. Not wanting to backtrack to the shelter we had passed a few miles back, I suggested we hike to a campground down the trail where Pep had parked his cycle and find a camping area there.

By 6 p.m., the three of us were in Montebello, where the fire department was holding a horse ride. Pep had made arrangements with one of the firemen to park his motorcycle, having given a little donation to their cause. When we asked if we could tent in the same area, the firemen not only said OK but even offered us some home cooking, inhaled by me as Pep sat in wide-eyed amazement. He was not used to being around a thru-hiker with an appetite that was in overdrive. One of the firemen even offered to take us part of the way up to the trail the following day, for it had been a two-mile walk down to Montebello, and I was not looking forward to a two-mile walk up to the trail.

May 27, Fish Hatchery Road (Montebello, Virginia) to Maupin Field Shelter (milepoint 820.7 north)

Up early, I found myself strolling around a fresh-smelling pine-forest camp area where a large number of horses – for the fire department's horse ride – were tied up behind our tent. "Happy Trails to you, until we meet again. Happy Trails to you . . ." Pep was also up, singing, or should I say, butchering, "Happy Trails." I guess the camp and horse atmosphere had overwhelmed him and prompted the sorry Roy Rogers impersonation, much to my distress and, I would guess, to the distress of any other campers within earshot. I figured it was time to move on.

Bill, a trail angel with the Montebello Fire Department, had offered to drive us as far as he could, up to within about a mile and a half of the A.T. At one time the dirt road was open and he could drive all the way up to the trail, but no more.

> *Hiker tips: I would not recommend Montebello as a stopping point for thru-hikers; the very small town was a good two miles off the A.T., and as I mentioned, the dirt road between trail and town is closed to traffic. Besides, the post office in Montebello closed at two o'clock p.m. and campsites were expensive. There was, however, a general store and phone if one were desperate for supplies, a phone, or both.*

After we got back on the trail and began hiking north, the first vista we reached for the day was Spy Rock. The location was said to be used by the Confederate Army to spy on Union troops during the Civil War. While standing on the enormous rock outcropping, I could certainly see how holding the area was a military advantage. One could see for miles in all directions.

There was an eerie quiet up on Spy Rock; the remnants of a stone campfire and the smell of smoke in the air made me feel as though I was in the midst of a Confederate encampment.

A hiker had scratched a note in the dirt, "Worth It," next to the A.T. just before Spy Rock. It was intriguing how hikers would take the time to leave notes for other hikers regarding the benefits of visiting a certain vista off the trail.

I was quickly jolted out of my mystic visions of Confederate soldiers by a group of junior high school girls who came staggering down the trail from an apparent night in the mountains. Their tangled, matted hair and blank stares told me they'd had enough of Mother Nature's wonders. One girl wobbled under the weight of a mini-van size pack, not to mention the two large rocks she carried in each arm! Why? Who knows! Only those who have shared in the delight of raising a junior high-aged girl could appreciate their unique thought processes.

As I hiked downhill toward the town of Tyro, I slipped, landing hard on my elbow! Although I did not break anything, my entire arm – from my shoulder to the tip of my fingers – was numb. That was definitely my hardest fall on the trail to that point, and it came on a very rugged and treacherous downhill stretch.

As we passed through Cripple Creek, the rain began again. Everything became very slick, making the hike down the side of the mountain even more difficult. We were close to 4,000 feet and headed down to 700 feet. Quite a descent!

"Badger look---!" is all I could get out of my mouth. He was gone! It all happened so fast that I couldn't do anything but watch with horror as he and his backpack went tumbling like a box turtle over the side of the mountain! Afraid to look and expecting the worst, I took my pack off and slowly crawled to the mountain edge. There, to my great relief, was Badger, lying face up like a spider in a web, in what appeared to be the branches of a small tree about ten feet below. With a grimace on his face and a slow, wary hand check of his extremities, my dazed but undaunted hiking partner shouted up, "I think I'm still in one piece!"

He untangled himself from the branches and crawled back up to the trail. He was bruised and scratched but otherwise appeared to be all right, considering he had just rolled over the side of a mountain. That was the worst fall I had seen anyone take on the trail, and Larry had certainly lived up to his trail name: he was one tough Badger! I had thought for sure that I would be setting a broken bone. With a smile on his scratched and bloodied face, he asked me, "What kind of score would you give me on my dive?"

With a nervous chuckle, I said, "A 9.9, but only because I don't give 10's. Besides, we have a lot more mountains to hike and you may take another dive."

Although we were joking, our nervous laughter could not completely hide the seriousness of what had happened and the thought of what could have been. Thank the good Lord for the small tree that prevented Badger from tumbling on down the mountainside!

We passed a trail maintainer. What a day to be working on the trail: windy, rainy, and cold. He was doing a great job, and with a grin oblivious to the terrible weather, he told us we had four more miles to Maupin Field Shelter. We were both tired and hungry. It had been a very tough and rugged eighteen miles, or – in hiker lingo – an ass-kicking day!

It was 6:48 p.m., and the rain poured down outside the Maupin Field Shelter as we arrived to find it empty. A note in the shelter encouraging everyone to go to Rusty's hostel quickly explained the lack of hikers. Rusty's was said to be a unique experience and well worth the extra mile or so off the trail, but we were just glad to be in the shelter as the rain pounded on the tin roof. Having nearly inhaled our cooked noodles for dinner, we settled in for the night. With a roof over our heads and a full belly, what more could a thru-hiker ask for?

After another typical day of adventure, laughs, and challenges, I was ready for a good night's sleep!

May 28, Maupin Field Shelter to Rockfish Gap (Waynesboro, Virginia) (milepoint 841.2 north)

Up at 6:30 a.m. on a cool damp morning, I tried my GORP mix

with a little powdered milk and water in an attempt to add a little variety as well as calories to my breakfast. It was OK, but I would not run to the store to buy it.

We had a big day planned with a destination of twenty miles north. In checking what I thought was a bruised heel last night, I discovered a blister under the callus on my heel that had been causing a nagging pain. Although I could not see much in the dark shelter, I did use a pin to try to relieve the pressure; but the callus was really thick and tough, and I was not able to get very much fluid out.

It was very cool as we headed out, but, I said, at least it was not raining. Wouldn't you know it, as soon as I said it wasn't raining, it began to rain! It looked like it was going to be one of those rainy days as we started out with rain covers on our packs.

Down at Reads Gap on Virginia Highway 664, the Blue Ridge Parkway milepost read 13.6. We really needed to be careful. It was very foggy; and the cars, although going slowly, seemingly appeared out of nowhere. We crossed the Parkway and hiked in a field of tall, wet, cold grass, and I was completely soaked after the first twenty yards. But I looked at the bright side: my pants were getting washed as I hiked. For that matter, everything I had on was getting a good washing, including my pack.

There was a lot of evidence of trail maintenance in the area. The volunteers did a great job! Now if they could only figure out a way to get rid of the rocks. Speaking of rocks, most of the larger rocks out on the trail had names like Spy Rock or Cash Hollow Rock. So yesterday, I had named one "Badger Rock" after his tumble, and now we were both taking it very easy over the wet, moss-covered rocks.

Badger and I arrived at Cedar Cliff to an incredible view of the fog! As I heard one of the locals put it, albeit not very originally, "The fog is as thick as pea soup."

We reached Humpback Mountain with a tough climb up and over the rocks. Crash caught up and passed us as he had done many times. A very fast young hiker with a light pack, he could not believe we kept catching up to him. I told him with a wink, "It's kind of like the Tortoise and the Hare, don't you think?" Although he was fast, he had a tendency to stop and dally around in some of the towns, whereas Badger and I just kept trudging along.

We were still two miles from the town of Waynesboro when I began to run out of energy and had some very tired legs. I guess I should have expected tired legs after a twenty-mile hike, especially after a couple of long days in a row. We planned to take it easy the next day and were looking forward to a big hamburger in town. In fact, all I had seen recently in the shelter logs were notes from hikers talking about food in town. Just reading about food made me hungry.

We were up on the crest of the Blue Ridge Parkway, where the cars continued to go by at a snail's pace, most with their flashers on. It was extremely foggy, which made the road crossings very dangerous. I constantly had to remind myself that I could not get across a highway as fast as normal with my forty-pound pack.

Out of nowhere, I literally bumped into another hiker, and I asked him how far the Waynesboro was. "You just passed it!" he bellowed with a laugh. "I can't believe that!" I groaned. We were following the only thing that we could see, the white blazes, and had actually walked right by the town of Waynesboro! Even after receiving directions, we still couldn't see or find anything. We were told there was a hotel in the area, but damn if I could see it.

It was already 5:40 p.m., and the day had been a nightmare. A woman in a convenience store told us a hotel was just up the road on top of the hill. We walked up but could not see anything in the soup-thick fog, not even a large hotel, so we walked back down. When I talked to the woman again, she said, "Oh it's up there. Didn't I tell you to take a left?" I had to hold Badger back; I think he was about to strangle her. So up the hill we walked again. Saying we were frustrated would have been putting it lightly. We were tired, wet, confused, disgusted, and basically just plain pissed off!

By 7:30 p.m. it wasn't getting any better. We finally made it to the motel, but Badger's maildrop – the supplies he had arranged for Pep to drop off – were not there, and to make matters worse, no one seemed to know anything or give a damn about it! Not knowing if Badger would need to buy supplies, we decided to get a ride to another hotel that was within walking distance of stores in town. Things continued to go from bad to worse. After we were dropped off, we found out the motel was very expensive, but the clerk was kind enough to tell us about another less expensive motel, "Oh, just a mile or so away," and even called to reserve us a room.

Fifty minutes later, we were still walking to the cheaper hotel. But it was not "just a mile or so away." It was more like three miles. Never again would I believe someone when they say, "Oh, just a mile or so!"

Two very tired and frustrated hikers finally made it to the budget motel on the outskirts of town and were told the only restaurant within walking distance was closed. So it was 8:30 p.m. as we called a cab to go find something to eat. So much for saving money on a budget motel!

May 29, Rockfish Gap (Waynesboro, Virginia) to Calf Mountain Shelter (milepoint 845.8 north)

As Badger and I prepared to head out, it was raining again; so we decided to do some laundry, hoping the rain would stop and also giving our legs a little more rest. The soap dispenser was not working in the self-service laundry, so a local trail angel drove us to a grocery store where we could get laundry soap and some other supplies we needed. He even took us back to our motel. What a trail angel! In a town the size of Waynesboro, which was larger than most towns along the A.T., at least in Virginia, we were really thankful for the rides.

The day before had been a long and disgusting day, to put it mildly. We did finally locate Badger's care package that morning. Turned out that the hotel would not keep it, so Pep had taken it to the visitor center next door to the hotel.

It was noon by the time Badger and I picked up his package at the visitor center and prepared to head back to the trail. I surely hated the thought of getting everything wet again right after washing and drying all my clothes, but I figured wet clothes were part of life on the trail. We had a difficult time just leaving the hotel. Our pre-arranged ride showed up; but the hotel clerk, who knew I had called for a ride, did not notify us that our ride was at the hotel, so it left. We ended up calling a cab to get us back to the trail.

The fog was gone as we left the visitor center in Rockfish Gap for the trail, and all Badger could do was shake his head and say, "It's hard to believe we could not see any of these buildings yesterday!"

> *Hiker tips: Be sure to stop at the A.T. visitor center in Rockfish Gap. It is open until 5 p.m. and had names of shuttle drivers and a list of places to stay, everything hikers would need to make their stays easier – everything we did not have. I was told that Waynesboro was the largest trail town on the A.T., and hikers definitely needed assistance getting around.*

I headed north, munching on a Baby Ruth candy bar. I had been eating everything in sight and still losing weight. Actually, I'd gone a little crazy back in town and bought too many food items – at least that was what my back was telling me as I heaved my overweight pack onto my shoulders.

I stopped and filled out a visitor card to the Shenandoah National Park as we headed north through a huge metal gate, and we laughed as I asked Badger, "Are those gates to keep bears in or out?"

We arrived at the first crossing of Skyline Drive at McCormick Gap, milepoint 102.1. What a beautiful view, and what a difference a day made! It was then I felt a sharp bite on my neck. I grabbed the little critter with a deathly squeeze as I threw off my pack. I had felt something fall on my neck a little earlier, but it only felt like a leaf or twig out of a tree. I don't know what type of insect it was, but it surely got me good.

We headed up Bear Den Mountain and spotted six to eight old, steel tractor seats mounted in the ground overlooking the valley, an indication someone else must have been impressed with the views.

"Gray skies are going to clear up! Put on a happy face!" I had done it to myself. I put another song into my head that I couldn't get rid of. That could drive a hiker crazy.

It was 5:30 p.m. as I finished eating, and I tried to decide if I wanted to use a bear pole or not. A young hiker came into the shelter toward evening, very excitedly, saying, "I just saw a bear crossing the trail a little ways back!" This resulted in a mad rush out of the shelter. Not to see the bear! Instead, everyone scrambled to hang his or her food on a bear pole!

May 30, Calf Mountain Shelter to Pinefield Hut (milepoint 872.0 north)

Another cool morning after a very cold night. I still had my warm twenty-degree down sleeping bag, and I was glad I did. I even put on my long-sleeve shirt and rain jacket just for extra warmth.

Hiker Tip: Potential thru-hikers take note of the date –
May 30 – and the need for a warm sleeping bag!

I was still looking for my first bear sighting, as we all got a good laugh from the young hiker who came into camp saying he had just spotted a bear. Apparently, he thought he had spotted another bear earlier in the day. "But when I got closer," he said, "I realized it was Woodchip with her large black pack cover leaning over picking some wild berries!"

Having added a bagel and peanut butter to my usual cheese stick and sausage, I finished off lunch feeling more full than usual. I was using peanut butter in a squeeze bottle, an idea picked up from another thru-hiker that was really handy on the trail, even if it did have the weight of a damn brick in my pack.

We talked to a southbound section-hiker during lunch. He'd left Harpers Ferry about eight days ago. Badger and I were really glad to hear that it only took eight days, for Harpers Ferry was where we had arranged to meet our wives in eight days.

Badger and I arrived at Blackrock trailhead on the Skyline Drive, and the sign listed an overview of the three-mile hike up to the summit.

It also warned hikers to "Watch for rattlesnakes" in the loose rock. I enjoyed crossing the Skyline Drive. Everyone was driving slowly, waving at us, and really enjoying the drive. After we filled up with water along the trail, we met a couple of day hikers from Washington, D.C., who were really decked out in the latest hiking gear. We dubbed them the million dollar hikers. As I told Badger, "They certainly had the Indiana Jones look, right out of the L.L. Bean catalog." The park was really well marked with concrete mileposts wrapped in metal bands listing the different distances. There were also trashcans at all of the gaps and at road crossings, so there was no excuse for leaving trash in the park. That also certainly helped lighten our loads.

We stood within ten feet of a deer as it slowly meandered away. They seemed to be as tame as ponies! In the park we hiked past a camper that was parked only yards from the trail, definitely the closest spot on the trail that I had seen anyone outside of the hiking community permitted to camp. It was an ideal place to park a camping trailer, as the camper could literally walk out the door and be on the A.T. with a truly beautiful view of both the trail and valley. The Loft Mountain camp store was also well stocked. A hiker really would not have to be carrying any food supplies, as there appeared to be a number of locations to pick up supplies right on the trail throughout the park.

> *Hiker tips: For northbound hikers, there was a sign indicating where the camp store is located, but do not follow those directions. Follow the A.T. north, and you will wind around to within a few yards of the camp store, saving you eight-tenths of a mile in blue blaze backtracking.*

As I headed north I walked past deer as thick as rabbits.

We crossed the skyline drive at the Ivy Creek Overlook, milepost 77, where an A.T. marker showed a map of the trail. It read, "The park hosts ninety-five miles of trail and the A.T. crosses the Skyline Drive 28 times. Traveling south on the trail you will travel over 860 miles to Springer Mountain, which will be more than two million steps. Northbounders have more than three million steps and 1280 more miles before reaching Mt. Katahdin in Maine..."

We hiked into the Pinefield Hut shelter, and I jumped over a little creek right in front of the shelter. Then I heard a splash and turned around to see Badger in the water. I started to laugh as I sat down in the shelter, where two sectional hikers were already sitting.

They asked me, "Aren't you worried he might be hurt?"

"Worried about Badger? Hell," I said, "I just saw him fall off the side of a mountain a couple days ago. A little water isn't going to hurt him!"

Sure enough, up he popped, with a Wisconsin Badger grin on his face.

After checking the *Data Book* we realized that we had just hiked another marathon day – twenty-six miles. No wonder our feet were tired. It was time for a hot dinner and some sleep.

May 31, Pinefield Hut to Bearfence Mountain Hut (milepoint 892.6 north)

We awoke to another very cold morning, and I was again really thankful to have my cold weather clothes. Two section-hikers in the shelter were not prepared for the temperature. One, who worked for the telephone company and went by the trail name of Dial Tone, said, "I thought I was going to freeze to death last night!" He was headed out to get a warmer sleeping bag.

At the base of High Top Mountain, we took a little break and changed into t-shirts and shorts for the warm climb to the top.

It was noon as we reached the top of High Top Mountain on a really gorgeous day, but the view was not as clear as I had hoped. I'm told it may be caused by pollution from the cities.

As we hiked north on the trail, I spotted a deer with a fawn. When they saw me, the fawn instantly dropped like a rock and lay completely motionless. The doe slowly crossed the trail in front of Badger and me in an obvious attempt to coax us away from the fawn. I walked up closer to the fawn to take a picture, and it did not flinch or move a muscle. I had been told that fawns did not have a scent and remained motionless to avoid danger.

We stopped at Lewis Mountain Campground for a break, and we hoped to get a few supplies from the camp store, but it had just closed. As the lady locked the door, she noticed me walk up and offered to open up long enough for me to purchase some supplies – more trail magic! I bought some snacks to go with my dinner and a pint of ice cream to hold me over until I got to the shelter. The clerk smiled as she mentioned that a few young thru-hikers had been in earlier and had bought some beer. She said with a wink, "You may be in for a noisy shelter tonight."

As I arrived at Bearfence Mountain Hut, (in the park they called the shelters, huts) there were three young thru-hikers by the trail names of Dog, High/Low, and Worm who were enjoying the evening with their beer. They offered me one, which I drank, as they proceeded to explain how they got their trail names. Worm spoke first: "I got my trail name because of the way I inch around the shelter in my sleeping bag while I sleep."

High/Low said, "I've had some real high days and a few low ones!"

Dog simply said, as he grabbed a handful of hair, "My shaggy long hair." Another hiker who had just come into the shelter was called Do It Yourself because he had made his own backpack.

It had been another great day on the A.T.: good weather, views, and knee-saving terrain. The Shenandoah Park had been kind to me as I finished day 63 on the trail.

June 1, Bearfence Mountain Hut to Skyland Park Lodge (milepoint 908.7 north)

I left the Bearfence Mountain Hut – in short sleeves, as it looked like it would be a warm day – and headed to Big Meadows Wayside for a mouth-watering hamburger. Then it was on to Skyland Park Lodge with the thought of getting a room for the night, which is always an extra incentive for the day's hike.

I'd had a fairly good night's sleep except for a mouse attack! Around 1:30 a.m. I was awakened by the sound of a mouse chewing on my food bag. As I didn't find any tuna cans with strings in the shelter to hang the bag from the ceiling to keep the mice from the food, I decided to take my food bag outside and hang it from a bear pole. To my surprise and great delight, I had to literally wade through a herd of deer grazing outside the shelter on my way to the bear pole. Much like cattle, they did not appear to be at all concerned. I actually had to push a couple of deer aside to get through the herd.

At Milam Gap, a sign warned backpackers not to camp between Milam Gap and Big Meadows due to the numerous reports of bears entering camps and harassing campers in the area. As we passed a cemetery within the restricted area, Badger asked with a laugh, "You think that cemetery might be the result of people ignoring the sign?"

As we hiked toward Big Meadows, a grouse ran beside me on the trail. I had never seen anything like it. Seemingly injured, it appeared to be limping and dragging its wing.

A second grouse flew out of the brush and landed on the trail directly in front of me, ruffling its feathers and hissing. I finally understood: first the limping grouse, then the aggressive grouse, both obvious indicators they had a nest of young close to the trail. Wasn't that something? I had hiked more than 900 miles, and the only animal attack I had to talk about was an irritated grouse protecting its young!

It was noon as we arrived at the Big Meadows Wayside to enjoy a big burger and fries. Lunch was great, but we had to hike a lot further off the trail than I'd anticipated, and I didn't care much for that. But being at Big Meadows certainly brought memories of visiting the area with my family years earlier. That visit brought my very first encounter with a thru-hiker and the realization that there was actually a white-blazed trail from Georgia to Maine.

We met two day-hikers, and as we chatted away, I noticed something. I pointed to one of the hikers' legs and asked, "Is that a tick on your leg?" He jumped and let out an "I'll be damned!" as he quickly brushed it off his pant leg. "Thanks, man! I'll need to keep an eye out for those little bloodsuckers."

> *Hiker tips: Having read about the tick problem associated with Lyme disease, I had taken a series of three shots over the past year in preparation for my hike and was glad I did.*

We arrived at Skyland Lodge, and I decided to treat myself to a cabin and a shower. I was also told that I could get a dinner at the lodge and that there would be some local entertainment in the lounge in the evening. I couldn't think of a better ending to a beautiful day of hiking.

Chapter 3
Skyland To Delaware Water Gap

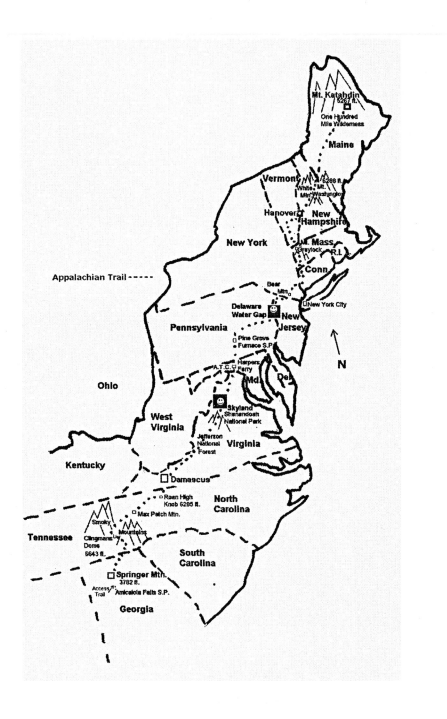

Mt. Katahdin
5267 ft.

One Hundred
Mile Wilderness

Maine

Vermont
5288 ft.
White Mt.
Mtn. Washington

Hanover
New Hampshire

New York

Mt. Mass.
Greylock
R.I.

Conn

Appalachian Trail - - - - -

Bear Mtn.

New York City

Delaware Water Gap
New Jersey

Pennsylvania

Pine Grove
Furnace S.P.

Harpers Ferry
A.T.C.

Md.
Del.

N

Ohio

Skyland
Shenandoah National Park

West Virginia

Jefferson National Forest

Virginia

Kentucky

Damascus

Roan High Knob 6285 ft.

North Carolina

Max Patch Mtn.

Smoky Mountains

Clingmans Dome 6643 ft.

Tennessee

South Carolina

Springer Mtn.
3782 ft.

Access Trail
Amicalola Falls S.P.

Georgia

June 2, Skyland Park Lodge to Range View Cabin (milepoint 928.1 north)

Got an early start as I left the Old Ash Cottage, my cozy little cabin for the night, at 6:30 and met Badger for breakfast.

Hiker tips: I would highly recommend the Skyland Lodge: food and lodging right off the trail and the best orange juice I've ever had, fresh-squeezed. I also had the apple cobbler with ice cream and it was delicious. I was certainly able to eat well through the Shenandoah National Park and, best of all, I did not have to carry any food supplies.

I passed the highest point of the Shenandoah Mountains at 3,837 feet. Some of the hikers joked that it was all down hill from there. Wouldn't that have been nice?

Badger and I arrived at Pinnacle Picnic Ground to find a water fountain and restroom right on the A.T. I told Badger, "If all of the A.T. were like the Shenandoah National Park, I bet there would be a lot more people thru-hiking." I did notice some bear scat around the picnic grounds. It would make sense that bears would be in the area looking for food. I was still anxiously awaiting my first bear sighting.

We stopped at the Panorama at Thornton Gap and had another burger with fries and a big milkshake. That made four days in a row I'd had ice cream. Heading for Thornton Gap and more food, I was practically eating my way through the Shenandoah National Park.

At Thornton Gap, a chatty waitress asked Badger, "You seen any bear yet?" He shook his head as she proceeded to tell him about a hiker who had been in the restaurant a week earlier after a bear ripped into his tent. It had destroyed everything in sight, including his metal water bottle that still carried the teeth imprints. She said the hiker told her, "That's enough for me! I'm getting the hell off this trail before I end up being some bear's dinner!"

My pack felt a little heavier as we headed back into the woods. I hadn't been able to resist the butter-pecan and chocolate-walnut homemade fudge they had for sale. I figured it would be a great evening snack in camp.

During a phone call to my wife, she told me that Horace Green, the trail angel who gave us a ride to the Homeplace in Catawba, had heard that Badger left his hiking pole there, so he went back to retrieve it. He'd contacted my wife with the hope she could return it to Badger when she next met up with us, and even volunteered to mail it to her. What an incredible trail angel!

We hiked up to milepost 28.5 on the Skyline Drive and were glad to be out of the woods for awhile. With no breeze, the bugs were driving us nuts. On the plus side, I really liked how they marked the springs in the Shenandoah Mountains with a big metal post right on the trail.

As Badger and I stopped for a break and a little fudge – I know, it was for an evening snack – a young fellow hiking south told us in an excited whisper, "Just saw a bear back on the trail!" That was all I needed to hear. I jumped up and headed north with my cameras at the ready, and Badger – a little more hesitant – close behind.

A bear sighting! My first bear sighting on the Appalachian Trail! It wasn't a particularly large bear, and it didn't let me get very close, but it certainly was an awesome sight in the wild.

We stopped at Elkwallow Gap in hopes of a soda and something to eat, only to find the grill had closed at 5:30 p.m. "Bummer," I groaned to Badger. While Badger and I drank a soda from a machine, a park ranger stopped and asked in a very official manner, "Have you seen or do you know the whereabouts of a hiker named Worm?" We said that we had met Worm a few nights back in a shelter but that was the last we had seen him and his hiking friends. We certainly hoped everything was OK as we hiked north, on the lookout for bears.

And we saw another one, which looked like it was a cub. Badger asked nervously, "If that's a cub, where do you suppose mommy bear is at?" To which I replied, "I don't know, but wouldn't you know it, as soon as we start to look for a campsite for the evening we see two more bears… could make for an interesting evening." No sooner were those words out of my mouth than I saw another bear scamper off into the woods.

We arrived at the locked Range View Cabin just after 7 p.m. and set up our tents for the evening. Having seen a couple of bears, we made sure that we cooked and ate our dinners a good distance from our tents and hung our food bags just as far away.

Seeing those bears reminded me of the local entertainer at the lodge who asked the audience, "Any of you want to see a bear?" Of course, the tourists all held up their hands (me included), so he told us in his down-home drawl, "All you need to do is take a big old, juicy McDonald's Big Mac and go sit out on a ledge tonight. You'll see some bears right fast!" We all got a good chuckle out of that. But I don't think there were any takers!

Ace and Alias, two young thru-hikers we had met on and off, hiked into camp and decided to join us for the night. They hadn't seen any bears so far, and they really felt left out when we told them about our bears.

I headed to bed wondering if we would have any black furry visitors during the night.

June 3, Range View Cabin to Jim and Molly Denton Shelter (milepoint 953.4 north)

It was early as I awoke and sat on the porch of Range View Cabin, eating breakfast as I enjoyed the beautiful view of the valley below with the mountains in the background. Hikers were not permitted to stay in the cabin and were asked not to tent close to the cabin, but nothing indicated we could not use the porch for breakfast. Ace and Alias were a little bummed out about all the talk of bear sightings and complained, "You guys are talking about seeing all of those bears and we've only seen a few lousy snakes!"

I'd slept well, considering a herd of deer meandered around our campsite the entire evening and I could actually hear them chomping on grass just outside my tent.

Arriving at Skyline Drive's milepost 21.1 after a two-mile hike and was heading to the third peak of Hogback, I stopped and talked to a trail maintainer. He asked how our evening had been and was surprised and seemingly a little disappointed when he heard that we had a quiet evening. "I can't believe you had a quiet evening," he said. "We had some hellish storms in the D.C. area that included hail and high winds!"

We were meeting a large number of day hikers, and I quickly realized it was a weekend. The days on the trail tended to run together after awhile. In the words of one thru-hiker, "Every day is a weekend when you're thru-hiking the Appalachian Trail."

Badger and I reached the north entrance to the Shenandoah National Park and were officially leaving the park. I'd enjoyed the park, and I take my hat off to the Potomac Trail Club for doing an outstanding job of trail maintenance. It's a great place for a five-to-seven-day hike. It's not as challenging as other sections of the A.T., but it can certainly give a hiker the idea of what the trail is like, and it's a great place to be introduced to the Appalachian Trail.

We hiked past a note attached to a tree by a hiker named Moses that read, "I want all of my friends on the trail to know that I fell and cracked my kneecap. I am off the trail but plan to get back on as soon as I can and still hope to finish the trail this year." A very unhappy reminder of how dangerous the trail could be.

Around 4:30 p.m. we arrived at U.S. Route 522 where I hoped to get a hitch into the town of Front Royal, Virginia, while Badger headed north on the trail to find a campsite for the night. I planned to meet up with him later.

I got a ride into Front Royal and found myself a big steak dinner and a few brews. While in town drinking a cold beer, I asked one of the locals how the town got the name of Front Royal. "There are a lot of versions," he said, "but the one I believe to be true comes from a story of a British soldier." Apparently as the soldiers were being trained, the commander became frustrated with one of them and ordered the soldiers to "front up" in front of a large royal oak tree, hence the name Front Royal. He added, "Front Royal was once called Hell Town, due to its reputation as being a very wild town during Colonial times."

> *Hiker tips: Front Royal is an easy hitch into town and has a lot of conveniences for hikers within easy walking distance. Combine this easy accessibility in and out of town and the many conveniences, and Front Royal makes a good food and resupply stop.*

To be honest, I might have had a few too many brews with my dinner. It was well after 7 p.m. when I got a lift back to the trail, and it was difficult to get going again, but I headed north to find Badger and the campsite. Before I hit the trail, though, I was able to stop for an ice cream cone. That made it five days in a row with ice cream, a backpacker's dream.

As the sun began to set, I was finding it difficult to see the trail. I wasn't sure if that was due to the lack of sunlight or that last Guinness. Badger and I had agreed he would put his bandana out on the trail if he camped anywhere off the trail, but I saw no sign from Badger or a campsite.

It wasn't good. It was 8 p.m. and there was still no sign of a camping spot. It looked as though I would be setting up camp in the dark. I guessed that I had missed Badger back on the trail and I figured it would be best if I pushed on to the next shelter, even though it was three more miles and that would put me in at about 10 p.m. I wasn't happy about hiking in the dark, but I was also not delighted by the thought of putting up a tent in the dark and not having any water source.

I located some water near the trail around 9 p.m. I gave some thought to setting up camp there, but I had heard other hikers talk about hiking at night, so I figured: what better time to give it a go? I only had about an hour until I reached the next shelter, and besides, it was a cool evening with no bugs. My challenge would be to not miss the shelter sign on the trail.

It became too dark to see, so I began using my headlamp on the rocky trail. I was surprised that I could see the blazes so well, but I found it difficult to see both the blazes and the trail at the same time with my headlamp. I continued to be extremely concerned that I would be so intent on watching the trail that I would miss the sign for the shelter. Then what would I do?

It was just before 10 p.m. when I spotted the sign for the Jim and Molly Denton Shelter. Never was I happier to see a shelter sign. And there was Badger. "Hey, Slayer!" he yelled. "Good to see you. I couldn't find a level spot to camp so I decided to hike to the next shelter." Like me, he had not planned to hike so far, but circumstances dictated we hike longer and we were both glad we did. The shelter had been recently built and had a beautiful wood deck with a shower not far away. I planned on getting some water and then heading to bed. It had been a very long day.

June 4, Jim and Molly Denton Shelter to Rod Hollow Shelter (milepoint 953.4 north)

My start was later than usual, due in part to the very comfortable and roomy shelter. Along with the cooking pavilion and nearby shower, there was even a spigot for water – not the typical shelter along the trail.

I hadn't been very impressed with hiking at night. I guess if it were really hot and there was a full moon, it might be all right, but personally, I found it difficult and not a pleasant experience at all. At least everything turned out OK.

Trailside shower, a rare but welcome find

Badger and I compared notes about the U.S. Government Zoological Compound we'd hiked beside most of the day before. It was huge! *The Thru-Hiker's Handbook* read that it covered thousands of acres and was home to many rare and endangered animals and birds from all over the world. Originally a military compound and U.S. Cavalry Remount Station, it supposedly had a sign that read, "No Trespassing. Violators Will Be Eaten." But we hadn't found the sign and obviously had not been eaten.

We were walking in dense woods, and the sounds of the birds reminded me of the sounds in a jungle. Combine that with all the vines hanging down from the trees and all the undergrowth, and one could easily believe he was on an African safari.

And then we missed the trail again! We'd been having a lot of trouble following the trail, due in part to all the rocks and in part to the many paths going in all directions from people taking short cuts. After about ten minutes of backtracking and searching, we again relocated the trail.

An interesting fact for history buffs is that the 27 miles of A.T. we were hiking followed the western boundary of the base of operations for the Mosey Rangers during the Civil War. John Singleton Mosey led a Confederate Parsons Ranger unit in the exact area from 1863 to 1865.

I hiked up to the Manassas Gap Shelter, and as I sat down to rest, I found a hand-written note beside a hole in the shelter floor: "Be aware, there is a copperhead that lives in this hole. 6-1-00."

"What the hell!" I hollered as I jumped up. "That is one hell of a way to let someone know about a snake -- after I'd already sat down!" I thought to myself. I then took the note and attached it to the side of the shelter so hikers could see it as they arrived at the shelter. I did notice that the note seemed to have been written in a hurry!

As we met day hikers headed south, I continued to be amused at their reactions when they asked, "Where you headed?" And we replied, "Maine!" They looked at us as if we had gone crazy.

I was moving a little slowly after not getting much sleep. I had been too excited from hiking in the dark and too apprehensive about not finding a shelter, to fall asleep very quickly the night before.

We arrived at Ashby Gap, Virginia, on U.S. Route 50. There was a little grocery store off the trail where Badger resupplied and headed north. But I was interested in a warm meal and was lucky enough to find a friendly local who gave me a lift down to the Blue Ridge Restaurant, where I had a nice open-face roast beef sandwich.

Hiker tips: Although the waitress at the Blue Ridge
Restaurant took my money, I got the clear impression

that she did not want hikers as customers. I might be wrong, but I don't think so.

Hitchhiking back to the trail from the restaurant was quite an experience, as a truck stopped to pick me up and the two Spanish-speaking fellows in it greeted me with, "No Engleese!" Against my better judgment, I got in and tried to explain that I only needed to go a mile. They only smiled and gave me a puzzled look. So I just waved at them to go until I said stop. Again puzzled, they simply shook their heads, smiled and said, "Si." We went racing off, and just a mile down the road I yelled, "Stop!" They both threw up their hands and stared at me as if I had gone out of my head and was about to shoot them. I motioned for them to pull over, and they shook their heads in agreement and swung the car to a screeching stop. Motionless, they sat in the car until I climbed out; then they shouted something in Spanish that resembled "loco hombre!" and drove off. Although I could not understand any more than that, it was probably for the best, for they flipped me the international hand signal as they drove away.

I was headed to Rod Hollow Shelter and traveling blind, for I had been using pages cut out of my *Data Book* to save on weight, and I was now beyond the pages I had with me. I planned to meet my wife in Harpers Ferry, West Virginia, in a few days, but until then, I would be without – to me and to many hikers – the ever important information from the *Appalachian Trail Data Book*.

It was a beautiful late afternoon, as the sun was setting and the temperature had cooled off. I also had a bag of chips and a bottle of Gatorade for the evening. Again, I was in hiker heaven. What more could I ask for? And then I came upon some fresh, steaming bear droppings! I hoped that the bear didn't like Gatorade and chips. It was going to have a real fight on its hands to get mine.

By the time I had my tent up and my water bag filled it was 8 p.m. There was a sign in camp that read, "Trail Shower" pointing down to the creek, and I thought, "Great, I'll be able to take a quick shower." But when I got to the creek, all I found was a measly little half-inch pipe sticking out of the creek about a foot above the ground. Obviously, someone had a terrific sense of humor or was a midget.

June 5, Rod Hollow Shelter to Blackburn Trail Center (milepoint 990.1 north)

We were on the trail and headed north to Harpers Ferry, West Virginia, on another beautiful morning. I felt very rested and had come to the conclusion that I simply slept better in a tent. As we hiked north, we came upon an interesting sign: "Hiker Notice: Warning, you are about to enter the Roller-Coaster. Built and maintained by the trail boss and his band of merry crewmen of volunteers. We will see you at the Blackburn Trail Center if you survive." Not what I wanted to read at 6:30 a.m. Apparently the Potomac Appalachian Trail crew had a real sense of humor. They were probably responsible for the one-foot high shower at the last campsite.

By 9 a.m. I was already one hot and sweaty hiker as I filtered water near Sawmill Spring. The roller-coaster trail was living up to its name and reminded me of Georgia with the many ups and downs. As I stuck my hand in the water, I couldn't help but notice how warm the water was and remembered with delight earlier in my hike when I'd iced my ankle in the streams and was only able to soak it for a few minutes.

"My God look at the size of that anthill!" I yelled at Badger as we passed two of the largest anthills I had ever seen. They looked like someone just dumped a couple truckloads of sand right by the trail. They were at least four feet high, and oh, were the ants active!

As we hiked toward the shelter, I said to Badger that I hoped we would get there before it rained, to which he responded brazenly, "Shit, I don't care if it snows. Let it come." I wasn't sure what that was all about. Maybe he was feeling a little cocky, or he might have been a little woozy. He had taken a hard fall a little ways back and had blood flowing from each elbow. That could have affected his judgment.

Headed down the mountain, we noticed – leaning beside a tree – a brand new hiking pole. Another hiker's nightmare: walking off without equipment after taking a break. There was no name on it and we had no way to know if the person was hiking north or south.

Hiker tips: I would suggest putting your name and address on as many pieces of equipment as possible. I had address labels printed, and taped them on everything that would hold tape.

Just passed Sam Moore Shelter and heard the strangest noise. Badger thought it was a bear cub crying, but whatever it was, we couldn't see it in the dense forest, and we were not about to go look and maybe become some mamma bear's lunch.

We arrived at the Bear's Den Hostel. We'd planned to hike down to a restaurant for lunch, but were told by hikers that the restaurant was not open on Monday, so we ate lunch with some hikers who were taking the day off at the hostel. Bear's Den Hostel is a beautiful 1930s stone building only 150 yards off the trail. The Potomac Appalachian Trail has fixed up the old home, which was once used by a Washingtonian as a summer home. It definitely was the cleanest and nicest hostel I had seen so far on the A.T. We picked up a few items from the hiker box just in case there were no food sources along the trail.

> *Hiker tips: A hiker box is a container where hikers put items they no longer need and think another hiker may find useful. The boxes can usually be found in just about every hostel along the trail. They are worth checking when you're low on supplies or want to lighten your load.*

Well, my string of days with ice cream looked to be stopped at five in a row, as the closed restaurant was my last chance for the day.

Near Crescent Rock, we met two electric company crewmen, one still in the utility truck and the other out on the treacherous rocky road checking how far they could drive. As I hiked by, the fellow checking out the road asked, "How far this here road go?"

With a shrug, I answered, "Hell, I don't know! All I do is follow the white blazes!"

Then the big fellow in the truck yelled, "I hear there are snakes up in these rocks! Even rattlesnakes! Have you seen any today?"

I replied matter-of-factly, "Not today, but I did see a copperhead yesterday!"

His eyes got as big as the headlights on his truck as he bellowed at his partner, "Get the hell out of those goddamn rocks and get back in the truck! This here fellow says there's snakes in them there rocks!"

I laughed as his partner scrambled across the rocks and jumped into the truck, hollering, "Let's get the hell out of here!" All that reaction, and they hadn't even seen a snake! I couldn't imagine how they would have reacted had they come across one. It was a nasty thought, but, oh, what I would have given for a rubber snake about then!

We had hiked more than seventeen miles when we got to the blue blaze trail leading to the Blackburn A.T. Center. Although three-tenths of a mile off the trail, it looked like it was going to rain, and when I had the opportunity to get in out of the rain, that was my choice.

It was right at 5 p.m. when we hiked down to the Blackburn Center. We really hit the jackpot. An old log summer home built by a doctor out of Washington, D.C., in 1910, the building was being restored and turned into a hostel by the Potomac A.T. Club. It was a fantastic place. We stayed in the bunkhouse and were the only hikers there. The caretakers, Courtney (Mogo) and Bob (Yukon Cornelius), had both thru-hiked the trail in 1998. I asked Courtney about getting some food for the night and she asked, "How's spaghetti sound?" My chin almost hit the floor. I couldn't believe what I was hearing, and all I had hoped for was some type of snacks. She went on to say they really didn't have food for hikers, but as there was just the two of us, she would cook up some spaghetti. What a wonderful gesture on her part! A kinder trail angel I had never met!

I took a solar-heated shower, and even though it had been cool and overcast all day the water was fairly warm. And as hard as it was to believe, Mogo offered me ice cream for dessert! My streak was still intact! Six days straight of ice cream and counting.

I called my wife, and she was all set to pick up Badger's wife at the airport and then head to Harpers Ferry. I arranged for us to meet them at Crampton State Park in two days.

A sign at the center read, "Springer Mountain is 991.8 miles from here. Mount Katahdin is 1,166 miles from here. The halfway point is Hunters Run Road just north of Tag Run Shelters. Total miles equals 2158.8."

> *Hiker tips: I would certainly recommend Blackburn Center to any hikers. Only .3 miles off the trail, the accommodations were great and the price was right: strictly donations! Hats off to Courtney Mann and Bob Stubblebine, the wonderful caretakers at Blackburn Trail Center.*

June 6, Blackburn Trail Center to American Youth Hostel (Harpers Ferry, West Virginia) (milepoint 1003.3 north)

After an enjoyable evening we headed out from the bunkhouse of the Blackburn Trail Center around 8 a.m. I woke up several times to the sound of rain pounding off the bunkhouse roof and thought how nice it was to be in the dry cabin with the warm, toasty wood-burning stove aglow.

Badger and I were about to cross another state line. Virginia had approximately 500 A.T. miles, more than any other state the trail passes through, so we were really happy about crossing into West Virginia and then moving right into Maryland. The A.T. actually travels through fourteen states altogether and we had only been in four states and were closing in on the halfway point. Obviously, we would be covering a lot more states in the next couple of months.

We crossed the Virginia-West Virginia line at Loudoun Heights, where a sign welcomed us to West Virginia. We had Jefferson County, West Virginia, off to our left, and to our right was Virginia.

It was 1 p.m. as we crossed the Shenandoah River into Harpers Ferry National Park and marked another milestone: we had hiked 1,000 miles.

Badger and I visited the Appalachian Trail Conference Center, where we registered as thru-hikers and had our pictures taken. The staff at the center numbered each picture as it was placed in the thru-hiker book. Badger and I were the 226th and 227th thru-hikers passing through Harpers Ferry headed from Georgia to Maine. I was surprised that there were not more hikers ahead of us. Staff members there told us that only about 60 percent of the thru-hikers starting in Georgia make it to Harpers Ferry. The exact distance of the Appalachian Trail for the year 2000 was 2167.1 miles; the mileage changes from year to year because of construction and re-routing. In fact, the trail was seven miles longer than it had been in 1999. The staff at the center also recorded thru-hikers' reactions to the places visited along the way and kept track of both negative and positive experiences. Not surprisingly, I wasn't the first to report a negative comment about the Blue Ridge Restaurant on U.S. 50.

> *Hiker tips: A very informative center with an extremely friendly staff, the Appalachian Trail Conference Center is something no hiker should miss. One other service provided at the center was a record of hiker names, addresses, and trail names for future reference.*

The staff members at the center even said it was OK for us to bring our packs into the office. Astonished, I said, "I've hiked over one thousand miles on the A.T., and this is the first place that has welcomed my pack!"

Back on the trail, we headed north through Harpers Ferry. We passed St. Peter's Catholic Church, built in 1833 by Irish Catholics who were working on the Baltimore and Ohio Canal. During the Civil War, the resident priest flew the British Union Jack as a symbol of neutrality, thus saving the church from destruction.

We hiked right through the heart of town, which included John Brown's Civil War Park. The town of Harpers Ferry was packed with historical significance, especially Civil War encounters. I was told that the town of Harpers Ferry was taken over by Union or Confederate forces seven different times.

After crossing the railroad bridge that spanned the Potomac River, the white blazes follow the C&O Canal Towpath for a short distance. After considerable effort, we located the blue blaze trail and a hand-written sign painted on a railroad bridge reading, "Hostel, proceed at your own risk." I could see why the sign referred to risk, as the blue blaze trail went right over the railroad track.

After a brief climb up the side of the mountain, we arrived at the Harpers Ferry American Youth Hostel. To my surprise, it was the same hostel that I had visited while on a biking trip along the C & O canal towpath with my friend Jim (Pep) and his son Lee. The rooms were much nicer, but I decided to tent outside for the night after I learned that a bicycling group was coming in later and that it might become noisy.

So, three dollars for a tent site and restroom facilities. It was hard to beat the price. Interestingly, the lady running the hostel seemed to be partial to thru-hikers, giving orange sherbet ice cream to thru-hikers only. That made seven days in a row.

The bicyclist staying at the hostel were touring battlefields on their bikes, certainly an interesting way to visit the Civil War battlefields. They really filled up the hostel, so I was glad to be in my tent.

Badger and I only hiked fifteen miles but had enjoyed our time in the Appalachian Trail Conference Center. We were looking forward to seeing our wives the following day and really exploring the town.

June 7, American Youth Hostel (Harpers Ferry, West Virginia) to Crampton Gap (Gathland State Park) (milepoint 1012.6 north)

We were headed out of the hostel bright and early after a restful night, except for the trains through the night that necessitated my putting in my earplugs.

> *Hiker tips: I would recommend the American Youth Hostel (AYH) to any thru-hikers, but be alert in looking for the signs to the hostel. We almost missed the sign painted on the railroad bridge from the canal path.*

Badger and I passed a section-hiker who told us about car-jackers in the area, warning us, "The thieves watched as hikers headed into the woods, then hooked up to their cars and were long gone before the hikers returned!"

"Welcome back to civilization," I grumbled to Badger.

We arrived at Crampton Gap and the Gathland State Park. A one-time retreat for George Alfred Townsend, the famous war correspondent, the park now has a large stone monument dedicated to all war correspondents. It was also the site of a large Civil War battle at South Mountain.

Connie and Alice arrived at the park about noon. We drove to Harpers Ferry, where we checked into the historic Hill Top Hotel that sat high above the Potomac River, overlooking both Maryland and

Virginia. As we enjoyed a wonderful dinner in the hotel taproom, we could actually see the A.T. and the C&O Towpath from the outside dining area. Yes, I had ice cream for dessert.

June 8, Crampton Gap (Gathland St. Park) to Turners Gap, Maryland (U.S. Alt. 40) (milepoint 1019.8 north)

Before breakfast, our wives got us to the self-service laundry to clean our clothing and gear. They asked, "How can you stand the smell of that stuff?" To which Badger and I both responded, "What smell?" I guess we'd been in the woods a little too long. We had a great (all-you-can-eat) breakfast at the hotel and then went to the Outfitters Store to get a few supplies.

We headed back to Gathland State Park for some hiking (can you believe it?) for the afternoon. Connie and I planned to drop Alice and Badger off on the trail at Dahlgren Church and then drive south, back to Gathland. We would then hike north and meet Badger and Alice somewhere in the middle of the seven-mile stretch and give them the car keys so they could pick us up.

We met the Badgers headed south around 3 p.m. and took a few pictures. As we were about to leave Connie asked, "Aren't you forgetting something?" We almost forgot to give them the car keys.

Connie and I reached the Old South Mountain Inn (near the Dahlgren Church), and although it's a little high-end for thru-hikers, we went in and had something to drink while we waited for Badger and Alice. Hanging on the lounge walls were numerous pictures of current and past presidents, as well as photos of Henry Kissinger, Bob Hope, and other celebrities. The close proximity of Camp David obviously encouraged dining by the many celebrities and dignitaries. After the Badgers arrived, we went into Boonsboro, Maryland, for a very nice dinner and then back to Harpers Ferry to the dessert bar at the hotel. Our wives could not get over how much food Badger and I had been consuming, or as my wife proclaimed, "inhaling!"

June 9, Turners Gap, Maryland (U.S. Alt. 40) to Raven Rock Hollow (milepoint 1036.7 north)

It was a bit late – 9:30 a.m. – when we left the hotel for Turners Gap after another great breakfast. Badger and I decided to get a good day's hike in while the wives did some sightseeing and shopping. We'd had a nice hike with Connie and Alice the day before, but they assured us that one day of hiking was enough for awhile.

I noticed in my *Data Book* that in five miles we would be crossing I-70 on a footbridge constructed just for the A.T. hikers. I remembered driving under the footbridge with its sign "Appalachian Trail" and promising, "I will be on that bridge some day." My wife urged, "Sure, sure; just keep on driving." The sign was a constant fuel to the fire that burned in me for many years until I finally got on the Appalachian Trail.

Before we headed out, I made a phone call back home to my cousin Keith, and we talked about his doing some hiking with me at a later date. I was moving faster than anticipated, so it would be more difficult to arrange, but I was hopeful that we could work it out.

Hiker tips: Hikers will be surprised at how difficult it is to stay in touch with friends and family. The window of opportunity for hikers to contact home can be very limited, making it extremely difficult to make connections.

We talked to a couple of thru-hikers who were doing the "Maryland Challenge," which is hiker lingo for a border-to-border hike through Maryland in one day, a distance of about 42 miles. One hiker left at 4 a.m., trying to complete the challenge. I tended to believe a hiker had to be a little crazy to attempt it. Of course, many of my friends believed I had to be a little crazy to hike 2,167 miles. I figured it was relative. It also reinforced the axiom, "Hike your own hike."

Since our wives had arrived, our appearances had changed drastically. We were sporting recent haircuts, and Badger had on a new shirt and shorts as well as a new pair of hiking boots. Alice shared, "The kids said they were tired of seeing him in the same old clothes in every picture he sent home." On the trail, other thru-hikers were really ragging us for our clean appearance. One even said, "I don't believe you guys are thru-hikers – you're too damn clean!" Regardless, it really felt good to be "decontaminated," as my wife put it.

We hiked by the Washington Monument. No, not the one in D.C. According to *The Thru-Hiker's Handbook*, the monument we hiked past was built in 1827 by the local people of Boonsboro and was the first monument to George Washington.

As we arrived at the footbridge crossing Interstate 70, the many questions I had asked myself years before flooded back: "How would it feel to be actually standing at this point on the A.T.? What sights would I have seen? What stories would I have to share at this juncture in my hike?" I was now at that point, and it felt great to be finding out the answers to those questions first-hand. With the Appalachian Trail sign boldly proclaiming the trail on the side of the bridge, many of the drivers passing under the bridge honked their car and truck horns, waved and shouted words of encouragement to Badger and me as we

White blazes over I-70

crossed. It was a great feeling.

It was after 5 p.m. when we hiked to State Highway 491 and found our wives waiting. "Boy, it's great being picked up after a day of hiking," I said. "You think you could do this more often?" Without hesitation, they replied, "Dream on!"

When we checked back into our hotel, Connie and I finally got the call we had been waiting for. We were the proud grandparents of a healthy baby girl born to our oldest son Bruce and his wife Christy. Caitlyn was our first grandchild.

June 10, Raven Rock Hollow (Maryland) to Pa. 16 (Blue Ridge Summit, Pennsylvania) (milepoint 1045.2 north)

It was early in the morning as we headed out for a short hike that would take us into Pennsylvania, another milestone under our belts and one we hoped to share with our wives.

As I continued to lose weight and inches from my waistline, I found the waist belt on my backpack could not be taken in any more, and I was forced to pad the belt by duct taping another section of my Z-Rest sleeping pad to it. The extra padding seemed to help, but I would only know for sure when I got all the weight back in my pack. I planned on sending several items home, which didn't seem like a great saving of weight; but as I learned early on in the hike, "ounces become pounds."

In talking with Badger and Alice about maildrops, we all agreed that proximity to the trail was more important than the number of days between drops, or for that matter anything else.

> *Hiker tips: It is extremely important to stress to those sending items in the mail that a hiker may get to the drop earlier than planned, so those mailing should be sure to have everything there a few days early. Nothing is more frustrating than hiking twenty miles and hitching a ride five miles into a town to find a package has not yet arrived. Plan carefully. I personally did not use maildrops too frequently. My wife and my son brought me supplies, as did my friends, Jim and Keith. When we were planning my hike, I specifically planned to use things that I could easily find in most grocery stores or even convenience stores. I was very happy with the outcome of my decision to limit the number of maildrops.*

We reached the blue blaze to Devils Racecourse Shelter. A sign indicated the shelter to be half a mile off the trail. For obvious reasons, I was very happy not to be staying in that shelter.

It was noon as we hiked into Pen Mar Park, a beautiful historical park with a great deal of picnic seating and a convenient concession stand. We met a charming elderly lady who told us that the park in earlier times had a large pavilion used as a dance hall as well as a stage for many notables of an earlier era, such as the famous cowboy singers Tom Mix and Gene Autry.

"You know," I told Badger, "just recognizing those two cowboy names really dates you."

Badger grinned. "How well I know, Slayer, how well I know," he replied.

As we were talking, Alice and Connie walked up. They had parked at the Pennsylvania/Maryland state line and walked the short distance south on the A.T. to the park to share lunch with us. Now if we could only figure out how we could get our wives to deliver lunch on a regular basis.

We met a fellow who was hiking with mirrors hooked on each of his hiking poles. I thought to myself, "Just when you think you've seen everything, up walks a hiker looking more like a truck on the interstate than a hiker!" But my thought soon turned into embarrassment as the hiker told us, "I am deaf and need the mirrors to check for people coming up from behind so I won't be startled." That was what I called not letting a handicap slow you down.

We crossed the Mason-Dixon line and were officially in Yankee territory, Pennsylvania.

It was early afternoon as we arrived at our final pickup point at State Highway 16 near Blue Ridge Summit, three miles north of the Pennsylvania line. We planned to return to the hotel for one more good night's sleep before the wives headed home and we headed north.

June 11, Pa. 16 (Blue Ridge Summit, Pennsylvania) to Quarry Gap Shelter (milepoint 1063.2 north)

It was already eighty-degrees and it was only 8 a.m., as we hiked north on the A.T. from Pennsylvania Route 16 and our wives drove west to Columbus, Ohio. Badger and I had really enjoyed sharing the beauty of the trail and the small towns with our wives, as well as the opportunity we had to introduce them to a number of the unique hikers we had been telling them about. We'd even hiked with them in three different states, not something we would soon forget.

But as much as I'd enjoyed hiking and visiting with my wife, it was nice to be back on the trail with a steady pace and nice not to have to worry about where and when to make connections. As I said before, towns are great, but they are also a real hassle. Or as one thru-hiker aptly stated, "Town stops are simply necessary evils."

I'd made some equipment adjustments during that last town stop. In addition to a lighter sleeping bag and some padding for my backpack belt, I put a donut insert into my boot in an effort to help my bruised heel.

We passed a group of Cub Scouts at the top of the mountain. One blurted out, with a sense of pride and forewarning, "You'll have a nice walk down, but just wait until you have to hike back up!" To which I smugly replied, "No chance of that, we're not coming back."

I could tell they didn't fully understand, but their leaders were quick to clarify: "Fellows, what you have here is a couple of thru-hikers. There's no turning back for them – they're headed to Maine!" Of course, the usual "Ooh's" and "Aah's" followed as did a multitude of questions from the wide-eyed future thru-hikers.

I was impressed how the leaders taught the scouts proper trail etiquette. As we approached the troop, I heard the leader shout out, "Hikers coming!" The troop then stepped off to the side of the trail in single file. It was really nice to see adults setting such fine examples and taking the time to instruct young people.

Badger and I passed two day-hikers from Washington, D.C., and I mentioned how hot it was. They responded, "If you think it's hot here, you ought to be in the city!" They had escaped D.C. for the mountains, much like many wealthy Washingtonians did in the early 1900s when they built summer homes up in the cool Appalachians.

We reached Chimney Rock Mountain wringing wet, and although I was tired and soaking in sweat, it felt really good to be hiking hard again. On our way down the mountainside, we passed through the biggest grove of mountain laurel I had yet seen on the trail. It was just beautiful, like walking through someone's backyard garden.

Mounted on a tree we passed was a wooden box with a notebook inside. We hadn't been able to find registers at the last few shelters, and now realized that boxes are used for registers in Pennsylvania. I wasn't sure if I liked the boxes better than shelter registers. I couldn't see a hiker having the time, or for that matter, taking the time to put down his or her thoughts during the day, compared to the opportunities to do so in the evening.

We hiked to the Rocky Mountain Shelter, and hanging in the shelter was the biggest bag of Powers Bars I had ever seen. It had to weigh every bit of fifteen pounds! The hiker who bought that bag of Powers Bars had to really love them, or maybe his dad owned the company. Either way, the weight obviously overpowered any urge to pack them any further.

Nagging injuries continued to pop up on the trail on a regular basis. We spent some time during lunch talking to the Duke of Earl. A retired attorney from Rochester, New York, he was having some ankle problems and had been told there was a slackpacker by the trail name of Admiral hiking south who he hoped could offer some medical advice. The Admiral was said to be a retired naval orthopedic surgeon, and the Duke of Earl was hoping to find out just how bad his ankles were. The Duke said he had hiked twenty-four miles the day before. "Maybe I just overdid the hiking yesterday," he said.

I told the Duke of Earl, "If you want my two cents, when you do twenty-plus-mile days, the old body starts talking to you, and you should listen." If I only could follow my own advice!

We hiked through Caledonia State Park, a very busy park. The many hamburgers and hot dogs on the grills had me salivating. There appeared to be some type of swimming pool with a concession stand nearby, and as I answered hiking questions from a couple of young boys, they volunteered to run and get me an ice cream cone. Well, maybe it was my suggestion. I gave them a couple of bucks, and they were gone in a flash. To be honest, I thought so was my money. In a few minutes though, they were back, but without the ice cream, saying, "Sorry, mister, but our parents are going home." At least they returned my money. I could have walked over, but I really did not have the ambition necessary to keep my ice cream streak alive.

I cooked my dinner in the Quarry Gap Shelter with so many bugs drawing blood that I felt like a human blood bank. Tennessee was in camp along with Old Boot. Both of them started out the first part of March. A father and daughter from Columbus, Ohio, were also in the shelter. I smiled to myself, as it was obvious the father was having a much better time than the daughter.

June 12, Quarry Gap Shelter to Pine Grove Furnace State Park (milepoint 1080.5 north)

We were up at 6 a.m. to get an early start on the trail and beat the heat, but we could not beat the no-see-ums (gnats). They were vicious as they swarmed both Badger and me! We'd had a rain shower during the night, and I slept well. Something about gentle raindrops hitting the tent always made sleeping better. Old Boot and Tennessee were out ahead of us. I guess they had the same idea about beating the heat. The design of the Quarry Gap Shelter – with a picnic table in the middle of the two small shelters – worked great for cooking and socializing but really cut down on the amount of room in the shelter.

This would be a big milestone day, as we planned to reach the halfway point on the Appalachian Trail. I really looked forward to crossing the midway point. Due to the actual distance of the trail changing each year, the exact midway point also changed each year but was usually in the vicinity of the Pine Grove Furnace State Park. I was told a small store at the park had started a tradition of sorts, called the "Half-Gallon Club." Thru-hikers headed north or south had the privilege of joining the club. Hikers simply picked out their favorite ice cream on arrival at the store and consumed the half-gallon of ice cream within a half-hour. Bingo! The hiker became a lifetime member of the club. A half-gallon, in a half-hour, at the halfway point to Maine or Georgia.

We reached Sandy Sod Junction, elevation 1,980 feet, where the mountain laurel was in full bloom for as far as I could see. Another beautiful day on a perfect trail of pine needles, as the fragrance of mountain laurel floated all around me.

Badger and I hiked up to the small and very old Birch Run Shelters, where the register had more of the characteristic hiker poetry: "Oh the rocks of Pennsylvania are beautiful indeed, but I've only been here two days and they have caused me to bleed! I fell head first into a

153

bunch, they sliced my skin and my arm; if I'd only landed on my head they'd have done no harm!" Another read, "Damn, I am only just into Pennsylvania! The real rocks haven't even started yet. I ain't going to make it through. Game over, man! Game over, man! Hollywood Mike!"

We ran into a southbound hiker with the trail name of Arkon, from Manhattan, New York. Badger had hiked with him until Arkon left for his daughter's wedding, saying, "My wife was not real happy with me being on the trail while she was making all the arrangements for the wedding, so I figured I better try and make the wedding!"

A unique and opinionated fellow to say the least, he told us some real horror stories about the hike ahead. Extremely upset with the rocks and angry as hell at whoever laid out the trail, he believed the planners had intentionally taken the hikers over, as he put it, "every goddamn boulder and rock they could find!" To add to his misery, when he went home to New York, he was on a bus for sixteen hours and said, "It was insane; the bus ride just about killed me! At one point I was in the middle of a drug fight, two dealers fighting over a customer!"

When he decided to return to the trail, he'd flip-flopped, starting in New York and hiking down to Damascus, Virginia. Being a southbounder, he was now able to give us a great deal of information – even if it was unsolicited – about the trail ahead.

We entered a section of woods that was totally divest of leaves, giving the appearance of a forest in the dead of winter. Even the pine trees were stripped clean, and as I began to look closer, I noticed on the ground hundreds – no, millions – of caterpillars! As I continued to hike along, I thought it was beginning to rain, but after stopping and listening more closely I realized it wasn't raining. Rather, caterpillar droppings were raining down on me! Rest assured, I did not look up with my mouth open. Badger knocked one off his leg, as there were caterpillars all over, millions of them chomping away on the remaining leaves, and the noise was deafening.

Then, as quickly as we entered the barren section of woods, we re-entered a forest of lush green leaves. I could actually see the line the caterpillars had reached. It looked like winter bordering summer.

It was 4:30 p.m. as we reached Pine Grove Furnace State Park, and I headed directly to the store for the halfway challenge. I selected a half-gallon of chocolate but the clerk warned, "I'm not sure if I would pick chocolate. That's a whole lot of chocolate ice cream to eat in a half an hour." So I chose Neapolitan instead. Old Boot and Tennessee were already there and bragged with Wiley Coyote-like smiles, "We've already eaten our half-gallon," which I didn't believe for one minute.

Mountain Slayer partaking in the halfway tradition at Pine Grove Furnace State Park while Badger, Old Boot and Tennessee look on.

But not to be left out and caught up with the challenge, I began to eat the entire half-gallon. I had to force down – and I do mean force down – the last spoonful. This was one of the biggest mistakes I had made to date on the A.T. My stomach was churning like a milkshake machine, and I was not at all sure if I would keep the "Neapolitan mistake" down. Badger being wiser, did not get caught up in the halfway tradition. And although he didn't say a word, I could see the "I told you so" written all over his face.

We elected to bunk at the beautiful, old, red brick Iron Master's Mansion hostel that was built in 1829 and served as the residence for the ironmaster of Pine Grove Furnace Ironworks. The ironworks manufactured cannonballs during the Revolutionary War, and the hostel was a stop on the Underground Railroad. The historic old home was well preserved, very clean, and well kept, and currently had 45 beds.

From my calculations I had only three more miles to hike to reach the exact midpoint of my 2,167-mile Appalachian Trail thru-hike.

June 13, Pine Grove Furnace State Park to Boiling Springs, Pennsylvania (milepoint 1099.9 north)

As I ate breakfast in the kitchen of the Pine Grove Furnace hostel,

I noted the following posted rules: "Mark your food with name and date or it will be eaten by others. Wash, dry and put away all dishes. You may use the food on the pantry shelves, but please make a donation so we can continue to provide for others. Kitchen is closed and locked at 9:00 a.m." The kitchen was very popular and quite busy throughout the evening and morning. A father hiking with his son had cooked some bratwurst and offered me one. Being a thru-hiker, I could not turn it down in spite of a stomach still churning from a half-gallon of ice cream. The Iron Masters Hostel could be rated right at the top of the hostels in which I had stayed: clean linens with a bunk, use of kitchen facilities, shower and laundry, all for a fee of $14. And above all else, the hostel was located right on the trail.

> *Hiker tips: I mentioned how nice the Iron Master's Mansion hostel was. Sadly, that was not always the case with every hostel. In one particular hostel, a hiker had all of his valuables stolen while staying overnight. Badger had been at the same hostel that night and said, "I noticed one particular individual that looked suspicious, so I decided to keep all my valuables under my pillow, and I'm damn glad I did!" Some hostels could also be loud and have unruly guests. The Place in Damascus on Saturday night immediately comes to mind. Interestingly, to date, with a couple of exceptions, the hostels seemed to get nicer as I traveled north.*

Badger and I were out on the trail and headed north bright and early. It certainly felt good to be hiking in clean clothes, especially on a nice cool morning. The bugs were even in hiding, ideal for hiking.

I'd had the opportunity to visit with Tennessee and Old Boot at the hostel. Old Boot hailed from Colorado and had been teaching eighth-grade history for about fifteen years. He got his trail name from a friend who gave him a flask which had an old boot engraved on the front. The Old Boot was an expression out west for someone who was experienced and knew what he was doing. Tennessee, in his late twenties, operated a bulldozer and had told his boss, "I've decided to take a hike. See you in five months." Oh, the independence of youth.

It was 8 a.m. when Badger and I arrived at the official midpoint of the A.T. According to *The Thru-Hiker's Handbook*, Woodchuck, a thru-hiker in 1985, had erected the marker. Of course, the exact midway point differed a few miles every year from the 1985 midpoint, and there was talk about moving the marker to the actual midpoint each year. But that would mean the marker would need some type of wheels, and I was not sure the exact midway point really needed to be marked.

I found a shirt by the side of the trail. Trail ornaments had dwindled but continued to show up occasionally.

I hiked up to a deserted mountaintop campsite, and it was the damnedest thing I had ever seen: a nice big tent still staked to the ground, lying in a heap. The collapsed, rain-soaked tent, with gear scattered in every direction, gave the appearance that the campers simply said, "To hell with it!" and got up and left. About fifty yards down the trail, I could see where the campfire had washed down the mountainside. That probably told the story – my guess was that the campers were caught in a storm strong enough to flatten a tent and wash their campfire down the mountain. Still, I had never heard of anyone just up and leaving all their gear on a mountainside. It was odd to say the least.

We were thinking about staying at the Kennedy Shelter; but just after we got there, a troop of Girl Scouts hiked in to set up camp for the night, so Badger and I headed north.

The two of us hiked into Boiling Springs, Pennsylvania, around 5 p.m. and stopped at the Garmanhaus B&B where Badger persuaded me to set up my tent rather than stay in the B&B. The owner, Mr. Garman, was kind enough to let us camp in his backyard for a dollar. That was a great deal, as the other campground was a good distance out of town and not very close to the trail, and we were camping within walking distance of a number of restaurants in town.

Then it was 7:30 p.m., and I sat in my tent in a pouring rain, kicking myself for not being in the nice warm and dry B&B just a few yards away. I guess hiking had affected my brain. I did have a good pizza sandwich for dinner even though my stomach was still a bit queasy. That might have had something to do with a half-gallon of ice cream.

June 14, Boiling Springs, Pennsylvania to Thelma Marks Memorial Shelter (milepoint 1121.5 north)

I was up early and packed a wet tent. I still couldn't believe I'd stayed in my tent with a B&B so close. The rain had stopped, but it was still overcast, actually perfect for hiking the next section of the A.T., which I was told was flat and unbelievably hot during the summer.

It had been very nice of Mr. Garman to let us use his yard for camping the night before. He charged a dollar so he could have a little control over who stayed. He said, "I just like meeting and visiting with the different thru-hikers." He asked thru-hikers to sign where they were from on his world map, which had many names on it. Obviously, a lot of hikers had used his backyard.

> *Hiker tips: Boiling Springs is a good stop, and I would highly recommend the Garmanhaus B&B, preferably inside. It's also a good spot to replenish your water supply. We were told there was no water for eleven miles.*

The rain started to pour down very hard as we crossed a small country road. A fellow headed to work stopped his car to ask if we needed a ride to get out of the rain. "Yeah, I yelled through the pounding rain, "a ride to Maine would be fine." He had a good laugh at that as he continued on his way, and I'm sure he got a lot of mileage out of that line among his co-workers. Although I was standing in the middle of nowhere, soaking wet with a forty-pound pack on my back, and he was warm and dry in his car headed to work, I told Badger, "I wouldn't trade places with that guy for all the money in the world!" Badger shook his head in agreement as we sloshed north following the white blazes.

As one could imagine, we had all sorts of uniquely designed steps to allow us to cross the many fences along the Appalachian Trail, but I had to admit that the small opening I saw that morning, cut into the bottom of the fence to allow dogs to get through, was a first.

We came upon a hiker who was exceptionally clean for someone carrying the gear of a thru-hiker, so I asked if he was a thru-hiker. He responded tentatively, "I guess so?"

"What you mean, you guess?" I inquired.

"Well you see, this is my first day!" he replied with a half laugh. Apparently he had just gotten off a bus after a long ride from Indiana, and had picked Pennsylvania to start his thru-hike to Maine, followed by a flip-flop to Georgia. A first-day, flip-flopping thru-hiker, to whom I immediately gave the trail name of First Day. Needless to say, he was all excited and had all kinds of questions, and of course, way too much gear. He was snacking on a big bag of Fig Newtons and offered us some. We thanked him, grinning. "Sure," I said, "anything to help lighten your load." First Day asked us the distance to the next shelter. Interestingly, considering all the equipment he was carrying, he did not have a *Data Book*.

> *Hiker tips: I would not want to tell future thru-hikers what they "must" carry, for that has to be a personal decision, but to my mind, the Appalachian Trail Data Book is one very essential item!*

We met the Admiral and a group of young hikers who looked to be in their twenties. They were carrying only hiking poles and water as they zipped by. Hell, they were practically running down the trail. Hiking the Appalachian Trail that way did not appeal to me, but, once again, "Hike your own hike."

It was well after 5 p.m. when we finally arrived at the Thelma Marks Memorial Shelter. I was glad to see the shelter. My tired feet were really taking a beating, as they'd gotten wet for the first time during my thru-hike. I had walked in my L.L. Bean Crestas for more than 1,000 miles on the trail, and I'd had them for more than a year and a half before starting on the A.T., so they'd done well: to have the lost waterproofing be the only problem after so much use was actually pretty good. It was too bad, though, that I didn't have the cold springs of Georgia to soak my feet in. Badger's feet were really hurting him as well; twenty-two miles in his new hiking boots was working him over.

> *Hiker tips: Boots, like many pieces of equipment,*
> *stimulated wide and varied – often emotional –*
> *comments among hikers. I chose L.L. Bean Crestas*
> *years ago and have never regretted the decision.*
> *They've performed great for me.*

June 15, Thelma Marks Memorial Shelter to Peters Mountain Shelter (milepoint 1136.9 north)

Badger and I awoke to a damp, drizzly morning. Rain and fog blew into the shelter during the night, and our shoes were wet, as were our pants and packs. It was never fun waking up to a cold, wet morning, but as I told Badger, "It sure beats waking up and putting on a tie." I had slept pretty well, but with my new fifty-five-degree sleeping bag, I ended up putting on a pair of socks and a shirt. It was cool enough to see my breath, and with the dampness I got chilled. I began to think I had made a mistake exchanging my old twenty-degree down bag for the fifty-five-degree one.

We hiked into the town of Duncannon, Pennsylvania, and stopped by the Doyle Hotel, an infamous and very old hotel used by many A.T. hikers throughout the years. But it was not open until 11 a.m. We weren't looking for a room. I just wanted to get a look at the hotel that I had heard so many stories about. Arkon, the hiker from Manhattan who seemed to have an opinion about everything, had stayed at the Doyle Hotel and said, "It was only a bit better than the shelter I stayed at last night!" From the looks of the run-down hotel, his observation was not as much of an exaggeration as I first thought.

As I hiked north on the trail through the town of Duncannon, I talked with Bill Fritz whose home was right on the A.T. He said he'd lived there all his life, and I could tell he loved to talk to the many thru-hikers who passed by his home. When we told him that we'd stayed in the Thelma Marks Shelter the night before, he asked in a low whisper, "You know a young couple was killed in that shelter six years ago?"

Startled, I said, "No, and to be honest, I'm glad I didn't know that last night!"

He moved closer to Badger and me and said, solemnly, "I had talked to the couple just two days before the murder just like I'm talking to you right now." The couple had told Bill that they were headed to Harpers Ferry to get married. In a hushed tone he continued: "What really made the hair on the back of my neck stand on end was the fellow who later murdered them was standing right there with them. The young couple was very friendly and talkative, but the fellow with them didn't have anything to say." Bill said the murderer was eventually caught, and it turned out he killed the couple for their packs.

Mr. Fritz had a huge stuffed bear in his yard, six feet tall if an inch. I had Badger take a picture of me with the bear, and as I posed, Bill warned with a grin, "That bear was shot just up the road from here." He winked and added, "Right in the area you're planning on camping!"

> *Hiker tips: Duncannon is an excellent trail town, as the A.T. travels right through town, which gives hikers the opportunity to get whatever food and supplies they need. We were able to get something to eat, and I picked up some Pepto-Bismol for the upset stomach I'd had since I finished off that damned half-gallon of ice cream.*

It was pouring down rain as I tried crossing Pennsylvania State Highway 225 without much success. The traffic was unbelievable. Then, out of nowhere, a woman stopped her car and put on her emergency flashers, halting traffic, and motioned for me to cross. Another nameless trail angel.

It continued to rain very hard as I hiked under some large power lines. I could hear them snapping and cracking overhead, and I figured I could be zapped any moment! I was not about to dally. I headed north as quickly as possible.

I hadn't seen Badger after he stopped to talk to a hiker he knew in town, but I figured he should have caught me and hoped he was OK.

It was 5 p.m. when I finally arrived at Peters Mountain Shelter. The beautiful new shelter was not marked with a sign and, in the fog and downpour, was extremely difficult to spot down the blue blaze side trail.

My watch read 5:40 p.m. and still no Badger. I began to wonder if he'd missed the side trail to the shelter. Trying to be positive, I figured he'd had a good long visit with his friend and was probably just taking his time on the wet rocks. I changed into dry clothes and enjoyed a sandwich from town, and downed another of the anti-diarrhea tablets I had picked up. Having diarrhea while hiking was not fun. Add pouring rain and it was pure hell! I sure hoped I didn't have a stomach virus or – worse yet – giardia.

There were two female hikers staying in the shelter, and as soon as I hiked up they informed me, "If you need water you're in trouble. It's one hell of a hike down to the water." Fortunately, a local had already told me about the long walk, so I had carried enough water for the night.

The two section-hikers were what was left of five Kentucky women who were hiking part of the A.T. The two – Mountain Momma and Bookworm – were staying out for a few more miles while the other three Kentucky women had left the trail to go back to work. They told me with pride about Momma Boots, a former Girl Scout leader in her seventies who got them all interested in hiking the A.T.

Badger finally hiked in a little after 6 p.m. He'd evidently missed a white blaze, which caused him to go in the wrong direction and forced him to backtrack to the trail.

Peters Mountain Shelter was a beautiful new shelter and was large enough for about twenty hikers. Besides Mountain Momma and Bookworm, the only other hiker there was Lightning Bolt, a thru-hiker from Brooklyn, New York. I had a nice chat with Lightning Bolt about the New York area and got more information about how my daughter, who lived in Brooklyn, could get out and meet me on the trail.

It had been cool the last few days. As Lightning Bolt observed, "It's like hiking in air conditioning!" We were expecting more rain, which was never pleasant, and, of course, more rocks. The rocks hadn't been as bad as I'd expected from listening to all the experienced hikers, but then I hadn't been in Pennsylvania very long.

June 16, Peters Mountain Shelter to Rausch Gap Shelter (milepoint 1154.4 north)

I had to put on wet clothes again – not something I enjoyed, to say the least. Usually my clothes dried as I hiked, but that hadn't been the case the last few damp days.

Hiker tips: Many hikers would wear their wet clothes
to bed, and the body heat inside their sleeping bags
would dry their clothes. I could never bring myself to

*do that, preferring to sleep in a dry set of clothes I only
used in camp and town.*

My stomach was beginning to feel a little better. I hoped I
wouldn't be taking as many runs into the bushes as I had the last few
days. That had been a real challenge, and no more needs to be said
about that.

The strangest thing occurred as I was hiking along the trail: a
friendly mouse joined me on my hike! Scurrying along ahead, every
once in awhile it would stop to take a look back, as if it were looking
for a hiking partner. It was the oddest encounter I had had on the trail to
date. My first inclination was to squash it, but then I thought, "What the
hell, let it be. We're well away from the shelter and it sure isn't hurting
anyone or anything." Was it a sign that I had been on the trail too long
when I started talking to, and fancying the company of, a mouse?

Sun! There was sunshine peeking through the trees on the trail. I
had not seen the sun for several days and was so glad to see it that I
actually took a picture of it shining into the woods.

I met a section-hiker; and when I told him my trail name, he
blurted out, "My God, I've been following you on the Trailplace
website! But I would never have recognized you from the picture
posted in the journal."

I told him, "That doesn't surprise me a bit, considering I've lost
over twenty pounds since that picture!" We both laughed.

It was break time. I needed some water, and Badger wanted to
check on a couple of silver-dollar-sized blisters that had popped up on
his feet over the last couple of days. He hadn't been complaining much,
but from the looks of those blisters I knew they had to be really
torturing him.

As we sat taking a break, I noticed some horseshoes tacked up on
trees next to the white blazes and a sign that read, "The Horseshoe
Trail." I had been told that, in an effort to protect the trail, the particular
section of the A.T. we were on was the only section on the entire A.T.
that allowed horses.

As we ate our lunch, we could hear some kind of machine gun fire
off in the distance. We didn't know what that was all about, but I
figured I would find out up the trail. With the gnats swarming like bees,
I could have used a machine gun just to eat my cheese and beef stick.

I hiked up on a strange sight. I had been hiking all day, not seeing
a thing, and then right next to the trail out in the middle of the forest
was a mailbox. It was in an area called the Yellow Springs Village Site,
which had nothing but a number of stone foundations and the lone

mailbox. The silence of the woods gave me the eerie feeling of days gone by.

We arrived at Rausch Gap Shelter, and I thought Badger was having a flashback from his military days when he said, "This shelter looks like a damn war bunker!" With its stone walls sitting low in the ground, it did give the appearance of some type of bunker. Actually, it wasn't a bad shelter except it was very dark inside.

In the shelter register, one entry told it all. "It was a nice all-you-can-eat buffet last night, sponsored by the mosquitoes. All biting bugs were invited, and I was served as the main course! Scratch! Scratch! Scratch!"

June 17, Rausch Gap Shelter to 501 Shelter (milepoint 1171.8 north)

A couple of section-hikers by the name of John and Nathan came in with a very well-behaved dog. The dog sat right down outside the shelter and didn't bother anyone. They were very conscientious about their dog, making sure it did not disrupt anyone else's hike. That showed that dogs can certainly share the Appalachian Trail; it all comes down to how considerate the owners are.

We headed to the 501 Shelter, about which we had heard a lot of good things, in particular about the solar-heated shower. It was a beautiful morning, but John and Nathan put a damper on it by saying they heard the forecast was for more rain.

The previous day Badger and I had passed a sign that read, "Old General." Having some very tired legs and no idea what that meant, we'd headed on to the shelter. John and Nathan's young legs allowed them to follow the sign, and they told us that the General was an old antique crane that was quite a sight out in the middle of the woods.

I avoided a real catastrophe. While airing out my tent at the shelter, I noticed the bag in which I stored my tent had a hole in it. Luckily, I noticed the hole in the bag before the constant rubbing against the metal tubing on my external pack created a hole in the tent; a single wall tent with a hole in it would not be too good.

We crossed Moonshine Road, and I had just mentioned to Badger that we had not seen any trail magic in Pennsylvania, when there, right by the road before a huge mountain, sat two jugs of water. And was it a coincidence that the two jugs of water were placed right beside the Moonshine Road sign? Who knows?

Badger and I talked to a section-hiker from New Jersey who had hiked 650 miles using a unique method of hiking. He would drive his car to a point on the trail where it crossed a road, drop his bike off there, then drive back to the starting point and hike to his bike, whereupon he would pedal his bike back to his car. Where there's a will, there's a way.

As we hiked on, I caught a whiff of my own odor. "Whew!" was all I could think. Without a doubt, I had to be the wettest, stinkiest hiker on the trail, soaked with perspiration from the top of my head to the bottom of my feet. I could certainly understand why the many non-thru-hikers gave us such a wide berth.

We passed a Ridge Runner coming from the 501 Shelter. He kindly left some snacks at the shelter and said, "Help yourselves to them if someone hasn't already finished them off." He also told us that Buckwheat was just ahead and Woodchip was probably a day or two ahead. He added, "There's a good chance of heavy storms tonight. Best get cracking to the shelter."

When we reached the 501 Shelter, we thought it actually looked more like a cabin than a shelter, with a large dome sunlight on top. There was a port-a-john and a solar shower; and the opportunity to use a phone at a home next door to order a pizza was a special treat.

I was also able to talk with my wife, and we finalized our plans to go visit our first new grandchild. Connie would be picking me up in a couple of days for a flight to California and a few days off the trail.

June 18, 501 Shelter to Eagle's Nest Shelter (milepoint 1186.9 north)

It was 7 a.m. as I left the 501 Shelter. It had rained quite a bit through the night, so I was again very happy I'd slept in a nice dry building.

A young thru-hiker named Sailor who was really sailing along (hence his trail name) was also in the shelter. We both agreed how nice it was to have a port-a-john just outside the door of the bunkhouse, quite a luxury compared to most of the privies at the other shelters. I laughed to myself as I thought how one's perspective changes when you've been out on the trail for months. I had some female friends back home who refused to use a port-a-john and would probably believe I had lost my mind as I praised the luxury of one, but I was comparing it to a shovel back in the Smokies or a box over a hole in Georgia.

Hats off to George Shollenberger and his wife Joan, who built the shelter and lived right next door, providing upkeep and hospitality at the 501 Shelter.

I met a couple of thru-hikers at lunch, Big Dog and AT Moses. They started out section hiking, and when they reached Harpers Ferry said, "Let's just do the whole thing!" AT Moses was a car salesman and simply quit his job. Big Dog maintained "a book called *Murder on the Appalachian Trail* got me interested in hiking the A.T." I was surprised to learn that the murder occurred at a shelter where I had stayed after my first twenty-six-mile day, the Wapiti Shelter. I wouldn't want anyone to get the idea that hikers were taking their lives in their hands by hiking the A.T., but it was a reminder that one has to be aware of the surroundings everywhere.

I arrived at the Eagle's Nest Shelter at 5 p.m.; and although I hadn't done as many miles as I'd wanted, I still figured to be on schedule to meet Connie at Pennsylvania Highway 309. One of the thru-hikers at the shelter was also thinking about getting off the trail, not unusual for hikers at this point as the miles started to drag on and homesickness took over many hikers' desires to finish.

Talk in the shelter was about backpacks and why hikers should never let their packs out of their sight. Apparently a thru-hiker was in a New York bus station and asked an employee to watch her backpack while she went to the rest room. When she returned, her backpack was gone; and when she asked the employee where her pack was, he just shrugged his shoulders. Another group of thru-hikers on the southern section of the A.T. hid their backpacks in the bushes while they went into town for dinner. When they returned, the backpacks were gone, and they found their hiking poles arranged in the form of crosses! When the thefts were reported, the police officer shook his head and chastised them: "You hikers will never learn. Some of the local boys hang around, see hikers come into town without their packs and head to the nearest bunch of bushes near the trail – the usual hiding place for packs – and off they go."

Another one of the hikers at the shelter was telling about Moxie, a hiker from England. I believe Moxie was the hiker we'd heard about earlier on the trail, the one a waitress had told us who'd been attacked by a bear in the Shenandoahs. The hiker told us that Moxie was just lying in his tent, having hung his food bag in a tree, when he heard a thump on the outside of his tent and thought it was a ranger checking on him. But before he could say a word, all hell broke loose as the bear slashed open his tent with its sharp claws and was showing teeth. Luckily, a friend had given him some pepper spray for the hike, which he really believed saved his life. The hiker quoted Moxie as saying, "The pepper spray only slowed the bear down, but enough so that I could get away." As it was, the bear shredded his tent and left teeth imprints in his water bottle.

One of the benefits of sleeping in the shelter, besides staying dry, was that I had been able to catch up on a lot of the trail talk, although I was not sure I wanted to hear any more bear stories. Nor did I want to read what I saw in the register, as one entry from a southbound hiker mentioned that the rocks were finally beginning to ease up. If that were true, I had a lot of rocks ahead of me.

Voyager, a young woman hiker from Cleveland, Ohio, was in the shelter talking about her boyfriend problems. As if I wanted to hear about boyfriend problems, right? But I did get a good chuckle as she announced, "When we split, he took the tent and I took the food!"

The compost privy at the shelter had a rather unique flushing mechanism: to flush the compost privy, one had to simply take a handful of wood chips that were provided in a bucket on a shelf above the seat and throw them in the hole. An environmentally sound outhouse!

June 19, Eagle's Nest Shelter to Eckville Shelter (milepoint 1210.7 north)

We got an early start on a beautiful, cool morning after an overnight downpour that seemed like it would never stop. Luckily, Big Dog had a radio and the night before had mentioned there was a good chance of rain in the area, so we'd decided not to hike on up the trail to tent.

I figured I had close to thirty-five miles to go before meeting Connie for our trip to California, and two days to make it. Fortunately, my pack was really light since I only needed one more day's worth of food, and the terrain was relatively flat.

It had gotten a little cool the previous night. I was really missing my down bag and planned to get it back a lot sooner than I had first thought. I'd also had a little trouble getting to sleep, but I didn't know if it was the cool evening or the fierce snorer we'd had in the shelter. Again, my earplugs had proven their worth.

Another great day for hiking: fairly cool, with low humidity, the sun peeking in and out of the clouds, and the birds singing away. My boots were even beginning to dry a little; they had not touched dust for a week.

As we hiked into Port Clinton, Pennsylvania, we found a peanut shop that filled my head with the smell of fresh roasted peanuts and the memories of the Great Darke County Fair back home. With the local restaurant closed, the lady working in the shop was kind enough to go into her back room and heat up some water for my instant noodles. I continued to be impressed by the nice people who went out of their way to be helpful along the trail.

Hiker tips: Hikers take heed: Port Clinton was a good

stop but not on Mondays, as most of the stores were
closed. But it's certainly an excellent maildrop and you
don't want to miss the peanut shop.

We met Stardust walking in town. Turns out he was the other half of the young couple having the little spat. He said he had been having problems with his feet so he was hanging around town for a few days. I wondered if the young Voyager was part of the reason for his not being on the move.

Badger told me that he'd met a ridge runner who told him that by the end of May, 3,000 thru-hikers had passed through Neels Gap, Georgia. We were numbers 226 and 227 at Harpers Ferry, West Virginia, so there looked be a lot of hikers behind us.

A few miles out of town, there were a number of trails leading off the A.T. due to a campground nearby, and following the white blazes became somewhat of a challenge. Badger and I had not seen a blaze for awhile, and we broke my cardinal rule on the A.T., which was, "If you haven't seen a white blaze within ten minutes, turn around and backtrack." Here, though, there were so many shortcut trails made by lazy hikers that we had no idea which trail to backtrack on! We eventually found a white blaze after a great deal of head-scratching and discussion as we wandered around.

We passed a family walking back from a rock outcrop called the Pinnacle, said by many to provide the best view in Pennsylvania. The family walking back had a teen-aged daughter, and I could tell she was not a happy hiker. Even though Mom and Dad seemed to be enjoying every minute of the beautiful day, if looks could kill, Mom and Dad would have been pushing up daisies. Apparently, the beautiful views of Pennsylvania were not high on her list of things to do. Oh, the fond memories of the wonderful times of a family vacation!

We arrived at the Pinnacle, and the view was definitely worth the hike of about fifty yards off the A.T. While scrambling over some rocks, I heard an "Oh, damn!" Badger was OK as he picked himself up, but he had a nasty scrape to add to his collection of bumps and bruises.

When we got to the Eckville Shelter it was full, but that was fine. It was such a nice evening that I preferred to tent. I finished off my dinner and soon had my tent set up after a long twenty-three-mile day.

Hiker tips: Another stop I would certainly recommend
is the Eckville Shelter. It had a nice restroom facility
along with a shower. The caretaker lived right next
door and had ice cream and soft drinks to purchase. I
stayed away from the ice cream, still a little gun-shy
after that half-gallon fiasco!

June 20, Eckville Shelter to Pa. 309 (Blue Mountain Summit, Pennsylvania) (milepoint 1222.2 north)

Early that morning we headed out of Eckville Shelter, and I had 11.5 miles to hike before meeting up with Connie at Pennsylvania Highway 309. I looked forward to the short hike (short being a relative term, since when I first started in Georgia, a hike of eleven miles would have been an all-day odyssey. Now, I considered it a short hike).

We made it to Dan's Pulpit, where, as stated in *The Thru-Hiker's Handbook*, "From time to time in recent years, a large male bear visits the 'pulpit' to preach fear to unsuspecting thru-hikers caught by surprise; no reported problems, but several converts." Badger and I got by without seeing the bear. We signed the register at the pulpit mailbox and headed north.

>*Hiker tips: Many hikers signed-in at the various trail registers, usually located in shelters, to assist others in locating them in the event of an emergency.*

Badger and I stopped for a break and visited with Pick. Pick was one of the few thru-hikers who did not carry a tent but simply used a tarp. It worked well for him, but it certainly wouldn't for everyone.

About noon we reached Highway 309, my stop for the day. Badger stopped to have lunch but would be hiking a little further north on the trail. I gave him a hearty thanks-for-the-memories handshake, wished him well, and warned him with a grin, "You be careful going over those damn rocks, Badger." I felt a tinge of sadness as he headed north and turned for one last wave. Badger had been a great hiking partner, and I doubted if I would see him again on the trail.

It was 3 p.m. when my wife arrived for our drive to Columbus, Ohio, and then on to sunny California by plane. It wasn't long before reality slapped me in the face when we stopped for the night at a hotel and found our car would not start. After several phone calls to AAA, we obtained a new battery and were back in business. As I told Connie, "On the trail, all I needed when I was low on energy was a Snickers bar." I knew I was back in the real world.

June 26, Pa. 309 (Blue Mountain Summit, Pennsylvania) to George Outerbridge Shelter (milepoint 1234.9 north)

Six days later at noon, I was back on the trail. Vicki and Al Hetrick, true trail angels and good friends, were good enough to pick me up at the Columbus airport and drive me back to Highway 309 in Pennsylvania. When we pulled into the parking lot of the Blue

Mountain Summit Inn, Al asked, "Just where is this Appalachian Trail?"

I pointed out the white blaze and said with a laugh, "You will probably see a thru-hiker or two coming out of the woods and cross right there while we eat our lunch."

No sooner had I spoken than, right on cue, out of the woods came two thru-hikers: Fix-It and Smoky. As it happened, I had hiked with them before; and as we waved and exchanged greetings, Al looked at me as if to say, "You set this up, didn't you?" Vickie and Al, continuing their trail angel ways, gave the two hikers their sandwiches and soft drinks for lunch, saying they would get something else to eat down the road. The smiles on Fix-it's and Smoky's faces said everything. I'd almost forgotten how great it is to get the unexpected trail magic.

It was 1 p.m., and what a difference! An hour ago I'd been in the hustle and bustle of fast-paced travel, and now I found myself walking through a quiet woods at a top speed of two miles an hour. Although I'd really enjoyed my time with the family, the peace and tranquility of the trail was very welcome. Daydreaming as I walked along, I almost missed a double blaze and knew I would have to be more aware of the blazes, especially since I was again hiking by myself.

I found my first day back on the trail a lot like the first day of my hike down at Springer Mountain, where I was starting out alone, excited, and somewhat apprehensive about what lay ahead. The one obvious difference was that I now had a much better knowledge of the trail and more confidence in my ability to take on whatever the trail had to offer.

I had been hiking through so many rocks that I quit using my hiking poles.

> *Hiker tips: I found it dangerous to have my hands in the hiking pole straps because, if the poles got stuck in the rocks, I wouldn't be able to let go of the poles if I went down.*

I'd only hiked four miles, and the rocks were really slowing me down. The plan to get in nine more miles began to appear a little more ambitious than I had anticipated.

When I met a young couple with two small children at a trailhead, I asked how they were doing. They blurted out, "Not good; our car won't start!" Sadly, they had no jumper cables and it wasn't even their car; it belonged to a friend. I wished them luck and promised I would send any day hikers I might meet over to the parking lot to help them out, all the while thinking how lucky I was to be back in the woods.

I made a stop at Bake Oven Knob Shelter to inspect my feet and my new boots. I did not want blisters if I could help it. One of my toes seemed to be rubbing on the side of the boot; and I remembered that when I had broken my other boots in, I'd had the same trouble with my big toe. That time I soaked the boots in water and put a ball-peen hammer inside the boot to push out the side of the boot to make room for my toe. Unfortunately, I hadn't brought the hammer, so the handle of my hiking pole would have to do.

In checking the register at Bake Oven Knob Shelter I noticed that Badger had signed it on the night I left for California. Fix-It and Smoky were at the shelter and still smiling from the sandwiches Vickie and Al gave them for lunch. I also saw in the register that someone commented on the A.T. Nude Hiking day, June 21st. Of course I had missed it, so I asked Fix-It and Smoky about the day. They told me: "You didn't miss a damn thing as far as we know. We didn't see a thing, literally!"

I got back on the trail, and soon there was thunder to the west. It looked like we were going to be getting a real storm, probably before I got to the shelter. Welcome back to the A.T.

More thunder and lightning in the west. It was getting really dark and looked ready to let loose at any minute. I was about two hours from the shelter, so I figured there was no way I was not going to get wet. On the positive side, I would get my boots wet and could stretch them out at the shelter, although I would rather have had my boots soaked without my feet being in them!

By a little after 5 p.m., the rain was really coming down, and I was soaking wet – literally soaked to the skin – as I trudged through the mud and goop. And my left knee was really starting to hurt. I wasn't sure what that was all about, but the pain was similar to what I had when I first started hiking down in Georgia.

Right in the middle of the downpour, I heard, ". . . Singing in the rain, just singing in the rain . . ." as Smoky and Fix-it passed me, vocalizing at the top of their lungs. Just then an enormous lighting bolt exploded not twenty-five yards from us! I laughed out loud as they both leaped high into the air, and their "Singing in the rain" quickly changed to "Let's get the f--- out of here!"

As I headed down the side of the mountain as quickly as possible, both of my knees were screaming with pain. I wasn't sure if it was caused by my new boots, by the five-day layover, or what; but I knew I certainly couldn't go much further with the pain I was experiencing. I arrived at the George Outerbridge Shelter at 6:30 p.m., and oh, how I was in need of a shelter. What a day! It had been quite a re-introduction to the Appalachian Trail.

At the shelter, Fix-It showed me a rash on his back. He said, "I laid down on a damn caterpillar, and it stung the hell out of me!" I gave him some ointment I was carrying that was really effective for rashes. I'd never seen a rash that big, however; it covered his entire back!

> *Hiker tips: My first-aid supplies were limited, but they did include "Bag Balm" (obtained it from my father-in-law, a long time dairy farmer), an ointment that worked for all type of chapped conditions and superficial abrasions. It's a must for every first aid kit.*

There were more bear stories in the shelter. A thru-hiker by the name of Ruth said she saw a bear eating berries on the ridge the day before. She said with surprise, "The bear didn't even stop eating as I walked by!"

June 27, George Outerbridge Shelter to Leroy A. Smith Shelter (milepoint 1251.6 north)

I stretched out my wet boot as much as possible, put on my knee brace, and figured the steep downhill I had right out of the shelter would be a good test. I planned to take it slowly. Evidently, getting off the trail for a few days had made coming back more like starting over than I had figured. I also had a big climb ahead and there was a seventy percent chance of rain. So, as I started out with the intention to hike sixteen and a half miles, I could expect rain, I had the trots, and my knee was hurting. But what the hell, it was better than working, right?

Just passed a sign that indicated route 309 was 15.3 miles south. That's where I'd started the day before. That was too many miles for the first day back on the trail, and I should have known better.

According to my map, there was a blue blaze winter trail that appeared to be much easier. It was tempting, but I decided to take the official A.T. I could see from where I was standing that the official trail went up and over a big mountain. Hey, I wouldn't want to miss any rocks!

I climbed up from Lehigh Gap, a difficult climb straight up a very steep incline. I had to stow my hiking poles to make it to the top. I certainly could understand why they had a winter route avoiding the climb. This section was a real butt-kicker and would be extremely dangerous in bad weather.

> *Hiker tips: I would suggest taking the official A.T. and climbing the steep rocks from Lehigh Gap if at all possible. Although very tough, it was fun and*

exhilarating but should not be attempted in bad weather.

Once on top of the ridge, I missed the trail by gawking at the wonderful views. Thank goodness I met another hiker walking back to the trail. He, too, had missed the blaze but had gone a lot farther down the wrong trail than I had.

I talked to a thru-hiker named Checkers who had just started the trail on Friday and was looking pretty sore. I told him that I probably felt like he did, and he responded with a groan, "I sure hope not." He went on to say, "It's really frustrating having everyone pass me by." My response was very simple: "Don't worry about it; hike your own hike."

Rocks! Rocks! Rocks! I had been told this was the worst stretch of rocks in Pennsylvania, and I had to agree.

A thru-hiker I met had started out at Springer Mountain, Georgia; but when he got to Waynesboro, Virginia, he was out of money, so he left the trail. He had been on and off several times since. When I mentioned that I had just gotten back on the trail after five days off and my knees were really hurting, he blurted out, "Tell me about it! It's a killer getting back on the trail after being off for a few days." I was a little frustrated by how my knees were hurting, but he seemed to think it was normal and just part of hiking. Having knee problems caught me by surprise. If anything, I thought the five-day rest would have helped.

Trail magic again surfaced at Smith Gap. A fellow with the trail name of Keystone Sarge was sitting in his car with a trunk load of snacks and a cooler of soft drinks for hikers. A former sergeant in the military from Pennsylvania, he drove seventy miles to provide the trail magic.

It started raining about two miles from the shelter. "Damn, I'm soaking wet again," I murmured to myself as I stopped to get a stone out of my boot and literally poured a bucket of water out of the boot.

I finally reached the shelter, thank God. I was never so happy to see a shelter in all my life. My knees were again screaming, and the blister on my big toe seemed to be growing as I watched. There were a lot of people in the shelter area, but only three of us were staying in the shelter. Most were tenting, probably because of a dead rattlesnake lying near the shelter and giving off a smell that would "puke a maggot," as one hiker moaned.

"I'll be damned, would you look at that!" Grandpa Bob said in his Jimmy Stewart drawl as a young thru-hiker sauntered into the shelter area wearing nothing but a smile! Actually, he did have his boots and a pack on, too. He also tied a t-shirt around his waist as he got closer to the shelter. A unique young fellow, Love Shack simply liked to hike without any pants. Everyday was nude hiking day for the Love Shack.

June 28, Leroy A. Smith Shelter to Delaware Water Gap, Pennsylvania (milepoint 1272.0 north)

I left the Leroy Smith Shelter early and hoped to get to Delaware Water Gap, a little more than twenty miles away; but more than likely I would stop at the Kirkridge Shelter fourteen miles north. A nice cool morning, the rain had stopped and it was forecast to dry off, which was music to my ears.

The Leroy Smith Shelter had a big picture of Mount Katahdin hanging inside, providing some encouragement for struggling thru-hikers, or for any thru-hikers for that matter! Someone in the shelter noted that Delaware Water Gap was less than 900 miles from Mount Katahdin. That was still a considerable distance, so I continued setting small goals – such as meeting with my daughter in New York – in an attempt to avoid the hiker blues and remain focused.

As I left the shelter, the clouds floated above the valley below with the snow-capped mountains peeking through, creating a view worthy of an oil painting. I used some moleskin on my toe, and it was the first time in my entire thru-hike I had used moleskin. Actually, I was not sure if I had a blister or just a callus, and I wondered if I didn't have the same problem that Badger had when he got new boots and found out his feet had swollen one shoe size? I'd purchased the same type and size boots I had always worn and even went to the trouble of breaking them in before my hike, but I began to wonder if I should have gone a size bigger. Then again, after talking to several hikers during the past two days, I learned that the discomfort of starting to hike again after being off the trail for an extended period was to be expected.

I met Steady Mike, another thru-hiker from New York headed north. An older fellow, he was emotionally down due to the wet weather and the rocks. He had started out the first of April, so he was making good time; but he said without hesitation, "I'm more than ready to get the hell out of Pennsylvania!" It seemed that many hikers were tired and mentally down. Maybe all the rain – along with the rocks and the limited views – had taken its toll.

Love Shack went flying by me, heading north in his non-attire. At the shelter he'd claimed he lost his shorts awhile back and just had not had an opportunity to get another pair; but to be honest, not many including me, were buying that story. Personally, I didn't care if he chose to show his ass on the trail; but from the cold reception he got in camp the previous night, I was sure he'd gotten some flack, especially going into camps where there were women.

Rocks! Rocks! Rocks! I couldn't wait to get out of the damn rocks.

I crossed Pennsylvania Highway 191 and only had half a mile to the Kirkridge Shelter, where I must decide whether I would stay or hike on up the trail the six miles to Delaware Water Gap.

I ended up hiking north out of the Kirkridge Shelter. I had walked in, fully intending to stay at the shelter, but once there, I got bored sitting around. I sat and thought about it, then decided, "What the hell, may as well go for it." I had six miles to Delaware Water Gap and planned to be there in three hours. It was mostly downhill, so I would see how my knees held up. I figured they'd be talking to me. There was a hostel and restaurant down at the Gap; so the thoughts of a bed, a shower, and a hamburger really spurred me on.

While sitting at the Kirkridge Shelter, I watched Fix-It draw a comical picture in the register that showed a local hiking club member sharpening the rocks with files and standing them on end for the hikers. He typically put drawings in each register. They were really quite good, and the one in the Kirkridge Shelter register was no exception.

I pulled a tick off my leg, which reminded me of a story about a couple hiking who found 200 ticks on their dog at one time! It was hard to believe, but they swore that it was the truth and that they had counted each and every one.

It was 6:30 p.m. and my knees were numb as I crossed Mount Minsi and finally arrived in Delaware Water Gap, Pennsylvania. It felt really good to be in town, and I was lucky to get the last bed at the Presbyterian Church of the Mountain hostel. It's in a good location, right off the trail with a pay phone across the street and places to eat within walking distance.

The shower felt great and the food was delicious after a twenty-mile hike. Although my legs were sore as hell and I had pushed a little too much, it was great to be cleaned up and in a comfortable hostel.

Chapter 4
Delaware Water Gap To Hanover

June 29, Delaware Water Gap, Pennsylvania to Blue Mountain Lakes Road, New Jersey (milepoint 1289.6 north)

I left the Presbyterian Church of the Mountain hostel after a good night's stay.

> *Hiker tips: With its bunk beds, shower and location just off the trail, I would highly recommend the Presbyterian Church of the Mountain hostel to any hiker.*

Mentally, I was ready to hike, but my feet and legs told me otherwise. They were hurting. It wasn't the best way to start the day; and with the next shelter twenty-four miles up the trail, I was not sure what the day would bring. Regardless, I was headed north, pumping down the Ibuprofen!

Although it was closed so early in the morning, the Delaware Water Gap National Recreation Information Center was right next to the trail and had a pay phone. An opportunity to call home always raised my spirits, and this was one of those mornings on which both my body and soul certainly could use a boost.

After walking under I-80, I headed into New Jersey and was only too happy to be headed out of those Pennsylvania rocks! If you would ask any thru-hiker for an opinion of the Appalachian Trail through Pennsylvania, I'm sure the first words would be, "Those damn Pennsylvania rocks!" Not particularly large or overwhelming, the rocks were simply relentless.

As I climbed back up into the mountains from the gap, it was a beautiful morning, cool and a little overcast, and just perfect for hiking. The birds seemed to be particularly vocal. I loved listening to the birds sing early in the morning.

I'd met a lot of new hikers at the hostel. One was a fellow about my age with the trail name of Copperhead. You probably can guess how he got his trail name: he apparently stepped on a copperhead snake early into his hike. Although he escaped without a tragedy, he indicated to me that "a clean pair of underwear was warranted after the episode!" Admitting to his tendency for misfortune, Copperhead also told me the story of how he got up one morning, put on his boot, and was stung by a scorpion! Nevertheless, he was back on the trail and headed north with a smile on his face.

> *Hiker tips: My son, who works as a forest firefighter out West, told me firefighters cover the top of their boots with socks in the evening to avoid those little devils. Probably not a bad idea anytime you're hiking.*

Later in the day I caught up to Lynn and his dog Dillon. I'd met them the second day out from Springer Mountain. Lynn had obtained the trail name Magic Thumb! He told me he got it for his ability to hitchhike into town even though he had a dog, which usually made it next to impossible to get a ride. So it was Magic Thumb and Dillon, and he said they rarely stayed in a shelter or a hostel. "We only stayed in two shelters so far," he said. "People just do not like dogs staying in the shelters."

I passed the Sunfish Natural Pond. It's a gorgeous pond, so peaceful and beautiful, and the only sound to be heard was that of the big old bullfrog croaking out his contentment with life. I think this would be a place to visit again. The word "pond" brings a misconception. After all, the pond was forty-one acres. In Ohio, we call that a lake! *The Thru-Hiker's Handbook* stated that Sunfish Natural Pond was a glacial pond, one of the seven natural wonders of New Jersey. Only a few hardy species of fish could withstand the naturally acidic conditions of the water, but pumpkinseed (sunfish) and yellow perch were plentiful. I was hiking right beside the pond – another step to the right, and I would have been in the water. I met a day hiker walking around the pond. We talked for awhile about thru-hiking, and her dream (like that of so many day hikers I've talked with) was to thru-hike the A.T. some day. She was hiking with her dog and gave me some good information about bears in the area. I'd been told by a number of hikers that I would likely see more bears in New Jersey than in any other of the fourteen states that the A.T. passed through. She mentioned that the bears were not really aggressive, but she did say, "They will come into camp after food. One actually came into my camp and took a dog chew right out of my dog's mouth." I'm not sure how she defines "aggressive," but that sounded damn aggressive to me!

Next I stopped by the Mohican Outdoor Center. There was a sign that read "Springer Mt. 1,277.3, Mt. Katahdin, 881.9." The sign was a little old, but the mileage appeared to be fairly accurate. It was hard to believe that I had hiked twelve hundred miles, although my knees would not have argued that point. It was a nice center with lodging for hikers. That made for a tough decision as my legs were really tired and aching, but I was not sure if I wanted to stop so early in the day. I had only gone ten miles.

It was 2 p.m. and yep, I decided it was too early to stop, so I headed north. Even though my knees were throbbing, I thought I would try to walk through the pain and see what would happen. I was heading north to sleep with the bears.

Just a mile up the trail, I talked to a couple of scouts and a scoutmaster headed south on the trail. They gave me some good information about a campsite and where to find water. Hearing it was just a little more than seven miles to the campsite, I decided to take it a little slower to give my legs a break.

A bear! The sight of another bear in the wild mesmerized me. The size of his head was hard to believe. I'd been told this was great bear territory, and here was the first bit of proof. I decided, then and there, that I would take every precaution in hanging my food for the night. Boy, that took my mind off the aches and pains!

Later, as I walked a ridgeline, I could hear roosters crowing down in the valley. It was really fascinating how the sounds from the farms carried all the way up the mountain and were so clear.

Break time was a stop at the Catfish Fire Tower. Just as I was starting back on the trail, I heard rustling in the bushes. Fully expecting to see a bear high-tailing out of the bushes, you can imagine my surprise when an enormous black snake slithered right across my feet! It had to be seven feet long! Thank God it didn't want any part of me, and I certainly felt the same about it. I couldn't even get my camera out in time for a picture, as it took me entirely by surprise. My reaction was very similar to Copperhead's, if you recall his comment about undergarments.

I crossed Millbrook-Blairstown Road and stopped to take a little break. An elderly fellow was out in his front yard doing some stonework and offered me some water. We had a nice little chat that eventually got around to bears. He said, "There are so many bears in this area, I'm afraid to have my grandchildren play outside in the evening." He went on to say that the state of New Jersey was considering a bear hunt simply to thin the number of bears, as they were becoming a real nuisance. After a very pleasant and informative visit, I headed north up into the mountains once again.

And there was another bear! I had just taken a seat on an inviting flat rock next to the trail for a bite of cheese and jerky when a sense of being watched engulfed me. A quick glance over my right shoulder confirmed my worst fear. There, sitting in a thicket, looking hungry and directly at me was the largest bear I had ever seen! "Look at the size of that bear," I whispered quietly to myself as it gazed eyeball-to-eyeball with me not more than twenty-five yards away. I quickly realized that this was not the best place for a snack. With my heart pounding the speed and force of a jackhammer, I ever so slowly returned the cheese and jerky to my pocket, eased myself off the rock, and slowly walked on up the trail. I wondered if the bear was following and if I was about to be a snack myself. Unable to resist the temptation, I took a quick look back and found the bear unmoved. Relieved and knowing full well that was the closest – at least I hoped it was – I would come to a bear on the trail, I paused for one moment to conjure up the last remaining shred of courage I possessed, then turned, and snapped a picture. My feet then overpowered any other urges I had, as I hastily moved on up the trail. It was interesting that I had seen as many bears in the last ten miles as I had seen on the entire A.T. before that! And in the state of New Jersey, too. Who would have guessed?

It was 7 p.m., and according to my *Data Book*, I was in the Blue Mountain Lake area and had hiked seventeen miles. My feet were

Lunch guest in New Jersey!

sore; they felt like someone had taken a baseball bat and hammered the hell out of them. But as I lay in my tent, pain was not an issue. After the close encounter with the bear, my heart was still racing with an unbelievable adrenaline rush. You can bet I hung my food bag far, far, far from my tent and slept with the figurative one eye open through the night.

June 30, Blue Mountain Lakes to Gren Anderson Shelter (milepoint 1303.3 north)

I had not brought an alarm clock along and never needed one, as I learned early on that when the birds started singing, I got up and moving. It hadn't rained anymore after an early downpour the night before, but I still had a wet tent that I attempted to dry off with my chamois before heading out. The single wall tent had served me well. My only complaint was the moisture build-up on the inside; but taking into consideration the light weight, I really couldn't complain. I also found another tick crawling on my arm the previous night. I'd come back from bushwhacking to hang my food bag, so that was probably when I picked it up.

As I headed north on the trail, my feet continued to hurt and felt as though someone was smacking the bottom of my foot with a board every time I took a step. I even checked to make sure I did not have a big blister on the bottom of my foot. No blisters; they were simply bruised.

Just scaled another cliff! I wasn't expecting that. Anyone who said the rocks stopped after the A.T. left Pennsylvania was pulling your leg.

I had been thinking about what a staff member told me at the Mohican Outdoor Center, for he kind of put everything into perspective for me. He asked me how it was going, and, being a little down, I starting complaining about my knees and new boots. As I told him where I had been the last few days, he just shook his head and said, "You walked twenty miles over those rocks, and you're only complaining about your knees hurting! Hell, I've had some people come in here actually crying, they were in such pain; and they ended up staying for several days!"

Back on the trail I spotted another three deer up ahead of me. I never tired of seeing deer or other wildlife on the trail.

I took a break on top of Rattlesnake Mountain, 1,492 feet high, with a beautiful view of the countryside. I believe I counted seven water towers sprouting up out of the green forest like mushrooms.

Didn't have any problems with bears the previous night, but I did hang all of my food high in a tree – even the toothpaste! I had heard that the bears would come into a tent just for the toothpaste. I jokingly wondered to myself, "Wouldn't you think the smell of a thru-hiker would be enough to turn most bears off?"

I met a hiker headed south who was looking for Brink Road Shelter, but he figured he missed the shelter when I told him I had not passed it. He was asked to drop off a package there for a northbound hiker named Duckman, so I told him I would take the package (my chance to do some trail angel work) to the shelter for him. He asked me with a grin how I liked the Pennsylvania rocks, but before I could answer, he laughed and said, "You know the only reason they have the rocks in Pennsylvania is so you thru-hikers have something to talk about!" It was a great line, one that I was sure he had used before. I also liked his answer when I asked how much longer I could expect to be hiking on the rocks. "You will slowly dribble out of them, just like you slowly dribbled into them!" I enjoyed talking to him. His last words were, "Keep on hiking! You make us old fifty-plus hikers proud!"

When I arrived at the Brink Road Shelter sign, I realized why the earlier hiker missed the shelter. It was two-tenths of a mile off the trail on a blue blaze. There's no way I would have been hiking to that shelter if I hadn't promised to drop off his package. Me and my big mouth!

I hiked back to the trail after visiting one of the most mosquito-infested shelters I had ever seen! A hiker at the shelter said that only a couple of people stayed in the shelter last night, that most hikers tented, and I certainly could understand why.

> *Hiker tips: I would avoid the Brink Road Shelter if at all possible. In addition to the gazillion mosquitoes, the privy was literally nothing but a box over a hole in the ground! Try that with mosquitoes buzzing every inch of your body!*

Passed a southbounder named Double Zero who told me, "I started the trail from my backyard in New Hampshire!" He also told me about a shelter that was not in the *Data Book*. "Thru-hikers are calling it the secret shelter," he whispered with a wink.

I then arrived at the Gren Anderson Shelter, and although I wanted to stay in the shelter, the mosquitoes were so bad that I decided to stay in my tent. In the shelter was a thru-hiker who was finishing up a hike he began last year before he contracted Lyme Disease and had to leave the trail. As I lay inside my tent on day 92 of my hike, I could see mosquitoes swarming outside and was very glad I had decided to tent!

July 1, Gren Anderson Shelter (New Jersey) to Unionville Road New York (Thru-Hiker Shack) (milepoint 1322.5 north)

Left the Gren Anderson Shelter early and was very glad I had set my tent up, as I'd slept well, even though mosquitoes had swarmed the shelter and campsite. I also really appreciated the ridge runner who'd left cookies and sodas in the bear box; they were great. New Jersey's idea of using a cooler-sized metal box mounted on concrete for storing food bags seemed to work well and made it much easier to retrieve food in the morning.

I continued to be impressed with the nice people on the trail. When I stopped for lunch in a tavern on U.S. Route 206, I ran into two section-hikers who volunteered to mail my journals and film home for me. They had planned to hike for five days but were leaving the trail after just two days because of blisters. They were fun-loving guys who were a little disappointed about not getting in as much hiking as they had hoped, but they were making the best of the situation with a few beers as they waited for their ride home. They were having such a good time when I left that I hoped they would not have one too many and walk off without mailing my journals and film! It was great to have help from time to time and wonderful to be able to trust complete strangers.

Story time: Jim, the southbound hiker who had Lyme Disease last year, was telling me about a hiker he had met at the 501 Shelter a few weeks ago. He was sitting in the 501 enjoying the unusually nice accommodation along with some snacks and soft drinks, when out of nowhere a hiker exploded through the door into the shelter, cussing and throwing his pack. The hiker then sat down to eat and continued cussing: "That no good son of a bitch! I'll kill that son of a bitch!" Suddenly he stopped, turned to Jim, and just as calmly as could be, asked, "So how was your day?" Taken completely off guard, Jim responded hesitantly, "Good. I take it yours has not gone well?" The hiker told Jim he had Tourette's Syndrome and to expect outbursts but not to worry. So all through the night, the hiker would let out with a barrage of, "I'll kill you, you son of a bitch!" and so on. And although he had explained his outbursts, Jim still found it very unnerving and told me, "I only had a corkscrew on my broken Swiss knife, but I had it lying right beside me the entire night!" Apparently no one in the shelter got much sleep throughout the night. Not even the caretaker next door seemed able to sleep, as Jim noticed house lights come on several times during the night.

I got the scare of my life when, walking along and thinking how New Jersey had so much more wilderness than I had anticipated, I accidentally stepped right next to a big black racer snake! It went scooting off, but my heart took an extra beat! I headed north watching the trail a little closer. As I did, a large wild turkey took off just beyond me! That was one big bird - looked ready for the Thanksgiving table.

I arrived at the Mashipacong Shelter and noticed the bear box had the lid torn off. I figured it had been vandals or one damn tough bear! I wasn't sure which I would rather it be. The register read that Badger was there on June 25, six days earlier. I headed north.

I ended up back at the Mashipacong Shelter! I'd headed the wrong damn way, taking off on a well-worn path in front of the shelter; but I soon realized I hadn't seen any white blazes for awhile. When I backtracked, I found that the A.T. went behind the shelter and was clearly marked with a white blaze. I needed to be more observant.

The bugs were getting nasty again; but when I went to put on my bug net, it was missing. I must have lost it on the trail. It wasn't good to be on the trail without my bug net.

I had a nice lunch at the High Point State Park Ranger Station and headed on.

Hiker tips: The ranger station was right on the trail. It's a nice place to get a drink of water and use the restroom facilities, but there's no food available.

At the High Point Tower observation platform, the highest point in New Jersey, I talked to a friendly fellow from the area that told me on a clear night one could see the Twin Towers of New York City.

I hiked out of the woods and entered a wheat field. As there were no trees for the white blazes, the trail maintainers had tied white plastic strips to the fence. Those led me to within a couple hundred yards of a large turn-of-the-last-century farmhouse, where there was a huge circus-type tent set up. The entire farm was rocking with country music. I got a number of friendly waves and shouts of encouragement from the fun loving crowd as I followed the A.T. through their pasture – dotted with cow patties – and headed back into the woods. It was fun to have the chance to hike down out of the mountains on occasion and see some of the local people and their homes.

I arrived at Old Smith Road a little past four o'clock. A sign there read, "Thru-Hiker Shack 100 yards," but the place was better known as the "secret shelter" to thru-hikers headed north. A unique shelter, it was more like a small cabin than the typical shelter. Along with a small front porch, it had a shower, bunk beds, and hot water available for washing clothes. Jim, a former thru-hiker, had recently built the cabin on his property and encouraged hikers to use it.

Also at the shelter were a couple of thru-hikers named Ruth and Country Gentleman. Toward evening, a fellow walked in carrying nothing but a little bag thrown over his shoulder, similar to what you would visualize a hobo carrying. We weren't sure what to make of the fellow as he told us in an unfriendly manner, "Had my pack stolen in Boston." He then headed up the hill and camped in the woods. A little leery of the suspicious character, we agreed that we should probably sleep with the proverbial one eye open.

Jim informed us we had entered New York and that we would be going back and forth across the New York/New Jersey state line for awhile as we headed north. He also said that we would soon start seeing southbound thru-hikers about the middle of July. Last year, he had about ten northbounders and ten southbounders staying on the same night; and he said that he found it rather unusual, if not disappointing, that the hikers each had their own group and did not talk much to those in the other group.

Again I decided to tent, due to all the nasty mosquitoes.

July 2, Unionville Road, New York (Thru-Hiker Shack) to N.J. 94 (Vernon, New Jersey) (milepoint 1336.0 north)

After a good night's rest I left the thru-hikers' shack. Only Ruth, the Country Gentleman, and I had spent the night, so it was very quiet and peaceful. Ruth and the Country Gentleman were carrying light packs and averaging twenty miles a day, so I figured I wouldn't be seeing them again. And we never did see the hobo hiker after he went up into the woods.

I hiked through the Vernie Swamp, where trail maintainers had installed a wood bog bridge that made it possible to cross the freshwater wetland without wading. Otherwise, it would have been a real challenge.

As I headed north on a beautiful Sunday morning, I hoped to find a church in one of the small towns. If not, I could take solace in the fact that I was, as many thru-hikers were fond of saying, "hiking in God's chapel" as I hiked north on the A.T.

I passed a sign indicating that I was about to cross New Jersey State Highway 284. That was good to see, as my *Data Book* said there was a deli down the road about a half-mile. I had plenty of time and was hungry for a warm breakfast, so I headed to the deli.

> *Hiker tips: The State Line Deli had a nice breakfast special: eggs, ham and a bagel, worth the extra eight-tenths of a mile. I also picked up a few supplies for on the trail, but a word to the wise: most of the little delis and restaurants wouldn't take a credit card. They wanted cold, hard cash!*

So far I had really enjoyed my hike through New Jersey. Farms, wetlands, road walks, hills, dells, and woodlands: there'd been a great variety, not to mention the stomach-pleasing delis.

I got back on the trail; and as I stepped over a large rock, there lay a snake. An extremely contrary reptile, it took several nudges from my hiking pole to finally get it to move one way as I went the other.

As I was standing on Pochuck Mountain Overlook, up walked a section-hiker and I inquired, "What we looking at?" Pointing his finger south, he said, "Look way over there in the distance and you'll see High Point Monument." When I told him that I'd been there the day before, he said, "You bull-shitting me? That's a hell of a ways from here."

"It sure looks that way, but believe me, I was there just yesterday," I replied with an undaunted smile. It continued to amaze me the distance I could walk in a day's time! The section-hiker was intrigued and asked all kinds of questions about thru-hiking. I could tell that White Blaze Fever had its grip on him.

It was noon when I reached County Road 565. The owner of the house right by the road was doing some stone work in his front yard; and when I asked if I could eat lunch under a nice shade tree in his yard, he gave me a friendly smile and said, "Sure, go ahead, most hikers do. You've got a big hike ahead of you!" We got to talking about the hike coming up for me as he worked and I ate, and he warned, "Look out for the bears we have around here; they're pretty big. One was in my front yard the other night, and I know it had to be at least 600 pounds!" He also told me I had about a thousand-foot cliff going up out of Vernon, New Jersey, the following day, but that the climb going down was actually tougher.

I'd been on Country Road 517 for a long time. It was the most road walking since I had been on the trail, and the hot pavement made for scorched feet. As I asked a local fellow for directions, he told me the A.T. had just purchased a big tract of land and soon the trail would be rerouted off the highway, none too soon in my opinion. He also pointed toward a big mountain north on the trail and said, "Look out for the bears up there; there's some big ones!"

It wasn't quite 7 p.m. when I arrived at a hostel run by the Presbyterian Church in Vernon, New Jersey, after getting a hitch into town from some section-hikers just getting off the A.T. A nice and clean hostel located in the basement of the church, it had a great shower and a few supplies.

July 3, N.J. 94 (Vernon, New Jersey) to Wildcat Shelter (milepoint 1353.4 north)

I arose at 6:30 on another beautiful morning. I'd been very fortunate to have some wonderful weather for a few days.

Hiker tips: The Presbyterian Church hostel had to be one of the cleanest hostels I had visited; I would highly recommend it. The hostel had been taking in thru-hikers for only two years but the staff was extremely efficient and gracious. There was even a gentleman named Peter who would pick up hikers at the church in the morning and drive them back to the trail.

On the way back to the trail, Peter, a church member who volunteered to shuttle hikers back to the trail, told me that the bear population had exploded. "Four years ago, there were about three hundred bears in the area, now it's up to fifteen hundred!" He lived out of town and often had bears in his backyard at night. With the number of bears increasing so fast, Peter warned me, "The bears are often seen at bird feeders or in trash cans, so you have to be careful." Hunting was not allowed in the area, and some of the older bears were well into the 600-pound range, he noted.

I was headed to Wildcat Shelter, which figured to be about seventeen miles north and across the state line in New York. Two hikers called Copperhead and Round-To-It were right behind me as we started the morning with a hike up the 1,340-foot Mount Wawayanda. I was still having a little trouble with my boot rubbing my big toe, but I was able to get some snow seal out of the hiker box at the hostel. That let me oil the boots well, and I hoped to stretch out the boot more.

When I hiked to the top of Mount Wawayanda, I saw a first: a white blaze with a blue blaze below it. I didn't have a clue as to what that was all about, but I had no doubt that I was following the white blazes. I had left Round-To-It a little ways back, sitting on a log smoking his pipe. His trail name fit him to a tee: he was in no hurry and hiked when he got "Round-To-It."

I arrived at Barrett Road where a sign read, "Need Water? Turn right at road crossing, go uphill to the yellow house with a red roof. The hose is on the back porch." It seemed to me that only on the A.T. would you find such gracious and trusting people.

After crossing Long House Road, I heard Copperhead sing out, "Would you look at that!" and soon saw the trail magic he was crowing about: a cooler with some Snapple pink lemonade and a note, "Enjoy – Running Water – thru-hiked in 1998."

Not long after, I reached the New York-New Jersey state line, which was painted right on a rock next to the trail. Copperhead proudly proclaimed, "Eight states down and six to go!" as I smiled and looked forward to Bear Mountain, New York, and a hike with my daughter Elizabeth.

We met a couple of section-hikers at the state line and told them we had just spotted another bear. One of them said, wild-eyed, to his hiking partner, "Let's get the hell out of here! I'm not one bit interested in seeing a bear!"

We arrived at the top of Prospect Rock to a beautiful view of the mountains and surrounding lakes. We could actually see water skiers on Greenwood Lake, as Copperhead pointed and with an ornery grin, said, "Check out that blonde on the skis." I laughed and said, "You certainly have better eyes than I do, or should I say a better imagination?"

Story Time: Copperhead was telling me about falling on a section of the A.T. near Palmerton, Pennsylvania. It was a very difficult section that required scaling a cliff, and it was raining as he crossed. He fell, sustaining a serious head injury. There happened to be a couple of hikers near by, Papa Bob and Steady Frank, who helped him get to the hospital. Ten stitches were needed to close the wound. Copperhead winced as he told me, "The worst part of the entire ordeal was calling my wife from the hospital and having to leave a message on the answering system that I was in the hospital!"

At New York Highway 17A near Bellvale, I said goodbye to Copperhead; he was going into Bellvale to meet a friend and slackpack for a day or so. I'd really enjoyed his company and hoped I would see him again on the trail. When he left, I still had two more miles to Wildcat Shelter, and I was out of water. But then, more trail magic! Just inside the woods were two gallon bottles of unopened water. I was set with water for the hike to the shelter.

I arrived at the shelter just after 4 p.m. with the Country Gentleman, Ruth, and one new face. The new hiker's trail name was Two Weeks And Three Days, a great trail name. He said, "I got my trail name from my wife. That's how long she said I would last on the trail!" We had perfect timing. Just after we reached the shelter, it started to rain.

Evening talk at the shelter got around to nude hiking day. There were a lot of stories about the hikers who took advantage of the day, although none of the hikers in the shelter had hiked nude or at least none would admit it. We were also seeing a number of U.S. flags in the shelters, and one of the hikers asked, "What's up with all the flags?" Someone asked her what day it was, and she didn't have a clue. She was embarrassed when she learned the following day was July 4, Independence Day. It was a good example of how detached from the outside world thru-hikers become on the trail. Time and dates become meaningless as hikers lose all awareness of weekends and holidays.

I took a look at the shelter register. Tennessee, the young hiker with whom I ate my half-gallon of ice cream (I was still feeling the after-effects of that bonehead move) had stayed in the shelter about a week earlier and wrote, "The mosquitoes are killing me, they are eating me alive! I met a section-hiker who gave me some Deet repellent, which literally saved my life!"

Hiker tips: I discovered another use for my silk
sleeping bag liner. Along with helping keep my

*sleeping bag cleaner and adding a little more warmth,
the liner was great against those nasty little
mosquitoes. Allowing air to flow through while keeping
the mosquitoes out, it worked really well, and I slept
just fine, even in the mosquito-infested shelter!*

Also in the register at the shelter was Love Shack's entry: "I told
my parents to pick me up on 8-5-00 at Mount Katahdin. That means
twenty-four miles a day without any breaks!" He was quite a hiker and
might be able to pull it off, but I loved Tennessee's comment about
Love Shack hiking twenty-four-mile days: "There are lots of ways to
commit suicide, but this is the first time I have seen hiking used!"
There seemed to be a lot more talk about Mount Katahdin in the
register. It appeared that as people got closer, they started to think they
might actually get there. Although I was not close enough to start
talking about Katahdin as if it were a sure thing, I had started to feel the
pull a little more.

Two Weeks And Three Days said that all of the water sources we
were seeing had been completely dried up the previous year. "The
hikers were completely dependent on water left by trail angels," he
said.

A brief trail commentary: Listening to and watching Country
Gentleman and Ruth in the shelter, I came to the realization that they
were prime examples of the end being more important than the means.
They were so consumed with thru-hiking the entire trail to the point
that nothing, and no one, on the trail was as important as them getting
to Katahdin. I was confident they would make it, but I really wondered
if they were enjoying any part of the trail? But again, as said so often
before, "Hike your own hike."

July 4, Wildcat Shelter to Arden Valley Road (Tiorati Lake) (milepoint 1368.8 north)

I hiked to West Monbasha Road where I was able to hitch a half-
mile ride to a deli for breakfast and then another ride back to the trail. I
really enjoyed the warm breakfast. The opportunity to eat at a few delis
enabled me to reduce my pack weight and at the same time enjoy some
great egg and salami sandwiches. I loved hiking in New York.

I had an opportunity to talk with an elderly man sitting on a rock.
He lived in the area and had often hiked many of the nearby sections of
the trail. He said he was thinking about hiking the trail to Vermont to
see his brother, so we talked about the A.T. north of his home. When he
saw my *Data Book*, he asked, "Just how far is it to High Point?"

I asked, "Do you mean High Point, New Jersey?"

With a slight grin, he said, "No, I mean High Point, *Jour-say*. That's how we pronounce it around here!"

Really got a kick out of that. I certainly enjoyed meeting the locals along the trail; and the encounter got me thinking about the question I had been asked on so many occasions, "What's been your favorite aspects about hiking the A.T.?" My response was threefold: First, the opportunity to hike every day. Second, seeing all the great vistas and wildlife. And third, the opportunity to meet and talk with the locals.

I finished some major boulder climbing on Buchanan Mountain, hand over hand! Tough, but fun.

When I arrived at East Monbasha Road, I found several jugs of water left by the "Tuxedo Trail Angels." I certainly appreciated the water on such a sultry day. My pants were totally soaked with sweat from my waist to my knees.

As I crossed New York Highway 17, there was a phone next to the trail, so I checked in to see how things were going with my daughter Elizabeth and our meeting at Bear Mountain.

Not long after that, I pulled my stupidest move yet on the trail! I was going through the "Lemon Squeeze", a section of the A.T. where hikers need to take their packs off and drag them behind them in order to squeeze between the rocks, and thought it would be great to get a picture of me squeezing through. I placed my camera on a rock and set the auto timer, but as I turned to walk back to the "Lemon Squeeze" for the picture, I heard a crashing sound. I turned around in time to watch my camera fall off the ledge and plummet into a deep crevice. After a great deal of straining, scratching, and crawling on my belly headfirst into a pitch black crevice, I was just able to squeeze far enough to reach the camera. If it had gone another two inches, I would not have been able to retrieve it! Still, it was broken. I was really irritated by the thought that I would have to be without a camera simply because I was too damn lazy to set my camera up using my tripod. If I'd made a dumber move on the trail, I couldn't think of it!

As I continued north on the trail, giving myself hell for being so careless, I got to thinking, "I was probably damn lucky I didn't come nose-to-nose with a rattler as I squirmed headfirst into that crevice!" There's always a positive, right?

I arrived at the Fingerboard Shelter just before 4 p.m. The shelter looked OK, but it did not appear to have any water sources.

An hour later, I threw my pack on and left the shelter. I'd walked down the side of the mountain more than a half-mile looking for water, only to find a lake from which I really did not want to get my water supply. After returning to the shelter, I sat for awhile and even had my

Therm-A-Rest out when it dawned on me, "What the hell am I doing sitting in this shelter without water when just a mile or so up the trail there's probably a better camp and water?" Although it was a gamble, I headed for a better camping spot.

I hit the jackpot! I met a ranger near Arden Valley Road, and he told me thru-hikers were allowed to camp at Tiorati Campground, just down the road. There were a lot of picnickers in the area, and it looked like a really good place to stay.

By eight-thirty I was ready for bed after a somewhat frustrating day, what with the broken camera and the lack of water. I'd been fortunate, though, to find a campsite reserved for thru-hikers with plenty of water, and just a short walk from the ranger station and Tiorati Lake. While eating a sandwich at the concession area, I'd had a chance to talk with a park ranger. He told me that "tiorati" was a Native American word meaning "sky-like" and that the lake and park were state-owned and used by people who typically drove fifty miles from New York City to boat, swim, and fish. Along with concessions, there were restrooms, showers, a swimming beach – free for thru-hikers – and a picnic area.

> *Hiker tips: The lake and camp area was just three-tenths of a mile down Arden Valley Road from the A.T. and certainly beat spending the night in a nasty shelter without water!*

July 5, Arden Valley Road (Tiorati Lake) to Bear Mountain Inn (milepoint 1381.2 north)

I was up early and on the road after a beautiful evening, happy that I'd made the decision to hike on to the Tiorati Lake area. Then I found myself grumbling, "What the hell? I must have missed the trail!" I knew there was a gate where I'd gotten off the trail onto the Arden Valley Road the day before, but I'd be damned if I could find it. So I turned around on the road and headed back. I'd passed it. Not a good way to begin a day's hike.

Back on the A.T., I headed north after a slight delay. Three big wild turkeys took off in front of me and gave me quite a start. They fly better than I thought they could.

On top of Black Mountain, I looked out over the countryside of New York. It was another beautiful view, and once more I could see the skyline of New York City.

At the Palisades Interstate Parkway, a big sign read "New York City 34 miles." The trail crossed right over the four-lane highway, and in the median between the east and westbound traffic were a lawn chair and a trail register! Many of the comments in the register said things like, "The biggest challenge of the Appalachian Trail so far has been getting across this goddamn Interstate!"

I arrived at the Perkins Memorial Tower on top of Bear Mountain and found more great views of the New York City skyline, the Hudson River, and the Graymoor Monastery to which Elizabeth and I planned to hike the following day. Ranger Mike, who worked at the tower and was an admirer of thru-hikers, was generous enough to give me a couple of sodas and a personal tour of the tower. The stone tower was built in 1934 as a fire tower. Mike told me, "I'll be waving from the tower as you and your daughter cross the Hudson and hike up the mountain tomorrow!"

It was early afternoon as I hiked down to Bear Mountain Inn. The beautiful rustic building next to the lake was built around 1915 using native rocks. The A.T. traveled right between the lake and the inn.

Beth arrived around 4 p.m. after an enjoyable one-hour train ride along the Hudson River, where she was able to see some of the tall ships that had come into New York for the Independence Day celebration. She seemed as excited as I about joining me on my hike, and we talked and planned for the next few days over dinner at the inn. One of the best parts of my hike for me had been sharing the trail with my family and friends. The opportunity to share some of the sights and experiences of the trail had been special.

Hiker tips: I would highly recommend meeting up with family for short periods of time if at all possible. It was certainly worth the hassle of arrangements just to be able to share the trail with them. I would also suggest doing this later in the hike rather than early, for I felt much more confident and relaxed.

July 6, Bear Mountain Inn to Dennytown Road Campsite (milepoint 1396.5 north)

As we headed out on the trail, I figured every hiker needed a trail name; so for my law-student daughter, I picked Mountain Law. Thus, it was Mountain Slayer and Mountain Law who headed north on the Appalachian Trail.

My pack was heavier now that Elizabeth had brought me more supplies. Bear Mountain actually had its own post office close to the inn, so I was able to mail home a few items that I would not need.

We left the inn and followed the white blazes north into a tunnel under U.S. Highway 9 and right through a trailside museum and zoo. According to *The Thru-Hiker's Handbook*, the museum – built in 1927 at the urging of Benton MacKaye, the Massachusetts naturalist who first proposed what became the Appalachian Trail – featured the oldest, continuously used nature trail in the country. The trailside zoo had numerous small animal exhibits as well as a memorial to Walt Whitman, and it was located at the lowest point on the entire A.T., 124 feet above sea level. I could now say that I had been on the highest point of the Appalachian Trail – Clingmans Dome in the Smoky Mountains – and the lowest. It was a great idea to route the A.T. right though the heart of the park. The only problem, the park was closed when we arrived. With a puzzled look, Elizabeth asked, "Now what?" I put my index finger to my lips. Without a word I threw my backpack over the fence, jumped up on the fence and in a hushed voice whispered, "Let's go." Although Mountain Law seemed a little tentative, she followed suit. "Nothing stops a determined thru-hiker," I joked as we headed north through the zoo.

As we crossed Bear Mountain Bridge over the Hudson, Beth told me that her taxi driver the day before had told her that it was the second oldest bridge in the state of New York. The oldest being the Brooklyn Bridge which she crossed on a regular basis heading to Manhattan from her apartment in Brooklyn Heights.

Once over the bridge we saw that the white blazes headed straight up into the mountains. It appeared that Mountain Law was going to get a good taste of mountain climbing really quick. Our packs were feeling heavy just from looking at the white blazes leading straight up into the mountains.

It was noon as Mountain Law and I visited the Graymoor Monastery, home of the Franciscan Friars of Atonement. Thru-hikers had been welcome to stay overnight for more than twenty years and were even offered hot showers and dinner. We had planned to stay for the night; but as it was early, we decided to head north. We ate lunch, checked for blisters, and headed back on the trail. Elizabeth was feeling good, so we decided to push on to the next shelter about eight miles north. That would mean a fifteen-mile day, a big day for a beginning hiker.

Captain America was at the Graymoor Shelter. He said he "blew out a knee." He'd been resting it for about three days and planned to stay a few more days in hopes he could continue without pain. As we talked, he asked where we were from. When we said Ohio, he asked, "You wouldn't happen to know a little town by the name of Anna, Ohio?" We both looked at each other and laughed as we said, "Yeah, just a few miles up the road from where we live." Captain America told us he had purchased an engine for his motorcycle in the little one-stoplight town of Anna, Ohio, and we all had a good laugh at how small the world really is.

We arrived at Denning Hill, and once again we could see the New York City skyline. It wasn't quite the view I'd had the day before, but Elizabeth was able to point out the Trade Center and its Twin Towers. We were making good time and hoped to get to Dennytown Road, where, according to my *Data Book*, there would be a tenting area and water. On the other hand, none of the southbound hikers seemed to know anything about the Dennytown tenting area which was not a good sign.

I almost missed a turn on the trail. I would have walked right by the double white blaze, so it was a good thing Mountain Law was on the ball. It was nice to have an extra pair of eyes! We'd both had a good laugh earlier in the morning as we passed a hiker still asleep in his tent with his food bag hanging on a little tree no more than two feet off the ground. But Mountain Law's laughter stopped abruptly when I told her about the bear attack in the Smokies – not something she wanted to hear before her first night on the trail.

In addition, we'd met a southbounder earlier who had bells on his hiking pole. Elizabeth asked, "What are the bells all about?" I told her that they let bears know a hiker is in the area, and her response was, "Dad, what did you get me into?"

We arrived at the Dennytown Road about 4 p.m. Mountain Law put in a big first day; we had hiked more than fifteen miles! I asked her, "Did you enjoy the day?"

"It was a good day," she replied as she rubbed her sore foot and stiff neck.

July 7, Dennytown Road Campsite to N.Y. 53 (Stormville, New York) (milepoint 1412.5 north)

It was 6 a.m. as we headed out on another beautiful morning. When asked how she slept, Mountain Law answered, "I slept well except for the bear visit during the night!" I guess I had told one too many bear stories. She believed I scared the bear away when I coughed. That should be good for a family story in coming years!

Elizabeth was a little stiff from carrying the pack and had a blister on her heel. We took care of the blister problem, we hoped, with some duct tape. As we continued to climb Shenandoah Mountain, Mountain Law said with a grimace, "I feel like the little mountain climber on *The Price is Right*!" We both laughed as I replied, "Just don't fall over the cliff!"

She mentioned how nice the cool breeze felt and how great the mountain views were. When you don't know the terrain, and with no control over the weather, picking out a place to meet for hiking is nothing more than a shot in the dark. We both felt very fortunate so far. The hike had been challenging yet doable for a new hiker, and the weather had been perfect.

Near the Clarence Fahnestock Memorial State Park, we crossed a trail area that was built up with stones in the low spots. I hadn't seen the trail constructed in this manner anywhere else; it was extremely well done, and I teased Mountain Law that someone knew she was going to be out hiking.

We finished a snack on top of the Shenandoah Mountain at 1,282 feet. We'd started below 600 feet, so it had been a heart-pumping ascent. I asked Mountain Law if she wanted to hike the rest of the way to Maine with me. Not very impressed with the idea, she responded quickly, "Over 700 miles to go? No way! I am not crazy!"

As we crossed the Long Hill Road, a UPS truck came to a screeching halt, throwing gravel and dust in all directions, with the driver slamming on his brakes as if he were going to deliver a package to us. It turned out that he just wanted to chat and ask some questions about the trail. I didn't usually see UPS drivers stopping for anything; they always seemed to be on the run. I wondered if this one's stopping could have had anything to do with the young attractive Mountain Law being on the trail with me?

We reached the Shenandoah Tenting Area where there was a hand pump for water. Mountain Law started pumping and quickly said, frowning, "Man, just my luck, no water." I pointed to a bucket of priming water near the pump and the sign: "Please refill the bucket when finished." Not having any experience with priming a pump, Elizabeth laughed and said as I poured the water into the pump, "I would have pumped on that dang thing all day!" We were headed to Stormville about five miles away, and the trail register told of pizza in Stormville, bringing a smile to Mountain Law's face and an added incentive to get there.

Elizabeth and I arrived at Ralph's Peak Hikers cabin, otherwise known as the RPH Shelter. The shelter had a sign noting the distances to various points on the A.T. They included the Connecticut State line, 26.2 miles; Mount Katahdin, 743.7 miles; Bear Mountain Bridge, 25.2 miles; and Springer Mountain, 1429.2 miles. It was interesting, although I wasn't sure how accurate the distances were. All I knew, I was getting closer to Katahdin with every step.

We arrived at State Highway 52 to Stormville, New York. "Interesting," I told Beth. "This was where I had planned to finish my hike with you."

"We still might!" she yelled half jokingly, as she tugged at the shoulder straps of her pack that were digging some pretty nasty grooves into her shoulders. The last three hours had worked her over pretty hard, so we decided to go on into Stormville and see if we could find a place to camp.

By 6:30 p.m. we were relaxing at Nick's Deli in Stormville. I'd talked to Nick when we arrived in town, and he set us up with a tenting site right behind his deli. We had hiked 15.5 miles for the day, and that was enough; again, it was probably too much for a new hiker. We had water and access to a phone, thanks to Nick, and food from the deli or even the pizza place right next door. Best of all, Elizabeth and I sat in Danny's Pizza shop and watched the Yankees-Indians game, being careful not to tell all the New York fans that Mountain Law was an Indian fan! I checked in at home and talked to Connie about getting a new camera in a few days. That would be good: the throwaway box camera I had been using was just not good enough.

July 8, N.Y. 53 (Stormville, New York) to West Dover Road (Pawling, New York) (milepoint 1424.7 north)

It was another beautiful, cool morning as we got back on the trail after staying in the backyard of Nick's Deli. We were headed to Pawling, New York, about 12 miles north, where I had made reservations at a B&B. I slept OK after putting in my earplugs, but Mountain Law said she didn't sleep well, probably due to the amount of noise throughout the night.

At the Morgan Stewart Shelter, we ran into Hoagie Dreamer and Slow Rider, a couple of young thru-hikers that we had seen off and on for awhile. Although they hadn't gotten started for the day, they joked about at least being up. Apparently they'd been having a tough time getting up and going in the morning.

As we continued north on the A.T., we crossed the Metro North Tracks, the exact tracks that Mountain Law would be using for her return to the city.

Later, we met a southbound section-hiker from Georgia with the trail name of Trail Walker. He had started his section hike at Mount Washington and was telling me about his experiences hiking in the White Mountains. I certainly was looking forward to the much-talked-about mountains.

Hoagie Dreamer and Slow Rider caught up to us and casually mentioned they wanted to pick up a maildrop in Pawling. Beth asked them, "Doesn't the post office close at noon on Saturday?"

"Yeah, it probably does, so what?" Then they looked at each other with dropped mouths and yelled, "Oh s--t, it's Saturday!" They took off on a dead run north up the trail.

We laughed until we had tears in our eyes. They had about a mile to the road, then another three or four-mile hitch into town, and it was 11:30 a.m.

We arrived at Route 20, which went to Pawling, a little after twelve. There were no hikers, so at least the two young hikers – or sprinters, if you will – got a ride into town. Right where the road into Pawling intersected with the A.T. stood a 300-year-old oak tree, the Dover Oak, which was said in the *Thru-Hikers' Companion* to be the largest oak tree on the A.T. Its girth four feet above the ground measured nineteen feet, five inches. The oak seemed a fitting spot for the end of Mountain Law's journey along the

Elizabeth and Dad in front of 300-year-old, Dover Oak, largest oak on A.T.

trail. When I asked her how many miles she thought she'd hiked, she answered with pride and exactness, "Forty-three and a half." Spoken like a true hiker. We were fortunate to get a quick ride into the pretty little town of Pawling, New York.

> *Hiker tips: Although a few miles off the trail, the little town is convenient for hikers, having all the necessary stops for hikers within easy walking distance.*

The B&B we were staying at had a pizza shop nearby as well as a laundry right across the street. We were also able to go to a 5 p.m. Mass, so all we had to do the following day was put Beth on the train (the station was right across the street from the B&B) and I would catch a hitch back to the trail.

I'd had a great time hiking with Mountain Law the last few days; and although she was sore, I think she also enjoyed herself. It had been very special having Elizabeth along on the hike for a few days, as it had been with my two boys earlier on. To spend time in the mountains with my children had been a very important part of my A.T. experience and something I would forever cherish.

July 9, West Dover Road (Pawling, New York) to Mt. Algo Lean-to (Connecticut) (milepoint 1445.4 north)

It was a little before 7 a.m. when I put Mountain Law on the train headed to New York City. I felt a twinge of sadness listening to the fading sound of the train whistle as the train rolled back to the Big Apple. Elizabeth had been one of the very first to sign my website guest book at the start of my hike. She signed, "Dad, I'll see you at Bear Mountain!" When I read that, I thought, "That sure is a long way off." I had found it almost impossible to look that far ahead. Now we had hiked Bear Mountain together.

I had a twenty-mile day planned, but my first challenge was to get a ride back to the trail. Within a few minutes a lady with two small children stopped on her way to church to pick me up. She went three miles out of her way to drop me off at the trail. A trail angel on her way to church, how fitting!

> *Hiker tips: Gear change information: I had been trying a different water system, the PurLife squeeze bottle filter, and it had worked well allowing me to avoid carrying large amounts of water. I had also changed my socks to adjust for the new hiking boots. I used a thick sock for my boot that was loose-fitting and a thin sock for my tight-fitting boot.*

As I hiked along, a little homesick, I got to thinking how lucky I was to have kids who were both willing and able to take the time to hike with me. They'd been good hikers too, allowing me to stay on schedule.

Every now and then I continued to hear the faint whistle of a train. The train system in New York was impressive. Elizabeth had taken the Hudson Line up from the city to Poughkeepsie, which was a short cab ride from Bear Mountain. We'd then hiked 42.5 miles north to Pawling, where she was able to take the Harlem Line back to Grand Central Station in the city. She figured she would be home about two hours after leaving Pawling.

I hiked past the Appalachian Trail train station for the Metro-North train near New York Highway 22. I'd been told it was the only place on the entire A.T. where the train actually stopped right on the trail. A small sign with a bench identified the trail and stop. I noticed that the train didn't stop there every day.

Near Hurds Corner Road, there was an iron arch over the trail with lettering that read, "Gate of Heaven." There was nothing else around, not a building in sight. Now I knew I was in God's country!

Another state was chalked up at Hoyt Road, the New York-Connecticut state line, and that made it nine down and five to go. I was feeling very good with 732.9 miles left to Mount Katahdin. The Connecticut welcome sign read, "Camp in designated sites only." I could only hope that Connecticut would be as good to me as New York had been.

It was a little after noon when I hiked up to Ten Mile River Lean-to, the first shelter area in Connecticut. It was obviously too early to be stopping, but it would be a long day with the next shelter nine miles away. It was interesting that they called the shelters in Connecticut lean-tos. I finished lunch with a couple of section-hikers who wished me luck as we parted company, saying with envy in both their eyes and voices, "You're headed to some of the best backpacking territory in the U.S., and we're headed home to work. It's just not right!"

When I entered the Schaghticoke Tribal Nation Reservation, a welcome sign warned, "Eastern Timber Rattlesnake, be very alert." A very good idea!

As I hiked up to the Mount Algo Lean-to, the mosquitoes were again swarming; and I quickly had my tent up and the good old mac and cheese cooking. Camping with me were a couple of thru-hikers I hadn't seen for awhile: Magic Thumb with his dog Dillon, and Tennessee. Magic Thumb was having a lot of back pain. He figured his body was wearing down and planned to take a couple of days off. Tennessee told me that Old Boot got off the trail back at Delaware Water Gap. A young ridge runner was also staying the night. A good group of guys, they all wondered where my good-looking daughter was. Word spread fast on the A.T.

My body was again telling me twenty miles was too much in the mountains; I needed to keep it closer to fifteen miles. My wife had pointed out that every time someone left after hiking the trail with me, I would put in big miles the following day. Looking back, I believe she was right. I guess it was my way of dealing with being a little homesick.

July 10, Mt. Algo Lean-to to Pine Swamp Brook Lean-to (milepoint 1462.7 north)

Up early and on the trail after a little rain during the night. Getting to the shelter had been a good decision. Connecticut had restrictions on camping. As the sign at the state line had indicated, hikers were required to stay at designated campsites or shelters.

I talked to a ridge runner who mentioned that the Schaghticoke Indians were a little unhappy with the U.S. government and had threatened to close the reservation section of the AT. The Appalachian Trail Conference had a re-route planned if that section were closed. Fortunately, that didn't happen, for it would have been a seven-mile detour for the hikers.

Near Thayer Brook there was a Ziploc bag hanging on a tree right beside the trail. Inside was a hand written note that read: "Help – someplace between here and Vernon, New Jersey, I lost a small army-green nylon bag containing a repair kit and a very important can of film that cannot be replaced. If you find please return to – " Another example of what all thru-hikers feared the most, losing something that could not replaced. So far I had lost a bug net, a water bottle, a tent stake and some clothesline rope. My wife would be impressed, actually more like shocked, that I hadn't lost more.

When I arrived at St. Johns Ledges, I estimated I had hiked 7.3 miles and felt kind of sluggish. I had to assume it was because of yesterday's twenty-mile day. Those always seemed to take a toll on me. I met a ridge runner by the name of Matt who was very informative. Ridge runners were often able to tell hikers what businesses were nearby, what was available in a town, and where to go to get supplies, and Matt was no exception. He told me where the post office was in Cornwall, Connecticut, and much more importantly, the location of a tavern that gave a free beer to any thru-hiker who signed the register.

I got a quick hitch into town, picked up my new camera at the post office, and then stopped at Baird's General Store where I purchased a big deli sandwich and a few other supplies. Then I relaxed while I ate my sandwich and talked to some of the locals, who said it looked like more rain. This prompted a quick hitch out of town (no time for the free beer) and back to the trail.

I made it to the Pine Swamp Brook Lean-to about 4:30p.m., where I set up camp and started dinner. When I arrived, there was a group of kids with a couple of adults packing up to leave, including one little girl who came back from the privy saying, "That thing stinks!" Her curled-up nose and general demeanor told me she was not long for the trail. I read in the register that the group of kids got to the shelter about 2 a.m. and kept the entire camp up all night! It looked as though I was fortunate they were pulling out, especially since it was so late in the afternoon. The register also told me that Copperhead had stopped by the shelter at noon, but it looked as though the mosquitoes and I had the shelter to ourselves for the night.

July 11, Pine Swamp Brook Lean-to to Conn. 41 (Salisbury, Connecticut) (milepoint 1479.1 north)

I headed out of Pine Swamp Brook Lean-to after filtering some water from a very unappealing swamp behind the shelter. It was a gorgeous morning.

At Sharon Mountain Campsite I had an excellent view of Lime Rock Park auto racetrack down in the valley. There was also some kind of wooden ramp that extended out from the side of the mountain a good ten feet and then just stopped! I'm not sure what that was all about. As pretty as the morning was, the mosquitoes really went out of their way to make my hike miserable.

> *Hiker tips: Be sure you have your bug spray (Deet) by*
> *the time you get to New Jersey.*

Just off U.S. Route 7, there was a gas station where I hoped to get a snack. An old sign on the trail just before Route 7 welcomed hikers to the gas station and listed some of the items they sold. The *Appalachian Trail Thru-Hikers' Companion* mentioned that there was no longer hiker service, but I thought, "What the heck, may as well go down for a soda. What could be the harm in that?" After walking the short distance to the station, I came upon a sign that read, "All information costs $2, this is not a world atlas information stand! Directions are only given to PAYING customers!" That should have been enough to turn me around right there, but it wasn't. Looking around the little station, I couldn't find any form of life except a big old dog barking as I took my pack off for a break. No sooner had my rear end hit the concrete than this angry-looking fellow walked out from behind the station with hate in his eyes. I greeted him with my typical, "Hello, how you doing?" and he immediately went on a tirade about hikers putting their packs in front of his doorway (my pack was leaning up against the wall of his station, far from any doorway). He continued bitching, and I immediately knew I did not want to hear anymore, so I put my pack on and walked away, saying, "Now, you have a great day." I even included a smile, free of charge! The cantankerous man, whose business had been passed by

201

(and I certainly could understand why), made the waitress at the Blue Mountain Inn look like a real caregiver!

I entered the small town of Cannon, Connecticut, incorporated in 1729. The locals told me that the ramp I saw up on the mountain was actually a hang glide take-off site. That made sense. And the racetrack was a 1.3-mile track, made famous by actor/race driver Paul Newman.

I hiked past the Connecticut Power and Light Company's Falls Village hydroelectric station right next to the Housatonic River. A turn-of-the-last-century building, it had a shower sticking out through the ivy over a small concrete pad, which would offer quite a reprieve on a hot summer day of backpacking.

I'd had an interesting morning hike, a little forest hiking but the majority had been skirting small towns and road walks. Not something I would want to do all the time, but it was a nice change of pace.

I hiked past the side trail to Limestone Spring Lean-to and had about four miles to the town of Salisbury, Connecticut, where I hoped to find a room, clean up, and put a little ice on my knee which had flared up again.

It was 3 p.m. when I found the White Heart Hotel, a handsome historic hotel to stay at in Salisbury. Salisbury is a quaint little trail town where I was able to do some laundry, mail a package, and get a good meal. I had hiked sixteen miles and after the two long days figured I would pamper myself a little with a comfortable bed and shower. I found out from some locals that Ethan Allen and the Green Mountain Boys once called the area their home.

July 12, Conn. 41 (Salisbury, Connecticut) to Mass. 41 (South Egermont, Massachusetts) (milepoint 1496.9 north)

I was up and on the trail early, munching on a granola bar for breakfast. My knee was still a little sore from the last couple big days, so I planned to take it easier by taking a few more breaks. Looking ahead, I had a maildrop coming up and it looked like it would fall on a Saturday, which was a real pain!

I'd talked to a couple of fellows at the ice cream shop in Salisbury. One of them was very familiar with the A.T. and had hiked north a number of times. He shared his excitement about hiking in the White Mountains and really had me looking forward to getting there.

It was another beautiful day and the forecast was for nice weather for the next two days or so. The weather forecasters were saying that it had been one of the coolest summers on record. You would not get any complaints from me; I loved hiking in the cool weather.

I met a couple headed up to Lions Head Mountain who were enjoying a breakfast by the trail. While I was talking to them, the group of kids who had been leaving the shelter the other afternoon hiked by. They were hiking without packs, and when I asked the little girl who had displayed such disdain for the "stinking privy" where they were going – as I certainly intended to avoid their campsite – she shouted with delight, "We're headed home!" She'd obviously had enough backpacking for awhile.

Approximately a mile from the Massachusetts state line I arrived at the top of yet another Bear Mountain, the highest point in Connecticut where, according to *The Thru-Hiker's Handbook*, a rock tower was built more than a hundred years earlier without the use of mortar.

At Sages Ravine I had officially crossed the state line into Massachusetts. That made the tenth state finished and four to go as I knelt down at the ravine to filter some water.

> *Hiker tips: I really liked the two squeeze water bottles I was carrying. The small bottle was kept within reach at all times for filtering and drinking as I hiked, while the larger one was used to filter larger amounts of water at night. I had sent my PUR Voyager water filter home earlier, saving the weight of the water filter, not to mention the weight of carrying filtered water.*

As I hiked along, I was thinking about my hiking buddy, Keith, who helped get me ready for my hike and had hoped to hike a little of the trail with me. The word from home was that he was planning to head out to the trail as soon as he finished painting his house. I bet he couldn't wait to get away from that job.

Met a ridge runner who surprised me when he said, "I started out working down at Amicalola Falls and remember seeing you there. You are the thirteenth person that I saw start the trail who's gotten this far!"

Noon came, and I had not made much progress. I guess I had been talking too much. After talking to the ridge runner, I ran into two more southbounders, Tinker Bell and Peter Pan. They'd started out from Mount Katahdin on May 10 and were doing very well. We exchanged information about places to stay. It was always beneficial talking to southbounders and getting information that only thru-hikers could share.

On top of Race Mountain, I was eating lunch when a group of young kids came hiking by. When I asked one how old he was, he held up seven fingers, threw out his chest and proudly proclaimed, "I'm this many!" They all had their little backpacks on and were having a great time, as evidenced by my ability to hear them well before I could see them!

I passed four more southbounders. That made at least six in one day! They were coming *en masse* now.

At an overlook I came upon a couple of day hikers. Knowing they were locals, I asked what they were looking at. One of them pointed off in the distance to a double hump and said with conviction, "That, my friend, is Mount Graylock." It looked a long way off as its double humps peered out above the clouds about sixty-five trail miles away, especially since I planned to be on that mountain in just five days.

Another group of young kids came along, this time from New York City. They were coming up the mountain as I was headed down. A particularly chubby little guy with a round red face was sitting on a rock next to the trail and gasping for breath. He asked me, "Man, are you headed back down this mountain?"

I said I was, and he immediately shouted, "I'm done; I'm going with you!"

I could tell he was really whipped and wasn't sure he was going to make it to the top of the mountain, let alone the next shelter. But when I told him that I was headed to Maine, his eyes grew saucer-sized. He said, "Oh my God, you're crazy! No way I'm going with you!"

I laughed so hard I thought I would fall off the side of the mountain.

A little after 5 p.m., as I hiked to Jug End Road and did not see one good camping spot anywhere, I decided to hike on to Massachusetts State Highway 41 and hitch a ride into South Egermont, Mass.

At the highway, the first person to drive by stopped to give me a ride into town and just happened to be the mayor of South Egermont. A great fellow, he suggested the Egermont Inn, even dropped me off there, and waited to make sure they had a room for me. A trail angel disguised as a mayor – that was a first.

It was late afternoon and I was cleaned up and lying in my room at the Egermont Inn. The people at the inn – a beautiful building from 1780 – were wonderful.

> *Hiker tips: All too often the owners of upscale inns didn't particularly want hot, smelly hikers as their guests. That was not the case at the Egermont Inn, where the staff told me they really enjoyed hikers, even though I walked up to the counter soaked in sweat. The price was also very reasonable and included breakfast. When I heard that breakfast was served at 8:30 a.m., I said I hoped to be on the trail by that time; and the*

owner promptly said, "We don't want you leaving on an empty stomach. I'm sure we can work something out in the morning." That was when I knew they were sincere about enjoying having hikers stay at their inn. I would highly recommend this stop to anyone hiking in the area.

July 13, Mass. 41 (South Egermont, Massachusetts) to Mount Wilcox North Lean-to (milepoint 1514.0 north)

Under way at half past 7 a.m., I needed to stop at a convenience store for some supplies, so I took my time walking through town until the stores opened and then headed back to the highway, looking to hitch back to the trail. When I'd called home from the inn the day before, I'd bragged on the phone to Connie about how fortunate I'd been getting rides; but the very next morning, not one person even slowed down as they saw me hitching. So, my hiking day began with a mile-and-a-half walk back to the trail. Nevertheless, it was still a beautiful morning, and I was back on the trail.

As I crossed South Egermont Road, I came upon a stone monument. It read, "Last Battle of Shays Rebellion, Feb 27, 1787." Appropriately, as the rebellion involved farmers, the monument was next to a cornfield. I enjoyed the many sites and monuments that I came upon along the trail. Many, like the one for Shay's Rebellion, were out in the middle of nowhere, and I doubt if I would have ever visited it if not for my hiking the A.T.

The mosquitoes were insufferable, so I stopped to put on some bug spray. Despite the mosquitoes, the wide variety of thick woods, swamp, and fresh-mown hay fields were making my hike through Massachusetts bearable.

I spent a little time at the Corn Crib, a farmer's market that had a little of everything; and I believe I had a taste of everything: milk, nuts, fudge, and a peach. And I wondered why my stomach was talking to me so much lately! An exceptionally friendly lady ran the market. She filled my water bottles with fresh spring water; and when I asked about the weather, she even called the weather service for me.

As I entered a thick forest, I thought I would appreciate the shade, but the roar of mosquitoes was incredible. The Deet I had applied kept them from biting, but the constant hum was maddening. I finally put in my earplugs just to stop the noise. They had turned a beautiful morning hike into pure torture.

I hiked out onto a cliff area where there was a breeze and no mosquitoes. With apologies to Dr. King, the words that came to me were "Thank God, free at last."

Two hikers passed by, first a southbounder and the other a north-bounder going south. Yep, a north-bounder going south! Buckwheat, a northbound thru-hiker I'd met early in my hike, was currently going south, saying, "I was getting in a rut and just decided to try something different." The other southbounder had the trail name of Mr. Clean. One look at his bald head and I knew how he got the trail name. He looked just like the genie in the old television commercials.

I reached the Mount Wilcox South Lean-to where I had planned to spend the night, but in the shelter was a note that read, "I should have taken Mike's advice. Do not stay here unless you have earplugs. I tented out behind the lean-to and about 11 p.m. they moved in – at least three porcupines. First I heard them moving through the woods, then into the shelter. The chewing and gnawing was still going strong at 3 a.m." I'd heard about this shelter. There was no way I was staying, so I headed to the Mount Wilcox North Lean-to.

That lean-to was about three-tenths of a mile off the trail, but it was late and I was tired, so I decided to hike off the trail to the shelter. I had only seen two thru-hikers and a couple of day hikers all day. Where was everyone? I figured I would be the only one at the shelter, but then I had to take that back, as I'd forgotten about all those damn mosquitoes that would be sure to keep me company.

Toward evening, a section-hiker by the name of Roamer hiked in, so at least there would be one other person for the mosquitoes to feast upon.

July 14, Mount Wilcox North Lean-to to U.S. 20 (Gaslight Motor Lodge) (milepoint 1529.6 north)

Had a much better night than I'd anticipated. The porcupines did not bother us, and I managed the mosquitoes with bug repellent and my sleeping bag liner. Roamer, a computer programmer originally from Maine, did not have his warm sleeping bag. Come morning, he said he certainly could have used it.

I was looking at a fourteen or fifteen-mile day; the twenty-mile days were really too much. The day before, my knee had been hurting well before I got to the lean-to. Upper Goose Pond Cabin or Lee, Massachusetts, were my destination choices for the day. I hadn't decided which one. I figured I'd wait and see how the day unfolded before making a final decision.

The day before had undoubtedly been the worst day so far for mosquitoes on the trail, and the morning didn't look to be any better. All along the way, local residents were saying that heavy spring rains in Massachusetts had really increased the mosquito population.

I continued to notice my energy level decreasing; my body was simply wearing down the longer I hiked, and I had at least a month more of tough mountains ahead. I realized I needed to try to replenish my energy level with more frequent rest breaks and more nourishing food.

There had been some interesting comments in the lean-to register. One was from a woman who had been off the trail for two weeks because of Lyme Disease. She was warning everyone to watch out for ticks and listed the symptoms: aches, pains, and overall fatigue. I laughed as I said to myself, "Hell, all thru-hikers have those symptoms!"

I hated to say this, but unless things changed real fast, I was going to remember Massachusetts for nothing but mosquitoes. Except for them, Massachusetts had provided a very enjoyable hike. Interestingly, each state had seemed to leave a lasting impression: Pennsylvania was rocks, New York was delis, Tennessee and North Carolina had the Smoky Mountains, Georgia had its ups and downs, Maryland was historical, Virginia had the Shenandoah, New Jersey had its bears, and West Virginia and Connecticut were ever so brief.

When I arrived at the Shaker Campsite after only four miles, my knee was hurting already. It was getting very frustrating!

I came upon an older couple out on a day hike wearing Wellington boots. When I mentioned that their boots reminded me of James Herriot and his stories about the Yorkshire Dells in England, they laughed and said, "You know, we were just talking about James Herriot and his books!"

Unexpectedly, I just walked within inches of a big skunk, and I mean inches! I wasn't sprayed and really didn't know why, but I surely was not going to stick around to find out. I needed to be more aware and observant; I was on top of that skunk before I knew it! I headed north at a quick pace.

As I headed north, I had a smile delivered to me from a most unusual source. There in the middle of a modest little wooden bridge, arranged with small stones, was a nifty little "smiley face." Someone certainly had a great sense of humor to take the time to design such a loveable face on the bridge. It certainly brought a smile to my face.

It was noon, and as I tried to take a break and eat lunch, the mosquitoes were so bad that I had to pull my blue silk sleeping bag liner over my head just to finish my sandwich. I bet that was a sight – me sitting on a rock eating a sandwich with a blue silk bag over my head!

As I passed a trail that led to the Upper Goose Pond Cabins, I thought about staying there, but I only had fourteen miles in and hoped to get in a couple more to keep the following day's hike at about 16-mile. My *Data Book* indicated a hotel just two more miles ahead where I hoped I would be able to get a room and ice down my knee. I continued north with a painful limp.

As I crossed the Massachusetts Turnpike on a very nice footbridge, the traffic below had horns blowing and people waving their arms and yelling, "All the way to Maine!" It energized me! It was interesting how so many people recognized thru-hikers and were so supportive.

I reached the Gaslight Motor Lodge where a large sign read, "Closed." I felt like someone just gave me a sucker punch to the mid-section. With my knee screaming in pain, I surely did not want to go any farther off the A.T. for lodging. A girl mowing the grass walked up and said her parents owned the lodge, but both of them were ill and they had closed it. My heart sank, and just as I was about to ask where the nearest lodging could be found, she said, "Let me see what I can do." She turned off her mower and walked into the house, emerging a few minutes later with a smile. "Come on in," she said. "We'll get you a room!" I guess seeing the total devastation on my face brought the trail angel out in her. She gave me a nice clean room at a very fair price. There were no eating places within walking distance, but I was just happy to have a bed to sleep in and some ice for my knee as I cooked up some macaroni and cheese.

July 15, U.S. 20 (Gaslight Motor Lodge) to Kay Wood Lean-to (milepoint 1545.6 north)

It was 6 a.m. as I awoke from a very good night's sleep, with no mosquitoes to serenade me or extract blood throughout the night. It had rained, too, so it looked as though I had really lucked out having a roof over my head. That thought came too soon, for just as I was prepared to leave, rain started pouring down. It looked to be wet all day; but for the moment, at least, I was relaxed and waiting for the heavy rain to let up.

An hour later it did let up some, so I headed north in my trusty Frogg Togg jacket toward the Kay Wood Shelter, sixteen miles north in the October Mountain State Forest, my goal for the day.

I had a planned maildrop in Hanover, New Hampshire, where the A.T. went right through the center of town, and it appeared to be none too soon to get some of my cold weather clothes back.

The rain finally stopped after I'd been hiking in it for about an hour and a half. It appeared to have sent the mosquitoes into hiding and cooled things off as well, making for a relatively comfortable hike. One real negative about the rain, however, was how the water ran off my raincoat, soaking my pants and running into my boots. My knee was really hurting again, even though it was very early in the day. It was a continued source of pain and frustration, especially since I had iced it down the previous night and had put an elastic wrap on it. I noticed a whiff of smoke in the air. I didn't know if someone had a fire nearby or if a shelter was close by and hikers were trying to dry things out.

By noon I arrived at the October Mountain Lean-to, where Armando, Angie, and Carmen from Brooklyn, New York, were finishing up lunch and shared some of their excellent pepperoni and cheese with me. Although it was a little spicy, it was very good and a welcome change from my typical lunch of some bland beef sticks, cheese, and crackers.

The short lunch rest did not help my knee much. If anything, it made things worse, as it got stiff and was more painful as I got back out onto the trail. I didn't know what to do for it and figured I would struggle on to the next shelter and make a decision from there. The thought of seeing a doctor had entered my mind. I had handled leg pain before; but this pain was becoming extreme, and I certainly did not want it to get so bad I would not able to continue.

I had not had a good day as I arrived at Blotz Road with three more miles until the next shelter. It seemed as if a trip to the drug store or even a doctor would be required to take care of my knee.

I hiked down to the Kay Wood Lean-to just after 4 p.m. The route was downhill the last mile or so and my knee was again screaming. The next day was a Sunday and there wouldn't be much open in town, but I figured I'd see what was available. I had to do something, as there was no way I would be able to go through the White Mountains with my knee in the condition it was.

I was in my sleeping bag before 7 p.m. It had become very cool, so the warm sleeping bag and dry clothes were a godsend after walking in rain all day. It looked like I would be hiking through the towns of Dalton and Cheshire the following day, so I had finished off most of my food, figuring I would have numerous options for resupplying. As evening moved on, it looked like I would have the shelter all to myself. I hadn't seen another thru-hiker for two days.

July 16, Kay Wood Lean-to to Mark Noepel Lean-to (milepoint 1545.6 north)

It was still rainy and cool as I left the shelter around 6:30 a.m. and headed to Dalton, Massachusetts, in hopes of a tasty breakfast. Two hikers had come into the shelter late the night before: Running Bear, a section-hiker headed south, and Piece-of-Cake, a young woman going north, and also section hiking. She got her trail name at the start of her hike when she looked at the map and said, "This will be a piece of cake." Of course, that was all it took.

My knee felt good, but I knew time would tell. I didn't mind cutting back on miles if I needed to, but I sure didn't want to have to leave the trail for any extended time.

Piece-of-Cake and I had breakfast at the Shamrock, a really nice Irish Pub and a first-rate breakfast stop. But then the difficulty began. I had a terrible time finding the trail north out of Dalton. After walking back and forth a number of times and talking to numerous locals, I finally found the trail through town. Just what I didn't need for my sore knee: extra miles of hiking on concrete, looking for white blazes on telephone poles! As I was finally heading out of town, a local stopped to chat and at the end of our conversation casually said, "Good luck on your hike south." I said that I was hiking north, but he confidently said, "Man, you're going south right now!" That was not what I wanted to hear, but I had walked around and talked to enough people that I was certain I was headed north. Or was I?

Then I met a hiker and his two young daughters at the north edge of town, and he assured me that I was going north. What a scare! That confusion really had me rattled. I couldn't believe that fellow told me I was going south, and I began to wonder if he did so on purpose. I would like to think not, but I'll never know. A couple of hikers did tell me the trail had been re-routed and that was why everyone was confused. Anyway, I headed north, and I mean north!

At the Crystal Mountain Campsite, as I finished off a sub sandwich that I had carried from town, Piece-of-Cake ambled into the campsite shaking her head in disgust. She, too, had been disoriented in Dalton. The person who helped her with directions said, "I'm amazed at the number of thru-hikers I find out on the street scratching their heads trying to figure out the right direction."

It looked as though the next shelter was about seven miles away and my leg was doing OK; but with a seventeen-mile day, I would reserve comment until the shelter. I had really slowed down. But it was a gorgeous day in the Massachusetts woods. The rivers were flowing robustly from the previous day's rain, and the sun was peeking in and out of the clouds. The only concern was my left knee, but no one said the A.T. would be easy, and I was confident I would work through it.

At a convenience store outside of Cheshire, Massachusetts, I stopped to pick up a sandwich, some snacks, and some Gatorade before my four-mile, 1,500-foot climb up to the shelter for the night. It looked to be the start of Mount Greylock.

It was a little past 7 p.m. when I reached the Mark Noepel Lean-to at 2,800 feet. My leg did OK. It seemed the uphill stretches were much easier on it than the downhill sections. God was looking out for Piece-of-cake and me, for just after we got into the shelter the skies opened up. Not just heavy rain, but some major bolts of lightning. It was really nice to be in a safe, dry shelter. We did have a porcupine munching away just outside the shelter; and as I glanced around the inside of the shelter, I could tell the little porker had been doing some major wood-chewing inside, so I quickly selected a top bunk for the night. We heard the porcupines gnawing away all throughout the night, but they didn't enter the shelter or get into any of our supplies. I had never been around such noisy little rascals.

July 17, Mark Noepel Lean-to to Mass. 2 (North Adams, Massachusetts) (milepoint 1571.9 north)

I left the lean-to bright and early, and headed for the top of Mount Greylock – at 3,491 feet, the highest point in Massachusetts – where, I had been told, breakfast was served at a lodge. Mount Greylock was noted for the inspiration it had provided to many writers including Henry David Thoreau and Herman Melville. As legend had it, the double hump on Mount Greylock provided Melville with the inspiration for his famous novel *Moby Dick.* After the summit of Mount Greylock, I had a major downhill toward North Adams, Massachusetts, which figured to be a real test for my knee.

Just a half-mile from the lodge I crossed Notch Road and met a couple of hikers talking about company profits as they walked along, apparently up in the mountains for some type of work session. As we passed, they nonchalantly asked, "Where you coming from?"

"Today or originally?" I responded, without giving it much thought.

"Well, I guess originally," one replied, a little puzzled.

When I said, "Georgia," all he could do was shake his head and say, "No shit!" I continued to find it amusing how people reacted the first time they met a thru-hiker. They found it difficult to fathom hiking from Georgia to Maine.

As I approached the top of Mount Greylock near the Bascom Lodge, I took note of an inscription that, for me, said it all:

"It were as well to be educated in the shadow of a mountain as in more classic shade. Some will remember, no doubt, not only that they went to college, but that they went to the mountain."
Henry David Thoreau

Owned and operated by the Appalachian Mountain Club, Bascom Lodge was built many years ago by the Civilian Conservation Corps. A friendly and helpful hut crew fixed me up with a great breakfast of eggs, pancakes, cereal, fruit and toast – all I could eat – even though the serving time was over for breakfast. It must have been the sad, pitiful look I gave them when I heard breakfast was over.

I headed down the mountain on a full belly. The descent of 2,000 feet in six miles would be a true test of my knee.

At the Wilbur Clearing Lean-to, the fog began to clear, and I had a spectacular view of the valley below as a magnificent hawk flew so close I could almost reach out and touch it.

With only about two more miles to Massachusetts Highway 2, which led into North Adams, I figured I would get to the post office for my maildrop with a little time to spare. But my knee was really aching again; the descent from Mount Greylock was tearing me up. I finally realized I could not go on and would have to find a doctor, a clinic, something. I was really down. It was the worst moment for me on the trail, both physically and mentally. I had hoped that cutting down on weight and miles would help, but the Mount Greylock downhill had proven to me that I was not even close to taking on any mountains, let alone the White Mountains that still lay ahead of me.

A little after 9 p.m., I lay in my bed at a motel just outside of North Adams, recounting the day's events. When I got down Mount Greylock and to Massachusetts 2, I attempted to get a hitch into North Adams. As I stuck out my thumb for a ride, a lady sitting on her porch yelled out, "No way you going to get a ride into town. They don't pick up hitchhikers around here." I waved and smiled politely, confident that with all the traffic, I would surely get a ride for the few miles into North Adams.

After a half-hour of cars screaming by me at breakneck speed, I walked up to the lady on her porch and said, "You know, I think you're right." She smiled and offered to call a cab for me, and I soon arrived at the post office in North Adams, which seemed to be a very large, spread-out town. When I asked in the post office if anyone knew where I could find a doctor, I was met with mostly blank stares and one quick mention of a hospital a mile or so up the hill out of town. Totally bummed out by the lack of assistance and the thought of a mile or so hike up a hill to the hospital, I walked out to the lawn to re-pack the supplies I had received in the mail and pondered what to do next. I knew I had to do something for my knee, but I could not go walking around the spread-out city looking for a hospital, and hitching a ride was next to impossible. I began to think that my best option was to walk over to a nearby pharmacy and see if there was something I could pick up there. I was desperate!

Just then a young fellow by the name of Tim came up and offered me a ride out to the hospital. He said, "I heard you in the post office and thought you could use some help." A trail angel if I had ever seen one! A little embarrassed by the very cool treatment I received in the post office, he wanted me to know, "Not everyone in North Adams is that callous." He had to go to work in about an hour and was just headed to get something to eat, and he wondered if I wanted to go get a bite to eat before the hospital. That is music to any thru-hiker's ears. I could have hugged him right on the spot, but I figured that was probably not the best thing to do. After a quick burger and fries, he dropped me off at the hospital and also gave me a card with a phone number to Papa John's Pizza where he worked, delivering pizzas. He said, "When you get finished here at the hospital, just give me a ring, and I will take you wherever you need to go in between my deliveries." A trail angel driving a pizza truck – who would have ever guessed?

After I waited in an examination room for an hour or so, a doctor finally came in and asked what seemed to be the problem. I said, "I don't know what's wrong. I've been hiking on the Appalachian Trail for 1,500 miles, and all of a sudden my knee is really hurting."

"Well, let's see," he said, while looking over some medical forms I had completed. "It says here you are 51 years old, and you tell me you've been hiking the mountains for the last three months, carrying a forty pound pack." He added with a dash of sarcasm, "I wonder why your knee is hurting!"

I felt foolish as the doctor pretty much summed it up: I simply had pushed too hard and was now diagnosed with acute tendonitis, and only a couple weeks' rest would cure my ailment. That wasn't what I wanted to hear, and I asked for other options. He just shook his head, muttering something about "these damn crazy hikers" and maybe I needed to talk to a doctor who would understand. He left the room.

I had no idea what he was talking about, but in a few minutes, in walked a doctor who immediately said, "Hey, I'm the White Rabbit! Who are you?"

"Mountain Slayer," I responded with delight, knowing I had a thru-hiking doctor!

"I bet you don't want to get off the trail," said White Rabbit. "Let's see what we can do." A doctor who'd hiked the A.T.! How lucky could I get? He understood my need to continue, set me up with a strong anti-inflammatory drug for my knee – Relafen – then told me I had to cut down my mileage, lighten my pack, and find a little stiffer knee brace for more support.

As he left my room I heard him tell the nurses, "Give that fellow all the free samples of Relafen we have," to which I heard a brief, "But doctor – " That was followed by a somewhat reluctant nurse bringing me a box full of Relafen. White Rabbit later offered me a ride to Domino's, which was right next door to a drugstore where I could purchase a knee brace and meet up with Tim, the Papa John's driver who had earlier offered to give me a ride.

When he dropped me off, White Rabbit's last words to me were, "Now, you do what I told you. I'll be checking up on you." I smiled and thanked him for all his help.

I then made some calls and found a motel that had reasonable rates and was willing to give me a lift back to the trail. Tim gave me a lift to the Chimney Mirror Motel, located on Massachusetts Highway 2 just outside of North Adams itself, in between one of his deliveries and would not take a penny for all his help. Great people, great trail angels!

So as I sat at the motel on what started out as a very depressing day, I realized that it had ended up being much better than I could have hoped.

July 18, Mass. 2 (North Adams, Massachusetts) to Congdon Shelter (Vermont) (milepoint 1586.0 north)

A little after 6 a.m., just as they promised, the people at the Chimney Mirror Motel dropped me off at the A.T. trailhead on Highway 2. It was a beautiful day for hiking, but the mosquitoes were again out in full force. There was a bad weather blue blaze at the Sherman Brook Campsite Shelter, but on such a nice day, I would again be following the white blazes. The blue blaze trail would probably be better for my knee, but my vanity would not permit me to take the easy way. I figured to follow the white blazes as long as I could walk.

I certainly understood very rapidly why there was a blue blaze trail, as the white blazed A.T. took me up over a mountain that reminded me of the rock climbs in Pennsylvania. I would still recommend the white blaze trail unless the weather was simply impossible. The boulder climbing was fun and not really that long. It was also a good test of the knee, which seemed to be doing OK, but it was early in the day.

As I hiked into Vermont, the welcome sign to the Green Mountains of Vermont read that the Long Trail was approximately 263 miles, and the A.T. shared the same trail for about a hundred of those miles. The Long Trail was said to be the nation's first long distance trail and was mostly completed by 1921. At Sherburne Pass, the A.T. turned east to New Hampshire and Maine while the Long Trail continued north to Canada. The Green Mountain Hiking Club maintained the Vermont section of the trail. Eleven states down and only three more to go.

> *Hiker tips: I wanted to take a time-delayed picture and couldn't find anything to put my camera on, so I Velcroed the tripod to one of my hiking poles, which I had secured in the ground.*

I talked to a southbounder named Ken, who had been on the trail for forty-three days. He said it had been rugged but great hiking. When I told him about my knee, he said, "Don't be in any hurry in the White Mountains – just enjoy it!" Good advice; now all I needed to do was follow it.

The Seth Warner Shelter was a good place for a break and lunch. Seven miles yet to my destination at the Congdon Shelter and I was beginning to feel some pain in my knee, but I was hoping it would not get any worse. Of course, I had hiked over some rocks and up about 2,000 feet, so I had to expect some discomfort.

I passed another group of youngsters and their advisor, also headed north to the next shelter. I was glad to be ahead of them, as shelter space could be at a premium on the very popular Long Trail.

Late in the afternoon, I neared the Congdon Shelter to see a large number of hikers milling around. The shelter looked to be full, but in any case, I was done for the day. Fortunately, the eight Girl Scouts I had passed earlier in the day decided to tent.

During the evening I had the opportunity to talk with two hikers just starting the Long Trail. One said he had hiked the trail ten years earlier when the shelter was a cabin. Apparently, the trail maintainers had cut a large opening in one side, making the cabin into a shelter.

July 19, Congdon Shelter to Goddard Shelter (milepoint 1600.4 north)

It had really cooled off through the night, and it was tough getting out of my warm sleeping bag. I continued to look forward to getting my warmer clothes back.

As I hiked north on the trail, I stopped to talk with Beat Feet, a southbounder. He was really kicking, doing big miles every day because he was running out of money. When I asked him about Stratton Mountain lodging, he said there was a caretaker up on top of the mountain to help out with information on lodging. He also high-fived me, saying, "Congratulations! That's the three-quarter mark for north-bounders!" I hadn't realized that.

Another southbound hiker by the name of Can-Do told me "thru-hikers can get a free gondola ride down the mountain to a lodge," which certainly appealed to me.

What a surprise! As I crossed Vermont Highway 9, I found a bulletin board at the trailhead with maps and messages. When I causally looked at the message board, to my astonishment there was a message tacked to the board with the words "Mountain Slayer" printed on it. I was shocked that there would be a message for me out in the middle of the Vermont woods. My shock quickly turned to concern, though, as I thought, "Something must be wrong at home!" But I was surprised, and relieved, when I read, "Mountain Slayer: I will be starting in North Adams on Wednesday (July 19). Hope to make it to the Long Trail Inn on the 24th. – White Rabbit." My trail angel doctor from North Adams was on the trail! I figured he would probably run right over me if his trail name were any reflection of his speed on the trail.

At Hell Hollow Brook I stopped for lunch and a rest. My knee was starting to flare up again. That usually meant pain for the rest of the day; I hoped it would not get too bad.

I passed two hikers, one age 75 and the other 73, out for a few days of hiking. I told them, "I can only pray I will be able to be hiking when I'm your age." Although they did not respond, I could tell by their smiles they understood what I was saying and knew how fortunate they were.

Three miles to go to the Goddard Shelter on a cool, slightly overcast hiking day in Vermont. Although it was still painful, my knee seemed to be feeling a little better. Life was good.

It was late afternoon when I reached the Goddard Shelter, finished off a scrumptious Lipton meal, and relaxed on the front porch, where a magnificent view of Mount Greylock bid farewell to the northbound hikers and beckoned the southbound hikers. I, along with a father-and-son team, Dave and Bob Mean, was staying in the shelter while the two 70-year-olds put up their tents and really made us all feel like wimps for staying in the shelter.

I learned that the gondola at Stratton Mountain stopped running in the late afternoon, so I planned an early start the following day to hike the sixteen miles in time to take the gondola down off the mountain.

July 20, Goddard Shelter to Stratton Mountain (milepoint 1616.7 north)

Early on another beautiful Vermont morning I left the Goddard Shelter. During the night I'd had one of those special moments on the trail that words can't describe: I got up about 1 a.m. to see a full moon that literally lit up the entire spruce-covered mountains as far as the eye could see. It wasn't difficult to understand how the view of Mount Greylock and the surrounding mountains were such an inspiration to the likes of Thoreau and Melville.

I probably resembled a traveling gypsy as I headed out of the shelter area with clothes hanging from every imaginable hook and clasp on my pack. With heavy dew and cool temperatures during the night, all the clothes I'd hung out to dry were still damp and needed a little afternoon sun to complete the drying process.

I hadn't seen much wildlife the past week or so. I figured the forest was too thick to see anything, for I was sure there had to be wildlife around. The absence of wildlife could also have been due to the heavily used Long Trail, the oldest long-distance trail in the United States. It's said to be where Benton McKay got his vision for the Appalachian Trail. But in the way things often seem to happen, I had just made a tape-recorder note about the lack of wildlife when I came upon some really big tracks crossing the trail. They looked to be from an animal the size of a cow, so I wondered if I could assume I was looking at the tracks of a moose headed north on the A.T.

Finished my lunch with two southbound hikers at Story Spring Shelter just after noon. Excitedly, they told me, "We saw one enormous moose a few miles back! It scared the hell out of us! It's the first moose we have seen on the trail." They also said that at the Stratton Mountain Shelter I would have two options: I could stay at the shelter or catch the gondola down to the resort community of Stratton. My major problem was that I had to be there by 4:30 p.m. in order to catch the last gondola down for the day, but at least I might have a couple of options.

My knee was really hurting again as I headed downhill. The pain was excruciating! This was a Thursday; and with Connie coming for a weekend visit, I planned to take a few days off and turn the visit into a mini-vacation, trying my best to turn a negative into a positive. We had never vacationed in the region and were looking forward to traveling around Vermont for a few days.

It was just after 2 p.m. as I arrived at the Arlington-West Wardsboro Road. I still had three and a half miles to Stratton Mountain, then another seven-tenths of a mile to the gondola. It was going to be close!

I passed two hikers who told me I had another hour to the top, so I wasn't sure if I would make it to the gondola before it took its final trip down for the day. I reached the top of Stratton Mountain at 4:15 p.m. I had really been hustling. The caretaker at the shelter thought I could make it, "If you get cracking!"

I did it! I just made the last gondola as it prepared for the final trip down the mountain for the day. As I'd heard, thru-hikers could ride free. I could have stayed up on top in a shelter for five dollars; but I wanted a shower and a meal and I wanted to make a few phone calls, so I decided to ride on down to Stratton Village.

July 21, Stratton Mountain to Spruce Peak Shelter (milepoint 1626.7 north)

Just before 9 a.m. and after a very restful stay and hearty breakfast at the Ski Lift Lodge, I got a ride back up the mountain on the gondola. At dinner the previous evening, I'd been able to talk the bartender into allowing me to use the lodge's whirlpool in an effort to rejuvenate my knee. Then at breakfast I talked to a local tennis pro who gave me the name and address of a doctor in Manchester who he said could help me out. I was also able to talk to Connie and make arrangements for the weekend, so all in all, a very beneficial stay.

Back on top of Stratton Mountain, the second highest mountain in southern Vermont, it had really cooled off. The gondola operator said the temperature was ten-degrees cooler at the top of the mountain than at the lower gondola terminal. I had the seven-tenths of a mile walk back to the A.T. plus nine or ten miles to the next shelter ahead of me. I hoped the medication, the whirlpool, some rest, a short day, a light pack, and my slower speed would all combine to help bring my knee around.

At the Stratton Pond Shelter, a caretaker was setting up compost privies. I had used a few of the compost privies in the South and they worked well; in other words, they smelled a lot better than the other privies. The caretaker had two college students working with him, and I watched as they hopped into a canoe without life vests and paddled toward the opposite side of the lake. It looked rather dangerous; and when I asked the caretaker about their not wearing any life vests, he said with a laugh, "Oh, this is a National Forest. They don't provide those kinds of luxuries!"

I thought to myself, "Luxuries? I had never thought of life jackets as luxuries!"

I arrived at the William B. Douglas Shelter where I had planned to stay for the night; but the hiking had been fairly level and my knee was feeling good, so I decided to hike on. When it started to rain, I began to think that I might not have made a wise decision.

I had hiked more than eight miles, the longest I had gone without pain since my knee started to act up. Could it have been the terrain? Or perhaps the ice and whirlpool I had the previous night? Maybe the medication had started to kick in? Or just maybe it was the Guinness I had consumed in the tavern? After all, as the Irish were fond of saying, "Guinness is good for your health!"

A big roar of thunder started at one end of the mountain and rolled right up and through me as it continued to the other end. I actually felt the vibration below my feet as the thunder roared past and the skies turned dark. The rain was on its way. The only question was could I beat the rain the next mile to the shelter? Sadly, my question was answered in a heartbeat as the rain came blowing up the trail like a hurricane!

I was wet to the bones as I sloshed up to the Spruce Peak Shelter just after 4 p.m. The good news was I had finished eleven miles of pain-free hiking. Still, I was only cautiously optimistic, knowing full well it was too early to be doing any celebrating. But I thought how nice it would be if my knee felt good enough when Connie arrived that we could get some sightseeing and hiking in at the same time. I was really looking forward to sharing the Vermont mountains with my wife.

July 22, Spruce Peak Shelter to Big Branch Shelter (milepoint 1646.4 north)

It was yet another beautiful morning as I hiked toward Manchester Center, Vermont, after a good night's sleep in the Spruce Peak Shelter, which was actually a cabin. A number of hikers had showed up late and among them was the one hiker I had really hoped to see again: the trail angel doctor "White Rabbit." He planned to meet his brother at the Long Trail Inn near Mount Killington, Vermont. He asked how I was doing, and I said that just in the last day or so my knee seemed to be getting much better. With a rabbit-quick grin he said, "Good for you! You know, my knees are really starting to talk to me!" We both got a little chuckle out of that.

He also mentioned that he'd seen his first moose just before getting to the shelter and that he had never seen one on his entire hike of the A.T. the previous year. We both concluded they were out there, just not easy to spot. Oh, how I would love to get a picture of one!

White Rabbit and I hiked out of the woods and followed the white blazes to the top of Bromley Mountain. It was interesting how the Appalachian Trail went right up the ski run of a ski resort. White Rabbit told me, "There's a five-state view of Maine, New Hampshire, Vermont, Massachusetts, and New York from a tower on top of the mountain when the clouds clear off."

Lady Luck was looking out for me, for on top of the mountain I not only found a warming hut that was not mentioned in my *Data Book*, but I also found a phone and was able to call Connie at home to make final arrangements for her drive out to meet me. And as luck would have it, I called her just as she was leaving our home in Ohio to start her long drive to Vermont.

As I left the warming hut on top of Bromley Mountain after taking a break, the sky had cleared enough that I decided to climb the tower and get that five-state view White Rabbit had mentioned. And I wasn't disappointed. The 360-degree view was fantastic as I could not only see where I was going, but also where I had been. With such a great view, the only thing that brought me down was the wind. It was really blowing up on top of the tower and turning very cold.

The weather had turned very cold, making for good sleeping if you were prepared. Woodsy, a section-hiker, said the other night a hiker had been trying to sleep with just a thin lightweight blanket. He got so cold he couldn't take it any longer and finally just left the shelter and started hiking to stay warm!

> *Hiker tips: It really got cold up in the mountains, even in the summer. Be sure to have a warm sleeping bag. Some of the hikers from the area said that the warmest it had ever been on Mount Washington, New Hampshire, was seventy-two-degrees. Mount Washington may be an exceptionally cold area, but it's certainly an indicator of how cold it can get high in the mountains.*

When I reached Peru, Vermont, I heard a great deal of shouting among some hikers "Do you see it? Do you see it? Yes, over there!" Of course, I was getting my camera out, thinking they were talking about some type of wildlife, possibly a moose! Instead, one of the hikers had left a pocket open on his pack, and he and his companions were looking for the Advil that had fallen from his pack. Although I was disappointed at not seeing a moose, I laughed to myself and figured losing Advil was critical to a hiker and justified the excitement.

Around noon I had just finished lunch when I looked down and noticed that I had been hiking with my belt pack open and my *Data Book* was missing. Knowing the importance of the book, I decided to backtrack and see if I could find it. Lady Luck continued to be with me, for I found it lying next to the trail only two-tenths of a mile back.

As I left the brand new Peru Shelter after a little break, I read in the *Data Book* that I had a downhill all the way to the next shelter, which would be a real test for my knee. I hoped to get in about four more miles in order to make the following day a seventeen-mile day.

> *Hiker tips: When I first started calling home, my wife had a very difficult time figuring out where I was or where I was headed, as many of the places I talked about were in my Data Book but not on any maps or information she had. So I had her order another Appalachian Trail Data Book 2000 just like mine, and we both found it much easier to communicate maildrops and other trail locations. She also became very good at figuring out where I was and anticipating phone calls by looking at the Data Book and seeing how close to a campground or town I would be on a given day.*

I came upon John and Brian, two young hikers on their first major hike. What I found intriguing was the way they sat down right beside the trail and cooked dinner at the oddest times of the day, whereas most hikers waited until they got into camp to sit and cook their dinner. When I inquired, they nonchalantly replied, "We were hungry, and this looked like as good a place as any other to eat!"

Around 6 p.m. I crossed Big Branch footbridge and figured the next shelter should be just up the trail. The Big Branch River was really running strong as I crossed, affording me an excellent opportunity to soak my knee as a precaution after my nineteen-mile hike.

July 23, Big Branch Shelter to Vt. 103 (North Clarendon, Vermont) (milepoint 1662.2 north)

I slept well again, due in part to the location of the Big Branch Shelter, which was right next to the river. The sound of running water always seemed to have a positive effect on my ability to sleep. I had a little extra incentive in the day's hike, as I was headed toward North Clarendon to meet up with Connie and get in a few light days of hiking and touring of the Vermont countryside.

Brian and John passed me and asked if I had noticed the Honda Accord back at the trailhead. They said someone had smashed the window and removed the radio. Some poor soul out hiking would return to a very unfortunate situation. That was really too bad.

A little later I again passed Brian and John on the trail; and yes, they had stopped and were eating again! Those boys surely liked to eat. Not long after that, Stubble, one of the thru-hikers who had been in the shelter the previous night, flew past me headed north. He had started his hike in mid-April, so obviously he was really moving along. A tall, lanky fellow with an Abe Lincoln stature and stride, he told me, "I've lost fifteen pounds since beginning at Springer, and I'm trying not to lose any more by eating everything I can get my hands on!" I knew what he was talking about, for I had lost twenty-five pounds and couldn't afford any more weight loss myself. When I first began dropping the weight, it was unwanted pounds that went away; and I thought it was great losing the belly I had accumulated over years of soft living. But as I continued to lose weight, I soon realized that my energy level was also dwindling. Without my realizing it, my body had become a "hiking machine" that needed much more fuel to keep it going than I had been injecting into it; so I too had begun to eat everything I could get my hands on.

I hiked with Stubble for awhile and learned he got his trail name by his inability to grow a beard, just stubbles. He planned to finish the trail by mid-August, hence his fast pace. To each his own.

I was able to congratulate a hiker on his completion of the A.T., and no, we had not suddenly been transported to Mount Katahdin. Power Man, a section-hiker for the past twenty years, was just about to complete his final section of the A.T. at North Clarendon, Vermont. I told him how I admired him and all the other section-hikers who had the grit and determination to come back year after year to complete the entire Appalachian Trail.

Mister Brown from Mississippi, who started on June 5, was another young southbound hiker I met. Oh, how I enjoyed meeting the southbound hikers and sharing all the different information.

Near Vermont Highway 140, with cars flying by, I finished lunch with the White Rabbit. I told him that a few days back I'd been crossing a highway; and when I tried to jog, I found it almost impossible, as if I had knots in my muscles. White Rabbit said, "I know what you're talking about. I had run marathons before hiking the A.T. but found after my A.T. thru-hike, I couldn't run for about a month!" Something about the repetitive use of certain muscles.

It was 3:30 p.m. as I reached Vermont Highway 103. I was talking about a ride with a fellow in the parking lot at the trailhead when my wife drove up! I was not expecting her until about 5 p.m., so that was a nice surprise and great timing. I threw my pack into the car and we drove to the Country Squire Inn near North Clarendon, Vermont, just a few miles down from the trail, to check in. Then we went out to eat at the little Whistle Stop restaurant down the road. As luck would have it, a few thru-hikers were having lunch, so Connie had the opportunity to meet some of the hikers I had been talking about. Granny and Pappy were preparing to hitch a ride back to the trail, so we gave them a lift. It was nice being on the other end of trail magic for a change.

July 24, Vt. 103 (North Clarendon, Vermont) to Governor Clement Shelter (milepoint 1674.6 north)

It was a late 9 a.m. start as Connie dropped me off at Route 103 for a short hike after a nice night's sleep at the Country Squire Inn. We decided to break up my hiking into short sections so that we could visit the Vermont countryside around Killington and, at the same time, I could get some light hiking in – just what the doctor had ordered. I had a seven-mile section mapped out for the morning, then would meet Connie for lunch. Later in the afternoon, after we did a little sightseeing, I could get in another short section of hiking before dark.

We had a beautiful day for hiking, and the forecast was for clear skies most of the week. Connie and I spent the early morning scouting out the roads that crossed the A.T., looking for good spots for her to drop me off and pick me up so that she would not get lost. It wasn't an easy task, as we soon found out. But the drive through the countryside was lovely and even included a visit to a rustic covered bridge.

Once I was back on the trail, I saw a sign at Gould Brook that read, "Hikers: Cold soda in the stream. Please put empty cans in a trash bag at the trail crossing. Enjoy your journey -- The Hiking Gnome." That was the first planned trail magic that I had seen in a long time. I really appreciated a little trail magic every once in awhile even though I'd heard some hikers call it an intrusion to their hike. But as one hiker said, "If you don't like the trail magic, just walk on by!"

I was again passing through my favorite hiking environment: cool shade and the soft cushioned trail of pine needles.

I crossed Cold River Road and headed north to Governor Clement Shelter. A little confused, I passed a large post with some white blazes painted over with brown paint. I wasn't sure which way to go and figured there must have been some re-routing of the trail through the area.

Just after noon I met Connie hiking in from the north. We planned to hike together back north to Governor Clement Shelter, where she had parked, to have a picnic lunch.

While doing a little sightseeing, we drove up to the Long Trail Inn, a popular stop among hikers on the A.T., and made reservations for the night. I decided to get another little hike in before the day was over, so from U.S. Route 4, I headed to River Road about five miles north. The Long Trail splits off from the A.T. on that section, bringing a grin from Connie and the comment, "Make sure you don't miss your turn out there, or I'll be looking for you in Canada!"

A little later, I hiked up to the junction where the Long Trail and Appalachian Trail split. Canada was 165.9 miles north on the Long Trail and Mount Katahdin was 469 miles north on the A.T. It was somewhat confusing, as both trails were marked with white blaze. Connie had joked about me going the wrong way and ending up in Canada. Little did she know how easily that could have happened! The junction reminded me of one of my favorite poems by Robert Frost, *The Road Not Taken*: "Two roads diverge in a wood, and I, I took the one less traveled by, And that has made all the difference." Aptly enough, it looked at the junction as though the A.T. was definitely the one less traveled.

Connie hiked south and met me a little before 5 p.m., and we again hiked the A.T. together back to the car. It had been great being able to do a little light hiking and spend some time on the trail with my wife.

July 25, Governor Clement Shelter to U.S. 4 (Killington Mountain, Vermont) (milepoint 1688.8 north)

After a pleasant stay at the Long Trail Inn, Connie dropped me off near the Clement Shelter after another drive around the countryside, scouting for drop-off and pickup points. The drive certainly offered a different perspective of the trail and the area that surrounded it.

The Long Trail Inn was very nice, with a long history of serving hikers; and the traditional Irish Pub was one of the few places that hikers could get a good glass of Guinness beer right off the trail. The inn had once been right on the A.T./L.T., but the trails had been rerouted south of the inn about a mile. It's a place where hikers can do laundry while they relax over an Irish stew dinner and Guinness in the pub. It's certainly worth the short blue blaze side trail. We met White Rabbit and his brother and joined them for breakfast. I was glad Connie had a chance to meet White Rabbit. I don't want to sound too dramatic, but he may have saved my thru-hike! I wished him and his brother good hiking as they headed north to Canada on the Long Trail.

Connie's visit had worked out very well, giving me a chance to eat better and more regularly and, more importantly, allowing me to lighten my pack and get in some low-mile days. It had been my hope that those changes would add up to a rehabilitated knee and an enjoyable hike through the White Mountains, for I was certainly looking forward to that.

It was late in the morning when Connie dropped me off, and I searched and searched but could not find the trail. Connie had dropped me off at the location where I was sure the A.T. crossed, but I'll be damned if I could find it. I couldn't believe it, but I was lost! Not paying attention when I got out of the car, I must have somehow missed the trail so I had no choice but turn back. Twenty minutes later I was still backtracking, with no sign of the trail and definitely lost. Had Connie dropped me off at the wrong location?

No, for I finally found the trail. I had just flat out missed it; walked right by it when I got out of the car. Obviously, when people dropped and picked hikers up at different locations, there could be challenges for both the hikers and their companions. White Rabbit had told me about his wife trying to find some of the little back roads with their motor home; he had some real horror stories on trying to make connections. He did the entire A.T. in about three months as his wife more or less followed him day by day in their motor home. She had to find the roads and pick him up at the end of each day – a difficult task, especially on the many unmarked gravel back roads.

I ran across another example of the unique, if a little bit crude, A.T. sense of humor as I arrived at the Cooper Lodge. There, standing majestically on Killington Mountain, was a privy aptly named "The Cooper Pooper."

It was there I met Moon Dance, the first southbound female hiker I'd had the opportunity to meet on the A.T. As we talked about what I would face on the trail, she moaned, "Those White Mountains really worked over my knees!" I did not want to hear that.

I also ran into Brian and John; and yes, they were eating again. About the same time, Connie walked in from U.S. Highway 4, so we all hiked the couple of miles north back to the highway where Connie and I had lunch at the Killington Mountain Deli. I wanted to get a few more miles in, so I hiked north for about four miles through pastures and hills on a beautiful evening in Vermont.

I had a good fourteen-mile day under my boots and was ready for dinner as Connie met me at the South Pomfret Road around 7 p.m.

July 26, U.S. 4 (Killington Mountain, Vermont) to Vt. 12 (Woodstock, Vermont) (milepoint 1706.5 north)

Connie dropped me off and I headed north from River Road near Killington Mountain. I had a seventeen-mile day planned, but there were no road crossings, so lunch looked to be a large deli sandwich I had in my pack. I'd already had a ham, egg, and cheese sandwich for breakfast from the Killington Mountain Deli and noticed how the regular meals were helping raise my energy level. I was getting a bit spoiled from eating so well and having Connie pick me up and drop me off at the various trailheads; but I planned to enjoy it while I could, for she would soon be back on the road headed home as I headed north on the A.T. with my mac and cheese!

When I looked at my schedule for the next week, I planned to ease back to thirteen or fourteen miles per day. I figured that would help my knee and allow me to enjoy the White Mountains.

I met my fourth southbound hiker of the day. They were really coming now. Two of them started June 1 and hoped to really start picking up their mileage. It had taken them two months to get to this point, and that made me wonder if it would be two more months for me to get to Katahdin. I hoped not!

Yet another southbound hiker and this one with a great trail name: You Can Call Me Dave. He started June 23. Now that sounded much more realistic than the June 1 start of the two previous southbounders. He mentioned the Presidential Mountains in New Hampshire took him a long time because of the weather. "Mount Washington had a temperature of fourteen-degrees," he said with amazement, "and I found it almost impossible to find my way!" And that had been only a few weeks earlier.

Still another pair of hikers headed south and amazingly, one of the hikers was a young woman hiking barefoot. She showed me the bottoms of her feet, which resembled raw meat! I was so shocked that I didn't even think to ask why.

It was a little before noon and I crossed a road. Hell, if I'd known the road were there, Connie and I could have had lunch together. Oh well, I figured she wanted to do some shopping anyway.

I came across a northbound thru-hiker by the name of John from Columbus, Ohio, who was about my age. His wife had been slack-packing him for quite awhile, and he now had an employee doing the same. His wife planned to rejoin him so he could continue to slack-pack all the way to Mount Katahdin. With weary eyes, he said, "I'm really tired of the trail and just want to get it over!" That wasn't the way I wanted to complete the trail. I'd enjoyed the lighter pack and Connie's company for a few days, but I was ready to get back to the solitude of the trail. Well, anyway, to each his own.

Soon I met three more southbound hikers. One young woman had two enormous knee braces on. She said she got off the trail in Hanover,

New Hampshire, to see a doctor, who told her to "Get off the trail for awhile and take it easy." That sounded familiar.

I caught up to the Keystone Rambler, who was headed north. A section-hiker from Pennsylvania, he had finished the trail to the south and hoped to get all the way to Mount Katahdin. I couldn't believe it when he told me he had hiked the Pennsylvania A.T. section four times! My only question was, "Why?" He just smiled.

Two more young southbound hikers came along. They, too, were saying the same thing: "Take your time in the Whites. They're great!"

It was just a little after 4 p.m., and my ride was patiently waiting by the side of the road. I was really getting spoiled.

July 27, Vt. 12 (Woodstock, Vermont) to Norwich, Vermont (milepoint 1723.7 north)

Connie dropped me off at South Pomfret Road and I was headed north with a plan that we would eat lunch together at West Hartford, Vermont. It had rained during the night and was sprinkling, with a forecast for light rain all day and into the next few days.

I reached the top of Thistle Hill where Granny and Pappy were camped. I had been able to give them some trail magic in the form of a ride when Connie first picked me up, and apparently, unbeknownst to me, Connie had given them another ride the other day. They wanted me to be sure and thank her again, saying, "We figure you know full well how appreciative thru-hikers are for rides," and I assured them I did.

At Thistle Hill Shelter, I had a beautiful view of the valley as the rain began to taper off. With some of the rain clouds still hanging over the lush green valley and the mountains reaching to the sky as a backdrop, it was a sight to behold.

A beautiful big doe bolted across the trail in front of me. I would have loved to have gotten a picture of a deer like that moving at full speed, but I was much too slow with my camera.

I met Connie for lunch in the little town of West Hartford at Rick & Tina's Country Store. Located right on the A.T., the store had a lot of supplies for hikers along with, as one hiker who was leaving exclaimed, "the best damn burgers and fries around!" The grill was opened early and there was a nice hot or cold menu, but I almost walked right by since it was not mentioned in my *Data Book*. Tina acknowledged that her business was not in the book and said she had called to request it be included to no avail. She also said that one hiker had walked into the store and was really upset because he had stopped just a half-mile from the store and prepared a Lipton meal for lunch, not realizing the store was so close. Tina laughed as she told me, "He just walked around the store cussing and shaking his head!" West Hartford was just a bump in the road, but it did have a tiny little library right on the A.T. with a friendly librarian who disappointingly told Connie, "We don't have a computer yet, but we're working on it!"

We left the little hamburger joint and I hiked up to the intersection of Tigertown and Podunk roads. There really is a Podunk Road!

I met up again with Miss America. I first had the opportunity to meet Miss America way back at the beginning of my hike. She had since left the trail because of ankle problems. She lives around the area and was just getting back on the trail and was headed north. Strangely, she was on one knee packing everything, right next to the trail, in the middle of the afternoon; so when I asked if she was OK, she bounced up and with that Miss America smile, said, "Yeah, sure. I just finished a nap by the side of the trail." Interesting to say the least. Oh well, hike your own hike.

At Happy Hills Shelter I met with Easy E and Frog, both southbound. They appeared to be having a great time on the trail, as both of them seemed to have a great sense of humor. When I told them about the cheeseburgers in West Hartford, they nearly ran over me as they raced toward the town.

Southey, another southbounder, told me a little about Hanover, New Hampshire. He said I could stay in a fraternity house near Dartmouth Campus. "But don't expect to get any sleep," he cautioned, "and it's not the frat guys making the noise. It's the damn thru-hikers up talking until four in the morning!"

Talking to all the southbounders was really getting me excited about the White Mountains. I surely hoped they were not overrating them. Connie was going to be wondering what happened to me if I kept talking to all of the southbound hikers, so I headed north at a quicker pace.

It was late afternoon as I followed the white blazes into Norwich, Vermont, along Main Street. I spotted my car but saw no driver. It was later than we had planned, and there was a craft shop just across the street from the car. I had no doubt that my being late was going to cost me some money.

Chapter 5
Hanover To Mt. Katahdin

July 28, Norwich, Vermont to Three Mile Road (New Hampshire) (milepoint 1733.6 north)

I was on the trail headed out of Norwich after Connie had driven me from the Sunset Motor Lodge, where we had spent the night.

From Norwich, Vermont, to Hanover, New Hampshire, I followed white blazes on the bridge across the Connecticut River and right through the heart of Hanover, onto the Dartmouth College campus, past the stadium, and out of town again. A positive aspect of the hike through town was all the opportunities to purchase food and supplies, not to mention finding an outfitter store right on the trail. I enjoyed a hike though a big town once in awhile, but I was sure glad the A.T. avoided most cities.

When I crossed the Connecticut River where the Dartmouth rowing team was practicing below, I noticed someone had painted a state line marker right in the middle of the bridge. Another state under my boots; twelve down and two to go.

An Outfitters store in town was not open until 9:30 a.m.; so when Connie picked me up from my hike at the end of the day, I planned on driving back and getting another tip for my hiking pole. It would be a small inconvenience for such a beneficial piece of equipment. I don't know what I would have done without the benefit of hiking poles.

As I headed north out of Hanover and turned left near a gas station, the trail seemed to disappear; but fortunately, a fellow who lived nearby told me with a scratch of his head, "Seems like I'm always giving directions to hikers. You would think someone would fix a sign there." He was a friendly fellow, and I could tell he really liked meeting the different hikers. He actually walked with me to the turn-off, chatting the entire time.

I crossed Swamp Footbridge, an elevated boardwalk that took hikers through a swamp with cattails as thick as grass. After a short time on the boardwalk, I was back in a section of forest and noticed green hoses running from tree to tree connecting them all together. I assumed they were gathering sap for maple syrup. It was probably more efficient, but I missed the old buckets.

I had an opportunity to talk again with John from Columbus, Ohio. He was hiking south at the moment and offered me an opportunity to do a little slack-packing with him when my wife returned home. I appreciated his offer and the lighter pack was certainly tempting, but I was just not interested in hiking in different directions and all the coordinating that was involved. Besides, as I told him, "I'm anxious to just strap on my pack and head north on the trail without all the hassles." He understood, although I don't think he agreed.

Arrived at Three Mile Road and no ride; I was there but not Connie. I hoped she could find the road, knowing I was a little early. Connie showed up in the next few minutes, and we drove back to Hanover to fix my hiking pole, to get some other gear that I needed, and to eat lunch.

> *Hiker tips: Lou's Restaurant and Bakery is a great place for lunch. It's right on the A.T. in Hanover.*

It seemed that every hotel and motel for miles around was booked due to a sophomore parents' weekend at Dartmouth. But Connie was able to find a room at an historic hotel, the Hotel Coolidge, in White River Junction about ten miles south. Named after Col. John Calvin Coolidge, the father of President Calvin Coolidge, it had been restored and was a special treat for both of us.

July 29, Three Mile Road (New Hampshire) to Firewarden Cabin (milepoint 1748.6 north)

We arrived early at Three Mile Road where Connie dropped me off for the last time as she headed home to Ohio and I headed north to Mount Katahdin. I'd had a great time visiting, hiking, and touring Vermont with Connie for the past few days. I hoped the time of fewer miles, a lighter pack, and better food had enabled my knee to recover enough for me to successfully hike the remainder of the trail. I believed it had. In any case, we'd had a wonderful time in Vermont and were already talking of a return trip some day.

I headed out with a full stomach after a hearty breakfast at the Polkadot Diner. There's nothing like bacon and eggs to start out a morning hike, and it was a meal I knew I would not see or taste for awhile.

While at the hotel, I'd talked by phone to my cousin Keith, and things were looking good for him to meet up with me somewhere in New Hampshire. We had planned to meet around August 7 if everything worked out for him. I really looked forward to sharing some of the sights and challenges with him on the trail, and I hoped he would be able to walk with me into Maine – if I got through, or rather, when I got through the White Mountains. I knew I had to think positively.

My pack felt as though I was carrying a damn Mack truck! I don't know what I was thinking; I had enough food and supplies for about four days, and that was way too much. It actually felt like it weighed more than when I left Springer Mountain in Georgia.

Springer Mountain in Georgia – now, that got me to thinking. It had been exactly four months earlier to the day – March 29 – that my wife had dropped me off on the trail and headed home. What a coincidence that it was four months later – July 29 – when she had again dropped me off and I was again headed north, this time with much more knowledge and confidence, but still the same sense of anxiety about the unknown. And also, much closer to Katahdin.

As I arrived at Holts Ledge to a fantastic view of the mountains ahead, I wondered, could they be the Whites?

I topped Smarts Mountain, and for the first time, was hiking with my bug head net on. The gnats were really bad for some reason, and the netting worked well over the top of my hat.

I stopped for a break on a very inviting rock; and while I enjoyed the afternoon, a mother and daughter hiked up, headed south. They had a lot of questions about thru-hiking, and it was good to talk to them since I needed a break anyway. I'd made a special effort to slow down and take a few more breaks in hopes of taking some pressure off my knee.

There were a lot of threatening clouds, and it looked like it could rain any minute as I hustled toward the next shelter. I reached the Firewarden Cabin just after 4 p.m. to find a friendly ranger by the name of Talks with the Animals. I loved those great trail names! Not a thru-hiker, the ranger simply got caught up in the thru-hiker mystique and selected a trail name. Hypothetical and Looking Glass, two young female hikers headed south, were also staying the night in the cabin.

July 30, Firewarden Cabin to Ore Hill Shelter (milepoint 1761.2 north)

I left the Firewarden Cabin early in the morning and after a rather intriguing night. Around 7:30 p.m., two young boys came barging into the shelter, soaking wet from the heavy rain. Part of a larger group called Outbound, they were really popping off and were very upset with their instructor and the rest of the group. They laughed about leaving the group back on the trail and about having some of the tent poles that would be needed by the others. Obviously, I was not impressed and came close to saying something, but thought "why bother?" and rolled over in my sleeping bag as I put in my earplugs. About midnight, in walked the instructor looking for the two boys. Of course, he was angered that they had left the group without permission, and I was surprised that he kept his cool as he quietly talked to them about responsibility to the group and so on. I'm afraid I would have kicked their skinny little asses out of the shelter and escorted them back to the group!

After an early morning start I was headed up and over a very rocky Mount Cube as two joggers ran by. Yes, joggers! I had no idea where they were running to or from.

Around noon near Warren, New Hampshire, I stopped for lunch and a rest next to a clear running brook. I had about five more miles for the day and figured to get to the shelter early, knowing I would need all the rest I could get for my climb the next day up Mount Moosilauke, the first mountain above the tree line for northbounders.

I met a southbounder in his sixties with quite a sense of humor. With a big toothy grin, he told me his trail name was Hillary. When I asked how he got that name, he simply pointed to his hat that had "Commander in Chief" written across the top. Obviously, I wanted to know more; but it looked like rain, so that was one story that got away.

Broke another water bottle while I was filling it at a stream; it was a good thing that I had two.

It was 2:30 p.m. when I hiked into Ore Hill Shelter, an early stop for me after hiking just thirteen miles, but I was determined to stop for the day no matter how bored I might become. Besides, I wanted to rest my legs for Mount Moosilauke and certainly did not want to carry the extra weight of a wet tent, as it looked like rain.

I encountered one of the most amazing privies on the trail. One of a kind, the Ore Hill Shelter privy looked like a large box with a "throne" centered on the inside. The entire front wall opened down like a drawbridge, with pulleys and weights allowing the user to easily pull the wall up or down creating a ramp. It even had two-inch wood strips nailed on the inside of the ramp enabling the user to safely walk up to and down from the "throne!" I felt a little ridiculous taking pictures of a privy, but I couldn't let the opportunity pass.

July 31, Ore Hill Shelter to Beaver Brook Shelter (milepoint 1776.5 north)

It was raining and had rained most of the night, not the kind of day I had hoped for as I headed out for a fifteen-mile day that included a climb of the 4,802-foot Mount Moosilauke.

In the shelter the evening before had been Little Feet, who was kind enough to share a bagel along with some peanut butter and jelly, both of which she squeezed from a bottle. When I asked how she got both the peanut butter and jelly in that squeeze bottle, she smiled and said, "Don't ask." Cruise Control and his well-behaved dog Shadow came in a little later, along with Back Draft, Uncle, and a few others.

The rain had stopped, but everything was wet and very, very slippery. The tree roots along the trail and the logs crossing the bogs were particularly treacherous! I was moving very slowly and tried to remain positive about all the rain and not get bummed out, but it was not easy as I continued to hope for good weather in the White Mountains.

I was getting close to Glencliff, New Hampshire, a few miles off the trail, and debating whether to call Lonesome Lake Hut for a reservation. I had hoped to stay in the hut in a couple of days, but heard that it was usually full and required a reservation.

Reached the top of Mountain Mist, 2,200 feet. It had been a great hike so far.

I just passed a sign that read, "Scenic View – Beware of Tourists."

Cruise Control and Shadow caught up to me. They were hustling to make it to the post office in Glencliff. It was open from 10 a.m. to 2 p.m., interesting hours that had inspired many "What the hell kind of hours are those?" comments in the shelter register. A friendly young fellow, Cruise Control was enjoying the wet weather as he wore a hat with an attached umbrella. Shadow was half German shepherd and half wolf with green eyes that seemed to look right through you. Cruise Control really loved that dog and had shared a story about him the previous night in the shelter, talking about a particularly challenging day when he was up early and headed north on the trail. When he stopped for a break, Shadow was not with him. Fearing he was injured or got caught in a bush, he hurried back on the trail to see what had happened. There in the corner of the shelter, he found Shadow sleeping the morning away. "I was really angry at first," Cruise Control said, "then just laughed, figuring the dog knew more than I did, and that was his way of saying slow down!"

I stopped in the little town of Glencliff to make a reservation at Lonesome Hut and found a little hostel where I was able to get a root beer and a Snickers bar. On my way back out to the trail, I met Little Feet headed into Glencliff, saying, "I've had enough for the day," so I told her about the hostel, which brought a smile to her face.

Back at the trailhead, Uncle was soaking his feet -- new boots! When I told him about the hostel and its snack bar, he also smiled and headed toward Glencliff. It's amazing what a little food can do for a hiker's mental outlook.

Then the old Mountain Slayer was back on the trail ready to kick Mount Moosilauke's butt! Would I be the Slayer or the Slayee? That was the question.

It was a little after 2 p.m. when I reached the summit of Mount Moosilauke, where a sign read "4,802 feet." I had started at 1,000 feet, so that was some climb. There was probably a beautiful view from the mountain, but I was totally fogged in and could not see a thing. As I hiked on, I realized that it was not fog that I was walking in, but rather clouds. I felt as though I were looking out the window of a 747 as the wind was really blowing and the clouds went flying by! The area was really barren: no trees, just scraggly remnants of scrub brush and rocks. It was a great climb but tough; and as I had met a couple of southbounders coming down all bundled up, I was sure they thought me crazy in only my wet t-shirt with so much steam coming off me that I resembled a locomotive.

One old boy coming down off the mountain really got me good. I mentioned I was disappointed about the weather and zero visibility, to which he quickly replied, "Why, it's clear on top!" My eyes lit up as I said, "Great!" He went on with a wink, "Yeah, they're even sunbathing up there!" I could hear him laugh for what seemed like eternity as he disappeared in the fog. I'd certainly made his day.

It was late afternoon as I headed down Mount Moosilauke after an inspiring ridge walk. I talked to a couple southbounders who were headed up, and they had already heard how miserable it was on top. When they asked if it was really as bad as everyone was saying, I told them, "Picture yourself flying across the mountain in an airplane, then eliminate the airplane. That's what it's like!" To which they replied, "Thanks for nothing," and headed up into the mist and clouds. I had heard that the weather was supposed to clear in the next day or so, just in time for my hike through the Presidentials, I hoped.

I finished dinner around 7 p.m. at a very full Beaver Brook Shelter. Those there included Uncle; Cruise Control and Shadow; two southbound brothers; a husband-and-wife team; and a very angry Dr. Seuss. Dr. Seuss, a young northbound thru-hiker who had zipped past me earlier on the trail, had lost his way across Mount Moosilauke. He had apparently missed a white blaze and ended up hiking down to some camp at the foot of the mountain before he realized he was off the trail and had to climb back up. He came in late, throwing his pack and cussing a blue streak! He was still cussing an hour later. In his defense, the white blazes were difficult to see, especially in the fog.

It was the end of another wonderful, but full and challenging day, the 124th day on the trail.

August 1, Beaver Brook Shelter to Lonesome Lake Hut (milepoint 1791.5 north)

Heading north down a steep mountainous incline, I left the Beaver Brook Shelter with the Lonesome Lake Hut as my destination for the evening. I'd heard an overnight stay there would cost $60 (there was a

10 percent discount for thru-hikers), which included dinner and breakfast with plenty to eat.

> *Hiker tips: Thru-hikers are often given the opportunity*
> *to work in return for lodging at the different huts in the*
> *White Mountains, if the hut crew needs help.*

The evening before, Uncle had kept us laughing late into the night, to the extent that I ended up using my earplugs again. Even Dr. Seuss was laughing by the end of the evening.

Two southbounders in the shelter had expressed a great deal of concern on how poorly the trail had been marked, saying, "On one section in the Whites we hiked for about a mile without seeing a blaze!" That blew my mind, for I had been totally dependent on the white blazes and didn't like hearing that, but I was glad I had been informed before I'd gotten to that section of trail.

Unwired, another thru-hiker, had one of the most unusual reasons for being out on the trail that I'd heard. He told me with a wink, "The only reason I'm out on the trail is because my wife told me she was going with or without me, so I figured I had better tag along." He and his wife both seemed to be enjoying the hike, stating in unison, "It's been tough!" I had to second that one.

We had the most awesome view of the sunrise from the shelter that I'd seen to date on the trail as the sun peeked out over the stunning Mount Washington at daybreak.

I was headed straight down the mountain on an extremely rugged section of the trail; and in a few places, the Appalachian Trail Club (AMC) actually cut wood blocks at forty-five-degree angles and somehow attached them to the sheer rock. The rock was mossy, wet, and slick; without a doubt I would have been sliding on my ass right off the side of the mountain if it weren't for the wood blocks. It had to have been a tremendous challenge to attach those ingenious wood blocks in such an unobtrusive manner. They even had reinforcement bars drilled into the boulders so hikers had something to hold on to. I'd laughed earlier when an experienced hiker told me, "It's easier to climb up Mount Moosilauke than to climb down." I was no longer laughing!

The climb down confirmed what I had already thought: I was definitely carrying too much weight and needed to lighten up at the next post office, even though I was extremely thankful for my winter gear.

I arrived at Kinsman Notch (noting how the low-lying areas between two mountains in the north are called a notch, whereas in the south such areas are referred to as gaps), which is said to be the end of Mount Moosilauke and quite an introduction to the White Mountains.

As I arrived at the top of Mount Wolf, the view was simply incredible, almost beyond description. Mountain peaks rose through the clouds in all directions for as far as I could see.

I came across some fresh moose tracks and thought, "What I would give to see just one moose." Just then, I slipped on some roots and went flat on my back! No harm done, but that was the quickest I had gone down since the start of my hike. Combine the incredibly slick trail with a lot of ups and downs and a lack of white blazes, and it all added up to some very slow going.

As I descended Mount Wolf, I went down again, this time taking a real tumble! I stepped on another root; and before I knew it, I was rolling down the side of the mountain. Luckily, my pack limited my capacity to roll very fast or far. I tried to avoid the many roots but found it impossible; the slope was nothing but roots, puddles, and rocks.

By shortly after 11a.m., I had not seen a blaze for a long, long time! Not good. I hated the thought of hiking without the white blazes. Normally, I would have turned around at that point, but I was gambling that I was on the section the two southbounders had talked about in the last shelter. It was a gamble I would hate to lose, for I surely didn't want to climb back up the trail! Besides, not having a map and seeing no other trails, I could only go forward if I weren't going to turn around.

I fell again and hit my forehead hard on a boulder. Blood began to ooze down over my eyebrow, but I could not tell how bad it was. I took my handkerchief out and wrapped it around my head in an effort to slow the bleeding. I hoped I would soon meet someone who could look at it. Of all days not to have met a single person on the trail!

Not far from where I cracked my head, I found a blaze. I'd never been so glad to see a white blaze in my life. I had been just about to retrace my tracks and could not express the relief I felt on seeing it. I almost fell to my knees and kissed the white strip of paint!

I came upon a creek and cleaned up the cut as much as I could with a little water and a moist wipe. Cruise Control caught up with me, and I asked him to take a look at my forehead. The first words out of his mouth were, "Oh, Man!" That was not what I wanted to hear. He said the cut was lying open but didn't appear to be particularly long.

"What the hell is a 'not particularly long cut'?" I half joked as he helped me put a bandage on. I hoped that when I got to the hut I would be able to take a closer look at it. It wasn't really hurting much – my hard head, I guess.

It was six more miles before the hut, but with Kinsman Mountain in between, the hike looked pretty formidable. Cruise Control wanted to work for his stay, so I told him to hustle ahead even though he offered to hike with me to the hut. It was so slick and steep that I found it almost impossible to stay upright. I had a reservation and was not interested in working, so I decided to take my time and just hope to get there in one piece.

I headed toward South Mount Kinsman's peak. At 4,358 feet, I was above tree line again, as the clouds and mist were rolling by on the barren mountaintop and I couldn't see more than a few feet in front of me. I fell two more times: it was one tough mountain. Actually, it was one tough day, and it wasn't over! But my knee was holding up well even after falling on it a couple of times, so there had to be a positive in there somewhere!

Crossed Mount Kinsman, but I couldn't see a thing in the fog; and the wind was so strong that it just about knocked me over as I fought to stay upright. I continued to strain to find any white blazes and finally found an old, faded-out white blaze. The wind continued to blow so hard that I couldn't even get the camera out to take a picture. But I had to admit it was exhilarating being in such an electrifying atmosphere!

As I arrived at the Kinsman Pond Campsite, I went the wrong damn way at first. Luckily, I went just a tenth of a mile before realizing I was on the wrong trail. A sign read that Lonesome Hut was only 1.9 miles, so I was feeling really good that I was over Kinsman. I just needed to take it easy and carefully inch the rest of the way to the hut.

I caught up with Cruise Control who was shaking his head, saying, "Man, this is tough!" Shadow, his dog, had always been able to do the trail, but there were a few places on Kinsman Mountain where she could not physically climb the boulders, so Cruise Control had to take off his pack and carry Shadow to the top. He then went back down to retrieve his pack and did the climb over. Talk about dedication to your dog!

It was late afternoon as I staggered up to the Lonesome Lake Hut, all in one piece. Well, at least I hoped so, for I had not yet taken a close look at my head.

I had a nice dinner with about fourteen other people. A day hiker named Carl had some antiseptic and surgical tape, so I pulled the wound together on my forehead while he taped it closed. He thought it could use a few stitches, but we both figured it was probably too late. My biggest concern was infection, and I was fairly confident we were able to get it cleaned before we closed the wound. I surely appreciated the two Lonesome Hut trail angels, Carl and his wife Paula, for helping me out with their medical supplies and care. The hut was nice but pretty rustic and without electricity. There was bottled gas for cooking and light; and the staff, made up of college students, was a friendly and fun group. The lodging itself was also pretty primitive: a couple of bunk beds with blankets and not much more; but for a hiker, having food, water, and a roof over one's head was like heaven.

August 2, Lonesome Lake Hut to Garfield Ridge Campsite (milepoint 1804.7 north)

It was sunrise when I received a wake-up call from Carlos, one of the crew workers, as he strolled from room to room strumming his guitar and singing that breakfast would be served at 7. I'd heard that each of the huts run by the Appalachian Mountain Club was unique in its own way, and the guitar wake-up call certainly validated that report.

After dinner the evening before, each of the college students working at the hut was introduced. They told a little about their duties and also shared a little history about the hut. I found it interesting that burros were first used to haul materials up to the hut site when it was built and that the crew still had to pack all of the food up to the hut and pack anything left back down the mountain – quite a chore. One of the crew members laughed as she said, "We love you thru-hikers and your unquenchable appetites. It sure eliminates the need for us to pack as many leftovers back down!"

Finished with breakfast and headed north, I had about three miles down to U.S. Route 3 where I would make a decision about getting my cut looked at by a doctor in town. Although I didn't want to waste a lot of time going into town, I wanted to be sure the cut was cleaned and taped well enough to heal properly. The next hut was only nine miles away; and although I loved the thought of food and lodging, I figured a shelter would work better for me, for I had planned on doing a few more miles than that. Anyway, I'd been told the Greenleaf Hut was a mile down off the trail.

A little sprinkle was coming down as I left the hut, and the weather forecast was for rain off and on all day.

I arrived at Route 3 and could not believe my luck. While I was standing at the intersection of the road and the trail, trying to decide whether to hike all the way into town to find a doctor, two southbound hikers walked up and said hello. They immediately noticed the bandage above my eye and asked how I was doing. I told them I was OK but was debating whether to go into town and get my injury looked at. With a smile, Julian said, "We're both doctors; let us take a look." Easing the Band-Aid off without disrupting the surgical tape, Julian, genuinely impressed, said, "Whoever fixed you up did a great job," adding, "and besides, it's too late to put stitches in it. The only thing a doctor could do now is give you some antibiotic." They suggested I continue on up the trail and watch closely for any swelling or redness around the cut.

Oh, how I was pleased to hear that! I could not thank them enough for their advice. It saved me a lot of time and energy. That was the third time I had run into a doctor at the most opportune time! The mountain gods were looking down on me again.

I hiked past a sign that indicated Liberty Spring Campsite was two miles north, and a southbounder told me "One hell of a climb is in front of you!" Not wanting to carry such a heavy pack, at the hut the previous night I'd gathered all my excess gear I wanted to send back home into one bag in case I got into a town with a post office. I surely hated carrying the extra weight, but it didn't look like I would be going into any town in the near future.

Met a nice young fellow by the name of Jeff out on a day hike, coming down from the Liberty Spring Campsite. Noting that I was a thru-hiker, he asked if I happened to have a journal on the Trailplace website, for he had been following a number of hikers there with the hope of some day doing his own thru-hike. I told him I did indeed have a journal, and as we chatted and I learned of his interest in hiking, I took a chance and asked, "Would it be asking too much if I asked you to mail my excess items home to my wife?"

The big strapping fellow proclaimed loudly, "Absolutely not! As a matter of fact, I would be honored!" It was always amazing where, when, and how a trail angel would come along. As Jeff continued south, he turned, waved, and said, "Good luck, you've got one heck of a mountain ahead," to which I replied with a grin of relief, "Yes, but my pack is a lot lighter, thanks to you!"

I ate lunch with Thoroughfare Gap at the Liberty Spring Campsite. He was one of about three hikers that I had seen on the trail in kilts. He started wearing the kilts around Harpers Ferry when he developed a really bad rash, and they worked so well he just continued to wear them, saying, "I get a lot of razzing, but I would rather deal with the razzing than the painful rash!" As he headed north, he too was trying to cut down on his miles and had also tried to make some reservations at the huts earlier but found out they were full, so I was unsure what the future would bring concerning hut stays. I figured I would worry about that when the time came. No, actually I figured I would not worry about that at all; I would just take things as they came and make the best of it. I was a little disappointed with the wet weather and lack of views, but decided not to worry about that either.

After dinner at the hut the previous evening, extra food had been set out for thru-hikers to purchase – all you wanted for just one dollar! When I told the crew members how nice that was of them, they reminded me they had to pack out all garbage, so they were very happy to give their surplus to the insatiable thru-hikers. After breakfast I finished off some peach cobbler and wrapped up a little spice cake for my snack.

> *Hiker tips: The huts enable thru-hikers to lighten their food bags; personally, I took full advantage of the food at the different huts and carried only one lunch and one dinner in case I couldn't get into a hut.*

Met a southbounder and talk got around to comparing falls on the rocks. It seemed everyone on the trail had a story of a "big crash" the day before.

I crossed the top of Haystack Mountain and met a hiker named Richard and his friends, who took my picture and gave me a sandwich. It was a great sandwich and I did not even have to Yogi it (that's trail talk for begging, after the cartoon character Yogi Bear). I think he took one look at my sad-looking, skinny butt and figured, "This guy needs a sandwich!"

It was an incredible feeling hiking once more above the tree line, walking along the ridge in the clouds and still unable to see anything below. It was simply awe-inspiring! It's difficult to put into words, but it was an incredible feeling even without a view. As I went along, however, the sun broke through, and I saw my shadow for the first time in days and was actually starting to get a few peeks of the valley below. Hiking along the Franconia Ridge above tree line actually gave me a rush. Things were looking up. It wasn't raining, and I was actually walking on dry ground.

By the time I was on top of Mount Lafayette at 5,249 feet, the fog had cleared off completely, which certainly lifted my spirits! Headed north and really pumped by the views, I could see nothing but the majestic White Mountains for miles in all directions.

I arrived at Garfield Ridge Campsite and settled in for the night around 8:30. It was a nice shelter with only two other hikers, one a graduate of West Point who playfully exchanged barbs with me when he learned my oldest son Bruce had graduated from the Naval Academy.

As I moseyed down to the privy, the bright stars in the evening sky were spectacular. I had never seen the sky so clear and bright!

August 3, Garfield Ridge Campsite to Ethan Pond Campsite (milepoint 1819.2 north)

I got another early morning start as I left Garfield Ridge Campsite, a campsite and shelter area that was maintained by a resident caretaker (hired by the A.M.C.) who introduced herself to us last night. There was a $6 fee to each hiker using the site; and to put it as politely as possible, the fee was quite the topic of negative conversation among the independent and free-spirited thru-hikers. I thought that due to the large amount of use in the White Mountains, a caretaker to help monitor the area and promote "leave no trace" camping was an excellent idea.

Galehead Hut was only about three miles north on the trail, so I hoped to stop and see if they had any breakfast items left.

The cut above my eye was doing OK. However, my perspiration tended to make it difficult for the bandage to stick. Although the surgical tape that actually held the wound together appeared to be holding.

It was a nice cool morning as the clouds cleared off and I could see what I believed to be the Galehead Hut sitting high in the grand White Mountains. It didn't take long to get there; and by the time I left, I had a belly full of food. For a donation of a dollar I had all the pancakes, oatmeal, bacon, and toast I could eat, dining in the galley with the very pleasant crew members. It was too late to make reservations at the Zealand Falls Hut, so I intended to stop and check for food when I hiked by. Not having a dinner in my pack, I asked Backdraft, an experienced thru-hiker who had worked for his stay at the Galehead Hut, where I could get another dinner. He looked up from pushing his broom and said with a nod, "Right here. How many do you need?" I offered to buy the Lipton dinner he handed me, but he refused, saying with pride, "We thru-hikers hang together!"

I ate my lunch on the trail: a bag full of pancakes and other goodies from breakfast I had stuffed in a Ziploc bag.

About half past one I arrived at the Zealand Falls Hut. The hiking seemed a little easier than the past few days, so I figured I would go on north to a campground at Crawford Notch. I did check at the hut and there was room for the night. It was very tempting, but the weather was great and I felt good, so I wanted to hike as much of the Whites as I could in prime conditions. The hut crew willingly radioed ahead and reserved bunk space for me at the Mizpah Spring Hut for the following evening

I hiked into the Ethan Pond Campsite shelter just before the rain let loose with a vengeance; it was nice to be in a dry shelter. As my Lipton dinner cooked, I cleaned my cut and found out that not only the

Band-Aid but also the surgical tape had fallen off sometime during the day. There was no swelling or redness, so I figured as long as I did not hit it again I would be OK.

Woke up once around midnight to the sound of rain hammering on the roof and thought how tough the hiking was going to be the next day, but at least I had reservations in a hut for the night.

August 4, Ethan Pond Campsite to Lake of the Clouds Hut (milepoint 1833.3 north)

I left the shelter early with my Frog Togg hood up on a surprisingly cool morning. I headed north toward Crawford Notch, only three miles, where I heard there was a snack bar that opened about nine o'clock. It had rained hard the night before and water was still finding its way down the rocky trail, but the sky looked to be clearing; only a few clouds remained.

The White Mountains had really lived up to their billing: very challenging, but magnificent views! And I had to agree that anything beyond twelve to thirteen miles a day was really too much. Interestingly, the Appalachian Trail was not the identifying trail in the Whites, so the A.T. was relegated to a back seat to the longer existing White Mountain trails. I also heard there was some bickering between the Appalachian Trail and Appalachian Mountain Club people over trail identification, location, and so on, but that was strictly hiker talk. All I knew was it would be much easier for thru-hikers if the A.T. were better identified in certain sections of the Whites. Specifically, the use of yellow blazes on the A.T. in the White Mountains instead of the white blazes I had followed since Georgia was very confusing. I had been told that the yellow blazes were thought to be easier to see in the fog and clouds, which could be true; but I personally missed the reliable white blazes. So far I had not been lost, probably more through luck than sense or skill, for I knew a number of very experienced hikers who had lost the A.T. at various times.

I arrived at Crawford Notch to find not only a snack shop but also a New Hampshire tourist center with a very interesting story. The Crawford Notch area was once the site of the Willey house where in 1826, a torrential rainfall caused a landslide that killed a husband, wife, five children, and two farm hands as they tried to escape. Sadly, their home was not destroyed; and if the family had stayed inside, they would probably have survived.

When I tried to call home, no one was around. I had hoped to let my wife know about my fall and that I was OK. I did get through to my friend Keith's home. I was told Keith was on his way, and his son asked, "How you doing? We heard you took a nasty spill in the White Mountains!" I had no idea how the word of my fall had reached home so quickly.

I'd been lucky enough to get a quick hitch down to the Crawford Notch; and when I was ready to head back, Dick Smith, a maintenance man, was kind enough to put down what he was doing and give me a lift back to the trail. He and his wife both work at the Crawford Notch State Park. They were from Florida and came up to New Hampshire every year to work at the Notch.

Talked to Sneaks at Crawford Notch. He took a real nasty fall the same day I did and said in all seriousness, "I thought I killed myself!" I laughed a little and he said, "No shit, I'm not exaggerating. I fell so hard that when I hit the ground I thought I was dead!" He really did mess up his shoulder and had to leave the trail. He was really down because he didn't think he would mend in time to finish the trail before Mount Katahdin officially closed in October. I certainly understood his gloom!

It had turned out to be a gorgeous day, the best day yet in the White Mountains. As I climbed Webster Mountain, the view was spectacular! What a great day! It was gorgeous, sunny and cool, perfect for hiking.

I found I was rock scrambling again, so I packed the hiking poles away and was climbing boulders hand over hand. I really enjoyed that kind of hiking, at least for a short distance!

I met Mr. and Mrs. Going Home, a great couple. They hiked the trail in 1993, in 1997, and again in 1998 and were section hiking when I met them. They noticed my cut and when I told them what and where it happened, they both nodded in acknowledgment, saying, "We know that area on Kinsman well. Back when we hiked in '93, a girl fell, broke her leg; and it was a nine-hour ordeal to get her off the mountain!" They also gave me a candy bar; former thru-hikers certainly know the way to a thru-hiker's heart.

As I passed over Mount Jackson, the views continued to be magnificent. The word out on the trail was that the entire weekend was to be clear. I could see Mizpah Spring Hut and Mount Washington from where I stood, and it was knock-dead beautiful! About halfway up Mount Washington, I saw several puffs of smoke and wondered if they came from the Cog Railway, the train route up the mountain that dated from 1869 that I had heard so much about. If so, it was surprising to me that I could see the train smoke eight miles away!

It was mid-afternoon when I hiked up to Mizpah Hut; and although I had a reservation for the evening, I asked if I could cancel. It was just too nice a day to be inside, and besides, the dinner menu featured rice! In addition, I had only put in nine miles and the next hut, Lake of the Clouds Hut, was only five miles further. So I was headed north, hoping there would be room. If not, I was told, there was a "dungeon" where thru-hikers could bunk.

> *Hiker tips: The dungeon was a small basement-like shelter under the hut that thru-hikers were permitted to use for a small fee.*

As the afternoon went on, I was really glad I had decided to hike on. The day could not get any better; it was just beautiful. The weather was so unpredictable that I could get up the next day and the weather would be poor again. And sure enough, as I hiked along Crawford Trail, which was also the A.T. marked in both white and yellow blazes, it was getting cold and windy. I even had my jacket and hood on. The Lake of the Clouds Hut was in view; and as the weather turned colder, I surely hoped there was "room at the inn."

I talked to four young hikers coming from Lake of the Clouds Hut, and they gave me the sad news that the hut was full. I hoped I could work something out with the crew. I surely didn't want to be in a tent on the mountain on such a frigid night.

Although there were no rooms to rent, the staff was short-handed, as four of the crew had been sent out on a rescue mission. With ninety guests, they asked me if I would help out with the evening meal in exchange for a place to stay. I jumped at the opportunity for a meal and a warm bunk.

After dinner the crew was introduced and then me as a thru-hiker, which resulted in my being bombarded with thru-hiking questions late into the evening. Although I wanted to get to bed early for an early start in the morning, the guests were so friendly and interested in my hike that I tried to answer as many questions as possible, making a number of friends and exchanging addresses in the process. It was 9:45 p.m. by the time I got ready for bed.

Before that, I talked to one of the crew members when she got back from the rescue. She said they needed a litter to evacuate the injured hiker who had broken both ankles, and I almost fell over when she told me it was very near Mount Kinsman, where I had fallen a couple days earlier! The hut crew said they were often called out on rescue runs, and each crew member was trained in emergency medical and rescue techniques. I think they enjoyed the challenge of rescue work once in awhile, but they were really tired when they returned. They thanked me for helping out in the pinch, but I really did not do much. It was actually fun helping out, and it was great to have a place to bunk for the night.

August 5, Lake of the Clouds Hut to Pinkham Notch (at milepoint 1848.1 north)

I was up early and left before breakfast was served, for I had a big day planned and wanted to spend some time at Mount Washington just a mile and a half north on the trail. The staff at the hut knew I wanted to get an early start, so they saw to it that I had some breakfast before leaving. What a great crew! The evening before I had walked into Lake of the Clouds Hut not knowing if I would even have a place to lay my head, and I ended up with a bunk in the crew's section! I headed north rested and with a full belly.

It was turning out to be a clear morning, but it was very cold and windy! I was bundled up from head to toe, including gloves, in my Puffball jacket and rain jacket, and with my hat pulled down over my ears.

Almost immediately after leaving the hut, I came upon a U.S. Forest Service sign that read, "STOP! The area ahead has the worst weather in America. Many have died there from exposure, even in the summer. Turn back now if the weather is bad."

I stopped to take off my Puffball jacket. Even though it was really cold, the jacket was just too warm to hike in.

> *Hiker tips: The Puffball jacket, made by Patagonia, is definitely the warmest jacket I know of for weight versus warmth. Although it was too warm to actually hike in, I found it a godsend for wearing around camp and on very cold evenings. It also worked great as a pillow.*

Looking back down at the hut from the trail, I was overwhelmed by the beautiful setting of the Lonesome Cloud Hut, high above the tree line on the side of the mountain with wispy clouds whisking by. It appeared nestled in the side of the mountain as if it were a natural part of the landscape. I found myself constantly stopping to look back at the 360-degree view of the Presidentials from Mount Washington undoubtedly the greatest view I'd had to date on my hike!

I passed a sign marking Mount Washington State Park & Crawford Path. Crawford Path is said to be the oldest, continuously used mountain hiking trail in America. It was first laid out in 1819 and had been used ever since.

A little before 8 a.m., I got to the summit of Mount Washington – 6,288 feet, and totally awe-inspiring. Although it's the second highest point on the trail – just after Clingmans Dome – let me assure you that the Mount Washington summit was second to none for its breathtaking view. There was a visitors' center and also a weather station which had once recorded the highest official surface wind speed on earth, 231 mph! And then there was the steam-driven cog train, (the oldest such railway in the world) that made a daily run bringing visitors up from Gorham, New Hampshire.

On the wall in the visitor center was a plaque dedicated to the many deaths in the Presidential Mountain range:

Deaths In The Presidential Range
This list of those who have perished on or near the
northeast's highest peak is meant not for morbid
curiosity, but as a pointed reminder – this can be a
dangerous place! Nobody on this list planned to die
here, but some did ignorant or stupid things that led to
fatal accidents.

The list consisted of one hundred and twenty-eight people, starting with the first death, that of a twenty-nine-year-old hiker from England back in 1849. The most recent death noted had taken place on Feb. 20, 2000, when a forty-two-year-old skier died in an avalanche.

The visitor center had a dayroom for hikers along with a telephone, snack bar, and a post office. Right inside the visitor center was a computer set to monitor the outside weather, so every fifteen seconds the screen was updated. While I watched the screen, the outside temperature was 41-degrees, the wind speed was 31 mph with gusts to 38 mph, and the wind chill was 15-degrees. It surely felt colder than that! The day's forecast was for mostly sunny skies with the expected temperature on the summit between 45 and 50-degrees. There were a lot of shivering visitors coming up on the cog train, some in shorts!

As I headed down Mount Washington, I saw a most unusual sight. I'd heard the noise of what I thought to be an airplane; and as I began to search the sky above me, I was shocked to see a plane racing across the sky below me.

I continued to meet day hikers coming up the mountain in t-shirts, practically running they were so cold! There I was all bundled up with gloves on, and they were just in t-shirts, an indication of just how dramatically the temperature changed from the bottom to the top of Mount Washington.

I talked to Nature Boy, a southbound hiker, who exclaimed, "I waited in Gorham four days for the weather to be good; that's how bad I wanted good viewing weather for my hike across the Presidentials!" I thought back to the words of the crew members at the Lake of the Clouds Hut. They'd told me as I left, "Eight out of ten days up here the weather is bad. It looks like you may have just lucked out, Mountain Slayer!"

I left Madison Springs Hut after another feast on leftover breakfast. But I also had good news and bad news. The bad news was that the crew at Madison Springs Hut told me there was no room in the lodge at Pinkham Notch. The good news was that for a time, I'd thought my camera was broken but realized the problem was my film: Connie had thrown me a curve and sent me twelve-exposure rolls instead of the usual twenty-four. When my camera stopped working up on top of Mount Washington, I thought it was due to the cold weather or worse, broken; but I was simply out of film.

About half past four, I hiked up to the Osgood Tentsite and probably should have tented for the evening, but I had it in my head to get to Pinkham Notch so I headed north. The A.T. was becoming very hard to follow. At an intersection of two trails, a sign read "A.T." but did not indicate which direction to go. Someone had carved an arrow into the sign; and it was a good thing they did, or I would have gone the wrong way.

I thought I had seen everything until I met the Tuba Man hiking south. The

Tuba Man headed south.

strapping young hiker was carrying a tuba in his backpack. Yes, a tuba!

When I asked how much his pack weighed, he said with a smile, "I'm not sure, but the tuba alone weighs 30 pounds!" He told me he was making a statement for the arts and enjoyed entertaining the other hikers in the shelter. I laughed to myself as I thought, "I sure hope you don't run into Ruth; she complained about snorers in the shelter! God knows how she would react to a tuba player!" He'd started hiking south from Katahdin in July and wanted to be the first hiker to carry a tuba all the way to Georgia. He boasted, "I'll make it, and you can be sure my tuba will make it also!" And you know, I never doubted him for a minute!

I hiked into Pinkham Notch and checked for a room at the lodge even though I had been told the lodge was full; and to my great joy and surprise, they'd had one bunk open up. Dinner had already been served, but I must have looked particularly pitiful and malnourished as they fixed me up a nice plate anyway. The hiking gods were again definitely looking down on me.

A little earlier I talked with a hiker staying in the lodge who had three generations of family hiking with him. They had made reservations months ago at the Lake of the Clouds Hut but could not get rooms for his entire family, so he hiked down to the Pinkham Notch for the evening. With a wistful tone in his voice, he said, "You know I started the A.T. this year about the same time you did, but only lasted three weeks. I got homesick and never finished!" Although he said he had no regrets about leaving the trail, I could see White Blaze Fever in his eyes and hear it in his voice.

The shower was great; it had been about a week since I last had an opportunity for a shower.

> *Hiker tips: Hiking through the White Mountains, there were really no opportunities to get a shower. The huts were nice for food and lodging but had no showers, except for Madison Hut which had an outside shower.*

I had my first chance to take a real good look at the cut above my eye, and it looked good. The surgical team of Carl and Mountain Slayer at the Lonesome Hut had done a good job.

Headed to bed after an awesome, but long, fifteen-mile day.

August 6, Pinkham Notch to Imp Campsite (milepoint 1861.2 north)

Got on the trail and headed north a little later than I had hoped, but I'd had a good night's sleep and a great breakfast. The bunk was great and the dinner the night before had been even better. Someone was definitely looking out for me.

I planned to get to Imp Campsite, only thirteen miles, but I'd been told it was really rugged. Then the following day, I hoped to cruise into Gorham, New Hampshire, to meet my hiking buddy Keith for a few days of hiking. Of course, all that planning would be dependent upon the weather.

There was a scale hanging right next to the trail at Pinkham Notch, and I was pleasantly surprised that my pack weighed a mere twenty-six pounds! Of course, that was with only a day or so of food and a liter of water, an economy made possible by the food opportunities I had at each of the huts.

As I was leaving, a woman called out, "Hey, Mountain Slayer!" She was one of the ninety people who had been at Lake of the Clouds Hut when I helped serve dinner and talked about my thru-hike. A lover of the outdoors, she said, "I just wanted to thank you and again tell you how much we all enjoyed hearing about your thru-hike. Good luck and God speed."

It was another beautiful morning as I crossed Wildcat Mountain and had a great view of the backside of Mount Washington. I could even hear the "chug, chug" of the old cog train climbing up the mountainside.

I topped Carter Dome and realized I had some heavy legs after a couple of big days, but I figured that with Keith coming in, I would be able to cut down on mileage over the next few days.

It was late afternoon on top of Middle Carter Mountain, and I continued to find myself looking back over my shoulder at Mount Washington, it was like making a new friend, then leaving and not knowing if you would ever see him again. What a great few days in the Presidentials!

Arrived at the Imp Shelter, where two young section-hikers were busy preparing their dinner. It was good to be in the shelter, for it again started to rain.

August 7, Imp Campsite to U.S. 2 (Gorham, New Hampshire) (at milepoint 1869.2 north)

It was very windy and rainy during the night and continued to be cloudy and overcast as I passed Rattle River Shelter Road. I was very happy to have gone through the White Mountains when I did. I had eight miles to U.S. Route 2 just outside of Gorham where I hoped to find Keith.

I was still on the Rattle River Trail section of the A.T. and was taking it really slow when I slipped and went down again! I'd told myself not to put my hand in the straps on my hiking poles while going down the mountain, but there I was, hands in straps when I fell. Landing flat on my back with my hiking pole stuck in the ground, I could not get my hand out of the strap and bent my Leki hiking pole ninety degrees. In trying to bend it back, I snapped it completely off, so packed it away and continued with one pole

I arrived at Route 2 outside of Gorham and headed to White Birch Campground, which I was told was about a mile down the highway, to meet up with Keith.

Walked for about forty-five minutes and found no campground. Evidently my information was wrong. Oh, how I hated it when someone would say "Just a mile or so down the road," and it was much further!

About noon, I couldn't believe my eyes as a Chevy Blazer with Ohio license plates went roaring by! Yes, I'd lucked out again. The Blazer made a quick turn and Keith pulled up with a grin, saying, "I had just set up camp and was going out sight-seeing. I didn't expect you until evening." A few minutes either way and we would not have connected.

So after a hearty hello, we headed to Gorham for some lunch and a stop at the Gorham Moriah Sports outfitter to get my pole worked on. They did not have the right section to fix it, but the shop owner was kind enough to find a section in a back room to replace it and without a charge. I couldn't beat that.

Back at the campground, Keith asked me to look over his gear, as he thought he might have had a couple unnecessary items. I promptly started throwing out gear left and right as he yelled, "Hey, I might need that!" Like all of us starting out, he had much more gear than was necessary, but he was very willing to go with my suggestions. Actually, his pack was still quite heavy even after my assault to lighten it up.

Our next challenge was to make arrangements for Keith to get his Chevy Blazer to a trailhead three or four days north on the trail.

It was late when we finally got the Blazer safely parked at Grafton Notch, Maine, but not until after quite an ordeal. We found out that not all those listed in hiking guides as shuttle drivers were trustworthy, to put it mildly. I had gotten an individual's name and phone number out of the *Appalachian Trail Thru-Hikers' Companion*, which said he lived in Gorham and ran a shuttle service. He charged $27 dollars an hour, which seemed a bit expensive to me; and when I asked him how much it would cost to drop us off at Grafton Notch, he could not give me a specific amount. That should have been a tip-off to me; but not having experienced any individuals who actually made a practice of ripping off hikers, and with his name being listed in the *Companion*, I trusted him to treat us fairly. Without going into great detail, the fellow drove us all around the area looking for the drop-off point; and when we got back, he said we owed him $80! When I questioned the outrageous fee, he got very belligerent and, to put it nicely, we had some words. The campground owner stepped in and cooled down the situation and told the shuttle driver never to come onto his property again. The owner then turned to me and said, "Sorry about that, Guys. You should have asked us; we would have worked something out." Live and learn.

Not wanting to be carrying any perishable food, we cooked the rest of Keith's bacon and burgers over the campfire and had quite a feast. Around 10:30 p.m., we had the hamburgers eaten and were inside our tents when the clouds opened up and the rain really let loose. It looked like Keith was going to get introduced to the challenges of the A.T. really quickly.

I'd had to laugh earlier in the afternoon as I was washing some of my clothes in the campsite laundry room. As we talked, I stripped off my shirt and threw it into the washer, and Keith looked at me with a dropped jaw and said, "Oh my God, look at you; you look like a picture out of a concentration camp!" I had not actually looked at myself in a mirror since Harpers Ferry, three months earlier, and I had to admit when I turned and looked at the mirror in the laundry that I hardly recognized my body. I was extraordinarily thin, to the point where my ribs could be counted without any problem.

August 8, U.S. 2 (Gorham, New Hampshire) to Gentian Pond Campsite (at milepoint 1881.0 north)

The weather was cloudy and spitting rain but pleasantly cool as Keith and I headed north. One of the fellows from the campground dropped us off and wouldn't take a penny. I guess he felt sorry for the way we were ripped off the day before. Just north of Gorham, the A.T. started out on the Mahoosuc Trail, and we were told it was a challenging section.

The sun was peeking out as we climbed Mount Hayes on what was turning out to be a lovely day with great views. We had some boulder scrambling early on where we had to stow our poles and climb, and as we took a break from that challenge, Keith checked for hot spots. He certainly did not want any blisters to start out his hike.

We talked to our first southbounder of the morning, Houdini, who had hiked the trail north last year and was going south this year. Keith and I didn't know if he was a glutton for punishment or just plain crazy! He told us where to find some good wild blueberries on the ledges ahead.

Moose sighting! What a thrill! That was worth the day's hike alone. My first moose sighting, and Keith was right there with me, a special treat. I was surprised by how long its legs were. We definitely heard it coming well before we saw it. It made a lot of noise as it went through the Mahoosuc Range about a half-mile from Mount Hays.

"What a great place to eat lunch!" Keith exclaimed, sitting on top of Cascade Mountain, looking out over the Presidentials on a sunny day. "And what more could a hiker ask for?" he added, patting his belly. "Fresh blueberries for dessert!"

We met another southbounder, Black Forest, coming from the tent site ahead of us. When we shared our moose sighting, he said to Keith with a hint of envy, "First day on the trail and you've already seen a moose? Hell, I've only seen one moose my entire time in Maine!" He asked Keith his trail name; and upon learning we were still working on it, he warned Keith with a smile, "You best hurry up! If you don't pick one, someone else will, and you may regret that!"

We had hiked about seven miles and Keith was feeling good. We thought we might try to get to a shelter for the evening, but that would be twelve miles for his first day, and probably was a little too much. We would decide when we arrived at the Trident Tentsite.

We hiked past Dream Lake, a beautiful lake worthy of it name, high up in the New Hampshire mountains. "My feet are starting to talk to me!" Keith said.

I nodded and said, "That's good. Pretty soon they'll be numb, and you won't even feel them anymore." He didn't think much of that.

Keith and I arrived to a full Gentian Pond Shelter a little after 6 p.m., I was shocked and felt bad because I'd told Keith a little earlier that the shelters had been pretty empty and we wouldn't have any problem in finding a space to sleep. A section-hiker named Ben, who was with me at Imp Shelter, told us he'd gotten to the shelter at 3 p.m. and it was full then. We did manage to squeeze in, since there was absolutely no room at the tent sites.

Sitting in the shelter eating our dinner, we had a beautiful view of the mountain range and could certainly understand why there were so many people at the campsite.

Constituting most of the crowd in the shelter was a group of young people and their adult leader. Keith and I were both impressed with the group's behavior in the shelter and their leader's consideration of other hikers. As we were relaxing in the shelter, and eating our dinner, their leader was conducting a meeting. She was considerate enough to move the meeting outside so we could have some quiet time and enjoy our dinner.

August 9, Gentian Pond Campsite (New Hampshire) to Full Goose Shelter (Maine) (at milepoint 1890.6 north)

As we were packing up to leave, a young hiker came sprinting back to the shelter, breathlessly exclaiming, "There's the biggest moose down at the pond that I have ever seen!" Keith and I followed him, and sure enough, an enormous bull moose was standing majestically out in the pond, munching away on some grass. What a beautiful sight!

We had two options for the evening's shelter: one at five miles and one at nine miles; it just depended on how we felt. Keith was a little stiff and sore, but that was to be expected.

Bull moose at Gentian Pond

"Oh, would you look at that. What a view!" Keith exclaimed as we sat down for a break on Mount Success. It was a unique and beautiful view above the clouds: we could see for miles and miles in all directions with the mountaintops peeking out above the clouds.

Keith was definitely getting the total A.T. experience, as minutes earlier we'd had spectacular views from Mount Success, and soon after it was pouring down rain and the trail was extremely wet and slippery.

Taking our time heading down Mount Success on a very wet and muddy trail, we met another southbounder by the name of Tiny Tim. He filled us in on the Mahoosucs, saying, "They are really tough. Just take your time and enjoy them."

As Keith and I rounded a bend in the trail, we heard whooping and hollering. "Whoopee! Hurray! I can't believe it! We did it!" A large group of section-hikers were celebrating the completion of Maine with hugs and handshakes. We also celebrated, since I was officially in Maine: my last state, and I had only 281.4 miles to go.

I entered my last state with mixed emotions: I was getting tired and worn down and looked forward to completing my hike at Mount Katahdin, but at the same time, it had been such a great journey that I hated to see it come to an end. It did appear that Maine was definitely the way to end a thru-hike. It seemed like everyone coming from the north was talking about how beautiful the state of Maine was to hike through.

Climbing Goose Eye Mountain, I slipped on a rock, cutting my hand. Keith also slipped a couple of times, skinning his knee; so we continued very slowly and very carefully. The section of the trail reminded me of the saying by thru-hikers in Maine: "No pain, no rain, no Maine!"

Keith pointed out to me that from the Goose Eye Mountain East Peak, we could look all around and see nothing but mountains for 360 degrees! The mountainside where we had unwillingly just left some flesh was such a challenge that enormous log steps had been installed to assist in the climb. The steps did not run very far but they did get us up one of the sheer-face boulders. We could only marvel at the trail maintainers' work.

Heading down Goose Mountain, we threw our poles ahead of us down the side of the mountain and climbed down to them. It was unbelievably difficult!

We took a break and talked with Little Bit, a flip-flopper who had started at Springer on March 4, hiked north to Waynesboro, then got a ride to Mount Katahdin and was headed south. She said that there had been forty people at her shelter the previous night! We hoped that wouldn't be the case for us.

It was the second day of hiking for Keith on the A.T., and near Goose Eye Mountain North Peak, he had a trail name. When I asked how much further he wanted to go for the day, he quickly replied, "No more than ten miles!" Ten-Mile was scraped and bruised and actually could be proud of the fact that he had hiked ten miles on a very challenging section of the A.T.

Ten-Mile was pretty jealous of Little Bit, as she had a beer packed away for a celebration at the Maine-New Hampshire State line. He said with a wink, "That beer sounded so good that I was tempted to knock her off for it!"

We arrived at Full Goose Shelter and Campsite around 6:30 p.m. and settled in for the night. Ben and several other section-hikers were also in the shelter; but fortunately, it was not crowded.

Keith was pretty worn out and we had the Mahoosuc Arm and Notch coming up the next day, a stretch considered by many to include the toughest mile on the entire A.T.! That presented even more of a challenge than Keith had had so far, so we planned to take our time hiking that section. The forecast was for the weather to stay about the same: just enough rain to make the house-sized boulders slick and treacherous.

I headed off to bed, ready for my first night's sleep in Maine. Fantastic!

August 10, Full Goose Shelter to Speck Pond Campsite (at milepoint 1895.7 north)

Keith and I left the Full Goose Shelter very happy that we hadn't tented the night before, as there had been rain throughout the night. But we'd had a snorer in the shelter who'd rattled the rafters and forced us to resort to earplugs. I laughed as Keith marveled at the snorer's volume and I shared with him, "You certainly continue to get the total Appalachian Trail experience."

We headed north to the Mahoosuc Notch as it started to spit rain, and that was the last thing we needed for the tough section ahead. We had to pack our hiking poles as we began the climb up the notch. Ten-Mile was game but indicated he was starting to feel some muscles he had not felt in a long while and wasn't sure how far he could go.

The Mahoosuc Notch is basically a ravine of gigantic, house-sized boulders that the A.T. goes over, under, and around. We had a 1,200-foot climb down as we progressed through, and then we would hike up 1,500 feet, all within five miles. It was really challenging and fun, but it was also dangerous, especially with the wet weather; and we were very deliberate and cautious as we climbed through.

Occasionally, there were different paths to follow. On one occasion, Ten-Mile found a cave-like space to crawl through toward the top. As he crawled, he yelled, "When my wife sees these pictures, she's not going to allow me to hike with you anymore." I figured he was right, but I was surely glad he was with me. Otherwise, no one would have ever believed me when I described the Mahoosuc section of the trail.

As we continued through Mahoosuc Notch, I heard Ten-Mile grumble, "This is not hiking; this is rock climbing!" Basically, the notch was one big boulder scramble after another. Finally through the notch, Keith and I stood in awe at the foot of the Mahoosuc Arm. It looked wicked as it went straight up the side of the mountain to 3,770 feet.

It was just past noon as I scrambled to the top of the arm and met two southbounders, Cheese Head and Northern Lights, on their way down. I asked them to let Ten-Mile know he only had a short distance to go before he reached the top. I had heard a little cussing from behind me as Ten-Mile followed me to the top, and I hoped the cussing was not meant for me. But I wouldn't blame him; it had been a long, hard climb.

We had a wonderful lunch on top of Mahoosuc Arm with a beautiful view out over the mountain and the pride and satisfaction of knowing the notch and arm were behind us. It was early afternoon as we hiked into Speck Pond Campsite, done for the day. It was a good spot to rest up after a big day and a chance to hang our gear out to dry.

Katherine, a friendly and chatty caretaker, was even willing to walk down to the pond with us (said to be at the highest elevation of any pond in Maine), to take a picture of Old Ten-Mile and the Old Mountain Slayer!

When we mentioned to Katherine that we were from Ohio, her face lit up as she said, "Cool! I attend Oberlin College in Ohio." She was working the summer as a relief worker for the shelter caretakers. The shelter caretakers stayed at a shelter site for ten days, then a relief caretaker would come in and relieve them for a short break. Katherine loved her job but did say that the hikers were always complaining about the Appalachian Mountain Club's $5 or $6 charge for a stay, calling her "the tax collector!" She handled the complaints very well. "I've heard them all and just give it back to them," she said with a shrug. Albatross, a southbounder who was also staying in the shelter, was complaining about how scarce the white blazes were on the trail, and I loved Katherine's comment: "Now let me see if I understand what you're saying – you want to see more paint on trees. Is that correct?" It was such a good response, it seemed to stop the crusty Albatross in his tracks!

August 11, Speck Pond Campsite to Grafton Notch (at milepoint 1900.3 north)

We were up and out of camp early. I'd slept very well, but Keith had been cold. He said, "I ended up putting every piece of clothing on that I had with me!"

Hiker tips: Ten-Mile was using a fleece sleeping bag to save on weight and had been told that it would be warm enough for the time of year in Maine. Well, it wasn't. He was really cold, especially his last night on the trail, even after putting on all the clothes he had brought along. If hikers plan to use the fleece, expect to have some cold nights and plan to wear all of the clothes you have along. The bottom line was: Ten-Mile was cold in his fleece, while in my fifteen-degree down bag, I was sleeping in a t-shirt

The only other hiker in the shelter had been Albatross, the sixty-five-year-old southbound hiker. He was up packing his gear at a very early 4 a.m., but what amazed me was that he didn't get on the trail any earlier than Keith and I did. Albatross said he had met Woodchip and Badger about a week earlier and added that Badger thought he might have a cracked rib, but he was still hiking north. That sounded like the same tough Badger I had gotten to know.

We had a beautiful day and planned on going to Grafton Notch, where Keith's Blazer was parked, and then head into town to clean up and resupply. We were happy to have survived the Mahoosuc challenge without any major injuries, and what a challenge it had been: everything I had been told and more! This day's biggest challenge would be a hike down the mountain from 3,985 feet to 1,495 feet. Ten-Mile and Mountain Slayer headed north following the white blazes.

I was trying to figure out how many more days I would be on the trail in order to start making arrangements for my return home, but it was hard to estimate with the type of terrain we had been covering. I had planned on fifteen-mile days and, as long as I stayed healthy, the end was in sight probably by late August or early September.

Coming through the Mahoosuc Notch had really worked my pack over. The pack cover had a number of tears in it, and the bag I kept my tent in also had a few holes in it. Thank goodness I noticed it before I had a hole in my tent.

Hiker tips: If I had it to do over, I would have gotten a waterproof pack for my tent. I believe it would have been more durable. Also, the external pack, which had worked great on most of the A.T., was not ideal for going through the Mahoosuc. It not only rode high on my back creating a balance problem, but the lower tubing on my pack scraped the rocks when I had to sit and scoot down the rocks on my butt. An internal pack would have been better in the sections that required scrambling over rocks, but the external pack worked

well on all the other sections of the A.T. Thru-hikers
have to make their own decision.

On top of Old Speck Mountain as we looked back at Speck Pond, Keith was amazed, as I had been throughout my hike, on how far we could hike in a day's time.

We could hear the sound of traffic on the road, so I knew we were closing in on the Grafton Notch trailhead. As we neared the end of our hike together, I told Ten-Mile he could not have had a more total experience of the A.T. He'd had both beautiful and lousy weather; had been cold, hot, and wet; had wonderful mountain views and fog; mosquitoes and bugs; rocks and dangerous boulders to climb, and relaxing forest hikes. Last, but certainly not the least, he also got to see a moose in the wild. Even most southbounders had not seen as many moose as we had the past few days. It all added up to four fantastic days of hiking.

A little before eleven, we hiked down to the Grafton Notch Trailhead at Maine Route 26. It was the end of the Mahoosuc Trail and the end of the A.T. for Ten-Mile, a very challenging thirty-two miles he would not soon forget.

After a few Kodak moments for remembrance's sake, we stashed our cameras and other gear in the Blazer and drove to an inn near Bethel, Maine, where I was able to do a little laundry and get re-supplied before Keith dropped me off in the morning.

August 12, Grafton Notch to Hall Mountain Shelter (milepoint 1916.6 north)

I was up early and back on the trail as Ten-Mile dropped me off after a good night's sleep and a hearty breakfast. We'd had a challenging four days on the trail, and I hoped my hiking buddy Keith had just as good a time hiking as I had. I really appreciated his driving all of the way to Maine from Ohio to hike a section of the Appalachian Trail with me.

My pack was much too heavy again. Would I ever learn? I had West and East Baldpate Mountain (3,810 feet) to climb right off the bat and had a sixteen-mile day planned, so I had a lot of hiking to do, and I cussed myself for having too heavy a pack.

The weather forecast called for more rain. There was nothing I could do about that, as I learned many miles back, so I would just deal with whatever came along. At least I was running on a full tank of fuel.

I was still climbing as I hiked in a section maintained by the Maine Appalachian Trail Club, which maintained the 267 miles from Grafton Notch to Mount Katahdin. At least all the bitching by other hikers about the AMC and its fees for huts and campsites would stop, I hoped. Personally, I appreciated the clean, well-maintained shelters and campsites within the Appalachian Mountain Club's jurisdiction.

As I headed north, I got to thinking about how fortunate Ten-Mile and I were to see a moose, especially the awesome bull moose at Gentian Pond. Being able to share the experiences on the A.T. with family and friends continued to be one of the unexpected pleasures of my journey from Georgia to Maine. I'd also enjoyed hearing some of Keith's observations. Like me, he was constantly overwhelmed by the spectacular views out on the trail. As he'd said over a beer in a pub on our last night together, "I expected the views to be good, but words simply cannot do them justice." I could not have said it better.

When I got to the top of Baldpate Mountain West Peak at 3,680 feet, I had ascended more than 2,300 feet in three miles and had thirteen miles to go. The clouds lifted and I had a wonderful view, or as Ten-Mile would say, "Oh my! Oh my! Look at that view!"

I spent some time talking to Whisper Light (he talked very softly), who had been out on the trail for a month and was really down and homesick. He asked, "How have you handled being out on the trail so long?"

With a slap on his shoulder, I said, "I just hike the blues away!"

He headed south with a nod and a whispered, "Thanks."

Came upon some moose droppings that reminded me of Keith saying he'd seen moose droppings in the Mahoosuc Notch. To me, that was incredible because I could not for the life of me imagine a moose going through the Notch. I laughed to myself at the comic picture I had in my mind of a moose with a backpack, climbing up and over the many house-size boulders. I guess I had been out on the trail by myself way too long!

I arrived at East B Hill Road, where I found a fellow with one leg sticking out his truck window as he waited to give rides to his hostel in Andover. Peg Leg, a trail name befitting his condition, was a friendly fellow who gave me a soda even though I was not in need of his transit service.

As I hiked through the Surplus Pond section, the overgrowth was so thick I almost felt like I was bushwhacking. I finally arrived at the Hall Mountain Shelter just after 5 p.m., and wouldn't you know it, there was not another single person at the shelter. Ten-Mile would not have believed me!

August 13, Hall Mountain Shelter to Bemis Mountain Lean-to (milepoint 1916.6 north)

On a beautiful Sunday morning I left the Hall Mountain Shelter with the intention of getting in another big day of hiking. I'd spent the evening in the shelter alone. Usually I enjoyed the company of other hikers; but after spending the last few nights in very crowded shelters, it was a nice change of pace.

I noticed on the shelter privy a sign that read, "Please close the door tight when leaving or the porcupines will eat this house down." I had not realized before hiking the A.T. that porcupines were so ravenous! Incidentally, the privy was not a compost privy. Caretakers at the AMC shelters were responsible for turning the compost in the compost privies, which was another reason to have a paid caretaker at the campsites.

A hostel in Oquossoc, Maine, spurred my interest, but it was seventeen miles north, so the shelter at twelve miles was probably more realistic for the day's hike.

I found Moody Mountain to be one heck of a tough mountain, more than I had anticipated. Metal bars were even attached to the side of the mountain to help hikers climb up, an indication of just how steep the trail was.

As I headed up Old Blue Mountain, I met my first southbound hiker of the day, Titanium Man. An older gentleman, he got his trail name by having two titanium knee replacements; and I wondered to myself, "How the heck is he going to get up and over Moody Mountain?" He mentioned he had a friend behind him and asked me to tell her he was just ahead. When I came upon his friend, a heavyset lady, she asked with quick, deep breaths, "How is the trail ahead?"

I said with a grimace, "It was a little tougher than I had anticipated but . . . ."

"The rocks, the rocks – are there any damn rocks?" she interrupted breathlessly.

"To be honest, there are rocks so big they placed iron bars on the mountain to assist the hikers up the mountain," I said.

She threw her hand to her forehead and screamed, "Oh, for God's sake!" as she headed south. Although I did not tell her, I really didn't know how she was going to get past that section of trail.

It was noon as I headed down Old Blue. It had been a tougher day than expected; and with ten miles to Oquossoc, the next shelter was looking better all the time. As I reached the top of Bemis Mountain, at 3,595 feet, there was no decision any longer: I was stopping at the next shelter. I arrived at the Bemis Mountain Lean-to at a little after four. I'd only gone thirteen miles, but it had been a long, hard day, and I was really tired!

As I lay in the shelter, I could not believe my eyes when the Vince of Wales hiked up and said, "How you doing, Mate?" Vince and I first hiked together on my first day on the A.T. It was great to see him, but I was surprised to see how much weight he had lost! He was hiking with a young fellow by the name of Indy, and we had a great time catching up on the trail news from each other. I was particularly interested in hearing about Badger, Woodchip, and Magic Thumb and his dog Dillon. Magic Thumb had not been feeling well when I last talked to him, and it turned out he had contracted Lyme disease as well as the contaminated water parasite, giardia. He was really sick for awhile but was now back on the trail, although having a tough time of it.

I was hoping to get to Rangeley, about seventeen miles north on the trail, the next day, as there was a small B&B there. Indy had a radio, and the weather forecasts told of rain coming in, another reason to find lodging if at all possible. The owner of Gall Pond Lodge had his card posted in the shelter; and there were some positive comments about the lodge from other hikers in the shelter register, so the three of us thought we would give it a try. I was feeling good, but really tired. The long days were taking their toll on me. I had been told the trail would be leveling off some, but it was still some very challenging hiking.

August 14, Bemis Mountain Lean-to to Maine 4 (Rangeley, Maine) (at milepoint 1947.1 north)

I left the shelter at 6 a.m. after a great night of reminiscing, during which, among other things, I learned Vince had lost 40 pounds! We were all headed to the Gall Pond Lodge in Rangeley, but Vince and Indy were still in the rack. For me, once the birds started to sing, I was awake. I was still not able to sleep late in the shelters.

It was another beautiful day in the Maine backwoods but felt like it could rain anytime. I hiked up to Bemis Stream, which was actually more like a river and one of the first stretches of water on the trail I had to ford. I was told to expect to ford many streams in Maine, for there were few bridges built for hikers.

A little more than two hours into my hike, Indy caught up to me. He was a very strong hiker.

I left the Sabbath Day Pond Lean-to after a break and a long talk with Bumble Bee. He started a thru-hike in 1997. He had to leave the trail because of tendonitis in his hip and was now section hiking, saying, "There's more than one way to skin a cat!"

The trail had been relatively flat for awhile, the first flat section in I don't know how long. It felt good just to be able to get out and stretch my legs on some flat land.

It seemed to be very desolate as I hiked through the thick woods and past many quiet, peaceful ponds. It felt so much like a wilderness that I half expected a Native American to come gliding across the pond in his canoe at any moment.

I looked at my map and figured I had two more miles before Maine Highway 4, which would put me there around 4 p.m. That would mean I'd hiked seventeen miles in ten hours. It had been a long time since I'd covered that many miles that fast.

When I arrived at Route 4, I had a nine-mile hitch into Rangeley. There were two other hikers trying to hitch a ride as well. That was not good, and I could tell they were not really happy to see me either; three's a crowd when it comes to hitchhiking, so I moved on down the road.

By 5 p.m., I was at the Gall Pond Lodge. I was able to catch a ride into Rangeley as soon as the other two hikers were gone; and Bob, the owner of the lodge, picked Indy, Vince, and me up in town and shuttled us out to his home on Gall Pond. He was a very friendly and talkative host. He was unable to provide meals due to the lodge's not being a licensed B&B, but he was very willing to shuttle us into town; so after a quick shower, we headed for town and a nice hot meal.

Although somewhat rustic, the lodge was a very warm, cozy place and the price was right! Bob was a very friendly fellow and had lots of stories to share with us as we visited with him in his living room. One of the stories that brought a smile to the group was about moose viewing, which had become, according to Bob, almost as popular in Maine as hunting. Bob told of an incident the previous year of a family out watching a large moose nonchalantly munching away on some grass in a pond when all of a sudden there was a loud crack, and – as Bob put it in his backwoodsy way – "The moose dropped like a rock in its tracks!" Apparently a hunter had shot the moose as the family looked on in horror! Having hunted deer back home, I failed to see the challenge of shooting a moose. They seem like such dumb animals. And to be perfectly honest, having hiked the A.T. for the past five months, and seeing all the animals in their natural environment, I no longer had any real desire to shoot any kind of wildlife. I hadn't become particularly judgmental about hunters, but I had changed my attitude toward animals in the wild.

Bob's tales of receiving letters from the various thru-hikers at the completion of their hikes were also amusing. He told how he often got letters in the mail from thru-hikers sending him pictures of themselves on top of Mount Katahdin. The problem was, he said, he never knew who they were because the pictures they sent to him were normally identified with their real names and he only knew them by their trail names. He also lamented, "The pictures are typically the same – a tiny fraction of a face peeking out from behind a ski mask as the hiker stands behind the sign of Mount Katahdin with hiking poles held high in the air!" It was really funny to hear him proclaim his frustration with what he was sure were thoughtful gestures on the hikers' parts. And when I thought back to the pictures I had seen of thru-hikers on Mount Katahdin, I realized he'd pretty well hit the nail on the head!

August 15, Maine 4 (Rangeley, Maine) to Poplar Ridge Lean-to (milepoint 1957.8 north)

Bob dropped me off at the trailhead on Route 4 outside of Rangeley. I got a later start than I normally did, but that was typical of a town stop.

> *Hiker tips: Town stops were nice and important for hygiene and food supplies, but they certainly took away from hiking time on the trail.*

As I left Route 4 and started up Saddleback Mountain, a sign advised hikers not to underestimate the time necessary to travel the next section, for the next thirty-two miles was extremely challenging. I had planned to divide the section to thoroughly enjoy the views and hoped it would be clear on top of Saddleback Mountain, for I was told hikers could see Mount Washington to the south and Mount Katahdin to the north!

Vince, Indy, and I were doing about the same miles, but we each hiked at our own pace, occasionally meeting along the trail for lunch or a break and usually meeting up at the same shelter each night. I normally headed out earlier in the mornings, and Indy and Vince typically caught up to me throughout the day.

I was getting down to the nitty-gritty, only 220 miles to Mount Katahdin. Every time I talked to Connie, she continued to ask for a summit date so she could make plans to pick me up; but I was still hesitant to give a specific date, knowing that so many things could be factors. I did go out on a limb and say that if everything went well, I would be at Mount Katahdin around August 28.

I climbed Saddleback Mountain as the previous night's rain streamed down the trail, and I found a couple more metal reinforcement rods embedded in the rock to assist hikers over the wet, treacherous rocks that had been smoothed by glaciers many years earlier.

The sun was beginning to peek out, so I figured the fog would soon burn off for my final view above the tree line as an A.T. thru-hiker.

I hiked to the top of Saddleback Mountain, 4,120 feet. There was no view of Mount Katahdin or Mount Washington, but at least it wasn't

Poplar Ridge, oldest lean-to in Maine

raining.

It was 3:45 p.m. when I hiked into Poplar Ridge Lean-to. According to David Field, who provided an informative and humorous register, Poplar Ridge Lean-to was the oldest lean-to in Maine and still had the original baseball bat designed floor. In other words, the floor was made up of small trees the diameter of a baseball bat placed side by side. It was a design that made for a rough night of sleeping!

We had a full house that night with Vince, Indy, a young woman southbounder named Windy, and one other late arrival who squeezed into the shelter.

The southbounder was a real talker, very opinionated. She seemed to disagree with whatever anyone said. The topic of trail magic came up, and everyone said that there didn't seem to be quite as much trail magic at this point for northbounders as there had been earlier in the hike. As the different reasons for that were discussed, she quickly interjected, "I believe there is just as much trail magic up north." Now this was from a person who was hiking south and had not hiked much more than 200 miles. Enough said.

Later in the evening, I got up to answer nature's call; and upon my return, Indy got me laughing as he told me about the biggest outhouse

Cribbage anyone?   *(Photo by Indy)*

he had ever seen on the A.T. With a look of amazement, he said, "The damn outhouse was so big it was a two-holer, and believe this or not, it had a cribbage board between the holes!" I laughed until my stomach ached when he added, "And the sign on the outside of the door read, 'Your Move'!"

August 16, Poplar Ridge Lean-to to Crocker Cirque Campsite (milepoint 1972.0 north)

It was particularly difficult getting started after an all-night rain. The morning was dreary, damp, and wet. As always, it was a special challenge to put on cold, wet clothes for the morning hike. But knowing I was down to approximately two remaining weeks was motivation enough to get me out of the sack; and besides, things were going well, and physically I felt great.

I crossed the Orbeton Stream and headed toward Lone Mountain. It was still wet and dreary but not raining, although it looked and felt like it could let loose at any moment. The gnats were out in full force, so thick I had to be careful not to open my mouth at the wrong time or I'd have some of the little critters for breakfast. That wasn't the type of protein supplement I was looking for!

267

I passed a father and son out for their first hike. The son looked to be eleven or twelve years old and seemed rather hesitant to start the trek. Not Dad – he was all pumped up! It would be interesting to talk with them in a few days; I was sure they would have lasting stories and memories.

A young southbound hiker came by with the trail name of Fancy Feet. She was coming from Sugarloaf Mountain, a ski resort about two miles north where hikers could stay in one of the huts on top of the mountain. She was moving pretty slowly, for she had started out early in the morning and here it was almost noon and she had only hiked two or three miles, but she was still positive about making it to Springer Mountain. She certainly had the proper mind-set.

I passed a nice plaque dedicated to the men of the Civilian Conservation Corps (CCC) who completed the final link of the A.T. in 1937. That got me to thinking about my dad and the stories he loved to tell about his time working for the CCC out West, planting trees in the late 1930s.

Met another southbounder with the trail name of Just Bob, who was flip-flopping. He'd hiked from Springer Mountain to Pine Grove Furnace in Pennsylvania, then got a ride to Mount Katahdin and was now hiking south. He said he figured that was the only way he would get his thru-hike completed before the weather turned too bad.

The trail continued to be very wet and slick, and I had gone down hard a couple of times. The logs used in the bogs on the trail were particularly slick; and remembering how I had broken one of my poles, I was definitely hiking with my hands out of the straps. That decision almost backfired when, on one particular fall, I was almost impaled by my own hiking pole as it went straight up into the air and came down like a guided missile, sticking in the ground just inches from my belly!

It wasn't quite three when I arrived at the side trail to the Crocker Cirque Campsite. I had been told there were some nice wooden platforms there for setting up my tent, particularly nice considering the rain we had had and the forecast calling for more. After a couple nights in crowded shelters, I was looking forward to staying in my own tent. I was also really tired, and I always seemed to get better sleep in my tent than in a shelter.

Vince was already set up when I got to the campsite; but there were other platforms, one of which I quickly laid claim to. A number of section and day hikers were using the two empty platforms next to my tent for cooking, so it was a little noisy; but it quieted down after a bit.

August 17, Crocker Cirque Campsite to Horns Pond Lean-to (at milepoint 1984.4 north)

I hiked out of Crocker Cirque Campsite early after a miserable morning, taking my tent down and packing it away in the rain. The wooden platform was certainly a benefit: even though I had a wet tent, at least it wasn't muddy. The platforms were basically constructed of two-by-six inch boards to make an eight-foot-square platform that was raised about ten to twenty inches off the ground. Metal eyelets were screwed into the wood, making it very easy to anchor a tent.

> *Hiker tips: My tent worked great on the platform, but Vince had problems with his tent, which required at least twelve stakes. It was a very nice tent, but it was heavy and required that many stakes to hold it down. But as Vince liked to say, that was "just the price you pay to be comfortable, Mate!" The weight of a hiker's pack usually got down to just that – comfort. It's really up to each individual hiker to determine how much weight he is willing to carry for the sake of comfort. I personally do not believe I would have ever stood on Mount Katahdin if I had carried the kind of weight that Vince carried.*

Although I intended to hike into Stratton for supplies, I wasn't sure if I was going to stay there overnight or get a few more miles in beyond Stratton. I had two mountains to start the morning off – North and South Crocker, both more than 4,040 feet – and I was sure that would get me warmed up.

As I closed in on Maine Highway 27, I met a southbounder and asked him about the trail ahead. He shrugged his shoulders and said, "Hell, I don't know! I've only been on the trail for fifteen minutes." With a big grin, he added, "And I'm still going strong!" That had me chuckling for awhile as I continued north on the trail. A good sense of humor would come in handy for him down the trail.

It was noon when I hiked out on Route 27 to get a hitch into town and had the scare of my life. I reached into my pack to get some money out of my billfold, which I kept in a special zipper pouch, and the billfold was gone! My heart sank. All my valuables – money, travelers checks, credit cards, everything – were in there. I had not had my billfold out since Rangeley and could not even begin to think where to start looking. My mind began to race, wondering what I would do in the middle of Maine without any money. It actually took my breath away as I frantically began to search with the dim hope of finding the billfold somewhere in my pack. After what seemed like an eternity searching my pack, and with my stuff lying in disarray all over the ground, there at the bottom of my pack, to my great relief, lay my billfold. What a scare! I was really lucky; just lying in the bottom of my pack, the billfold could have fallen out in any of the shelters when I hung the pack up.

Hiker tips: The pouch, attached to the inside of my pack, worked very well for my valuables. That is, it worked well when I zipped it closed!

By a little after two, I headed back on the A.T. after a great burger at the Stratton Diner; but I also felt the strain of carrying food for four days as I headed toward Monson, Maine. I'd been able to talk to my wife on the phone while I was at the diner, and she mentioned that Badger and Woodchip planned to summit Mount Katahdin in the next day or so. That was great to hear; and although I was a little envious, I surely was happy for them and hoped to be doing the same in about twelve to fourteen days. Connie also told me Ten-Mile had made it home safely and was sharing some great stories of our hike through the Mahoosucs.

It was late and turning cold as I arrived at Horns Pond Lean-to, one of several shelters in the immediate area. There was a large shelter for thru-hikers and a couple of smaller ones for day hikers. I met a couple section hiking. She was from Maine, so they were not letting the poor weather get them down. But it surely was cold! The caretaker said with a shiver, "It's 44-degrees right now, 42-degrees last night, and they're calling for frost tonight." And there sat dumb me without gloves. I'd sent them home because of the extra weight, all six ounces! I could not believe I'd done that! Thank goodness I had everything else with me to stay warm.

Hiker tips: I knew of some hikers who used socks as gloves as a way of saving weight. Personally, I preferred my fleece gloves with wind bloc. They were also waterproof and kept my hands warm and dry, and they were very light.

It was really a nice camping area but the cold was nasty. I headed straight to my sleeping bag. It was nippy, nippy, nippy!

August 18, Horns Pond Lean-to to West Carry Pond Lean-to (at milepoint 2001.9 north)

On a very cool morning, I hiked north from Horn Pond Shelter, but it was nothing like the previous night, during which Indy – in his 40-degree bag – had all his clothes on and was looking for more. Although there had seemed to be a little heat given off by the friction between the two groups of thru-hikers in the shelter. The closer to Mount Katahdin the northbounders got, the more excited they became; and their constant talk of completing the trail seemed to grate on some of the southbound thru-hikers, who were not nearly close enough to their finish to share in the enthusiasm. It was difficult for me, a northbounder, to understand or explain, but the tension was there. There could have been other factors involved, and certainly the past few days of very cold weather would cause any hiker to be a bit irritable.

I passed over South Horn and was headed to West Peak, the highest peak of the Bigelows at 4,145 feet. There were no views, but the weather was nice and cool for hiking as I continued to look for the positives.

Knowing I would probably be one of the first up and out of camp in the morning, Vince asked me to wake him when I left because his watch had quit working the day before. Indy, on the other hand, would sleep in and still catch up to me by noon. The only way I could get good miles in every day was to start early; and when I told one of the southbounders how far I planned to hike, she looked at me and remarked in an irritated tone, "Well, good luck. We could only do ten miles!"

I saw a beautiful sunrise when I got up, but I was hiking in clouds and the opportunities for good views seemed to come and go. As one of the Maine day hikers had aptly joked, "If you don't like the weather, just wait a minute and it will change!"

As I stopped for a break on the West Peak summit of Bigelow Mountain, the wind whirled the clouds, giving me one breathtaking view after another. I couldn't believe the number of lakes! I don't believe I could have thrown a stone off the mountain without it landing in a lake – there were lakes as far as the eye could see.

I arrived at the Avery Memorial Campsite, named for Myron H. Avery, the man who, according to *The Thru-Hiker's Handbook,* turned Benton MacKaye's vision of the A.T. into a reality. "A native of Maine, Avery was the first person to hike the entire A.T. (in sections during 1928-37)," the handbook said. "He wrote the first guidebooks, designed the first shelters, and selected the original route for much of the trail."

Just down from the campsite was a natural water spring with a wooden box covering it, presumably to keep the water clean – a good idea.

I topped Avery Peak as the weather cleared and the clouds diminished, giving me what I believed to be a view of Mount Katahdin off in the distance. I think I could even see Mount Washington to the south, but I didn't know for sure. These were definitely the best views I had had since Ten-Mile left, and it was one heck of a nice way to finish off my hike above the tree line with spectacular views in all directions. I certainly was going to miss the above-tree-line hiking and the awe-inspiring feeling that accompanied it.

As I drew nearer to Mount Katahdin, a lot of people had been asking me how I felt about my hike overall. With my hike not yet complete, I found it difficult to allow myself to think about the trail in terms of completion; yet the one thing that immediately came to mind, as corny as it may sound, was my rekindled faith in mankind. In other words, I would not soon forget the many people who had gone out of their way to help me as I followed the white blazes. People like Tim, the pizza delivery man in North Adams, who volunteered to drive me wherever I had to go; and Jack, down in Johnson City, who picked me up twice, drove me to a hotel, and washed my laundry, just to name two of many. There also had been a couple of jerks, but they had been few compared to the many helpful people I had met!

I met another flip-flopping thru-hiker. The option of flip-flopping seemed to be more popular as I hiked north and the window of opportunity for completion of the A.T. at Mount Katahdin began to close.

Yet another southbounder was Mr. G., who was also flip-flopping the trail. With a slap on my back, he grinned and said, "I left Mount Katahdin twelve days ago. You're getting close enough to smell it!"

It was noon on top of Little Bigelow Mountain, at an elevation of 3,010 feet, when I stopped for lunch on a nice flat rock. If God had created a better place to eat lunch on a more beautiful day, I certainly didn't know where it would be!

I marked another milestone. At Long Falls Dam Road, someone had painted in large bold numbers in the middle of the road, "The 2000-mile mark."

Around 4 p.m., I hiked into the West Carry Pond Lean-to after a long seventeen-mile plus day, but I felt great. A bit later, Vince came into camp rubbing his neck and declaring, "I knew I should not have done it! I knew it, knew it!" When I asked what he was talking about, he explained, still rubbing his neck, that in the last shelter register he wrote, "Mountain Slayer, Indy, and the Vince of Wales are on their way north to Mount Katahdin and nothing can stop us now!" He continued in all seriousness, "I think I jinxed us! Yes, I bloody well jinxed us!" Oh, how we laughed, but Vince didn't think it was very funny. Actually, he'd taken a very hard fall, so hard that he moaned, "I thought I had broke me friggin' neck!"

As evening settled in, I moseyed down to the West Carry Pond, hoping to see a nice sunset. It certainly was a gorgeous night in the backwoods of Maine.

August 19, West Carry Pond Lean-to to Pleasant Pond Lean-to (milepoint 2020.8 north)

I left the shelter extra early so I could reach the Kennebec River by early afternoon. The ATC furnished a canoe ferry to cross the river, but hikers had to be there by 1:30 or they were out of luck. Before the establishment of the canoe ferry, hikers would ford the river, which had resulted in the drowning of a hiker a few years back. That spurred the club to offer the ferry service. "Kennebec" is a Native American word meaning "long, silent river," but apparently the river was not always silent, especially since a power plant upriver released water at any time, which would cause a drastic and unexpected rise in the water level!

According to the *Appalachian Trail Thru-Hikers' Companion*, just north of the shelter the A.T. followed the route that Benedict Arnold had traveled with his army when he tried to capture Quebec. It traversed a bog where logs had been laid at times to assist hikers, but they could be extremely slick after a rain and proved to be very difficult to hike on.

As I continued my hike along Carry Pond, I had a fleeting glimpse of a large bull moose that made quite a racket as he raced through the woods with his enormous rack banging against the trees.

By noon, Indy and I arrived at the Kennebec River where a sign read, "Dangerous, hazardous crossing! The water may rise 2-4 feet without warning! Bottom rocks are extremely slippery. Please use ferry!" The river did not appear to be very deep, but it was extremely wide; and I welcomed the opportunity to ride across.

It was not long until Steve Longley arrived with his canoe and ferried us across to the north side of the river one at a time. A friendly and chatty fellow, he knew how to impress me by saying, "I'm taking you over in the same boat that brought Earl Shaffer over the Kennebec." I loved hearing that. He really enjoyed talking with the many thru-hikers and knew the way to their hearts: he'd painted a white blaze in the bottom of the canoe, so, as he put it, "The pure thru-hikers could rest easy, knowing they were still on the trail!"

We had a great hot lunch at a little lunch stand that Steve told us about near the little town of Caratunk. And when I say "a little town," I mean it. There wasn't much more than a post office that I could see. No matter. I was headed back to the trail with my belly full and hoping to get in about six more miles.

When we arrived at the Pleasant Pond Lean-to, we had hiked 19.7 miles, a big day but not a particularly challenging one; and I felt good. I did not have to make dinner; my belly was still full from the lunch stop, so I took a walk down to the nearby lake to enjoy the evening sunset. There I met Smoke and Prima Lady. They had attempted a thru-hike the preceding year but had been unable to finish before Mount Katahdin was closed for the winter, so they were back for their last 120 miles.

> *Hiker tips: According to what I had heard, park*
> *rangers officially closed Mount Katahdin on Oct. 15.*
> *And even though there was talk of hikers reaching the*
> *summit after that date, I would strongly suggest hikers*
> *not take the chance.*

Indy and I had a good laugh at Vince's expense. Before we headed down to the Pond, Indy gave me a wink and asked Vince, "Now, do I have to take this damn trail register with me so you don't jinx us again?" Vince shook his head and said sadly, "I think it's too late, Mate. The damage is already done!" We laughed all the way down to the pond.

August 20, Pleasant Pond Lean-to to Moxie Bald Lean-to (milepoint 2034.9 north)

It was 4:15 a.m. when I awoke to the lonesome call of the loons on the pond. I really enjoyed hearing their mournful cry. It's a sound that will forever bring me back to the Appalachian Trail every time I hear it.

An hour later it was raining again, but I remained warm and dry in the shelter. I found it intriguing that Vince and Indy elected to sleep in their tents, saying they didn't want to be bothered by the mosquitoes. From what I could tell, the mosquitoes were almost non-existent and certainly less of a problem for me than packing and carrying a wet tent the rest of the day. Again, "Hike your own hike."

As I packed up and was ready to head out, it was pouring down rain, so I figured no sense in getting too excited to leave since I was only hiking thirteen miles today.

As the rain slowed I became antsy; and as I headed to the trail, I heard Vince call out from inside his tent, "What time is it, Mate?"

I yelled back, "Six-forty-five, Mate!" and heard a most unusual question, "Yes, and how hard is it raining?" I thought to myself, "Now, what kind of question was that from a person who had been in a tent throughout the rainy night?"

It definitely was one of those nasty mornings as I hiked up Pleasant Pond Mountain on slick, rain-soaked rocks.

Hiker tips: I was currently hiking with maps instead of just the Data Book pages that I used exclusively early on. I was told that the New Hampshire section of the trail was not very well marked and, as I was hiking by myself, I thought it would be a safe thing to do, even though they were obviously more weight than a few pages out of my Data Book. Surprisingly, I found a benefit I had not considered – the maps were much more specific on water sources and I was able to carry less water, knowing a specific water source was not far away. Thus, I got a weight saving that I had not even considered.

I also had to commend the Maine Appalachian Trail Conference, which had done a great job of putting up signs telling hikers of certain locations and points of interest. I had heard more than a few hikers mention their appreciation of the effort.

I met an interesting southbounder by the trail name of Shipwreck. He told me with a frown, "I was so lonely on the trail that I got a dog for company about four days ago." The dog was nine years old, about the size and shape of "Ole Yeller," and I could tell the dog was having a tough time by the way it was panting incessantly. I did not want to be bossy but felt compelled to suggest, "For the dog's sake and maybe yours, I would not try and take it through the Mahoosuc," and wished him luck as he headed south; for he and the dog were going to need all the luck they could muster and then some.

I passed a couple of day hikers coming down the mountain with a big basket of blueberries. Bald Mountain was loaded with blueberries, and I had to be careful how many I ate so I would not get sick on them. In no way did I want another eating fiasco like I had at Pine Grove Furnace when I inhaled the half-gallon of ice cream in one sitting. My stomach still reminded me of that idiocy every once in awhile.

It was a little after noon as I topped Moxie Bald Mountain and oh, was it cold! I had a beautiful view, but it was so windy and cold I elected not to eat my lunch on the mountaintop as I had planned but save it for the next shelter. Instead, I pulled out a Baby Ruth; and to my surprise, it was so hard, it was like taking it out of the freezer!

Hiker tips: I would highly recommend that you take the summit trail to Moxie Bald Mountain, not the blue blaze, weather permitting. The view made the extra effort worthwhile.

I made it to the Moxie Bald Lean-to as the rain came pouring down. There were three hikers in the shelter already, and gear was stacked to the roof, taking up half the shelter. They told me the gear belonged to some hikers out on the lake, and without looking up from making their dinners, told me in no uncertain terms the shelter was full. I didn't say a word but simply gave a nod and sat down to contemplate my options as the rain continued to pour down.

Being cold and wet from the rain, I was not happy about the news of a full shelter; but what really got my goat was the extremely rude and obnoxious manner in which I was told. The fellow in the shelter – I came to call him Sad Sack – had two kids with him; and it was very obvious that he was not happy to see me, as he told me the shelter was full before my pack hit the floor!

After about ten minutes of an uneasy quiet and with no one else appearing, I asked if he was sure there wasn't room for one more. He coarsely replied, "No way, we're full!" While I waited for the rain to subside, no one in the shelter offered to move any of their gear, even though I was standing there shivering in cold wet clothes. I found this behavior very unusual; typically fellow hikers went out of their way to help another hiker, especially in inclement weather. Eventually I cleared a space under the overhang of the shelter to eat a snack and wait out the storm.

As the rain let up and I was feeling not at all welcome, I decided to hell with it and set my tent up away from the shelter just as another rain shower came blowing in. Not wanting to get everything in my tent wet, I went back to the shelter to change into dry clothes and discovered Sad Sack wanted to chitchat now that I had my tent set up outside and was no longer a threat to stay in the shelter.

Not at all interested in his sudden desire to converse, I changed clothes and went back to my tent to lie down. In about an hour or so, I heard a group of people talking as they walked up from the lake to the shelter, and I overheard Sad Sack immediately inquire if they were staying in the shelter for the night, to which they responded they had no intention of staying.

One would think that Sad Sack, knowing I was interested in getting in out of the rain, would have let me know there was room in the shelter, but not a word. Vince and I walked back up to the shelter to prepare our dinners and struck up a conversation with the canoeists who had been out on the lake. They were very friendly, offering us some food and saying they would clear out their gear in the shelter to make room for us, much to the chagrin of Sad Sack.

As the evening progressed, it soon became apparent what Sad Sack's problem was, as he told us he had been a thru-hiker earlier in the year and had quit before getting out of Georgia! All night long he kept explaining why he had left the trail, even though no one in the shelter had asked or, for that matter, had expressed a desire to know. It was obvious to all of us in the shelter that the trail had gotten the best of him and he was having a real problem dealing with that.

Another Vince story: As I went out to brush my teeth after dinner, I nodded to Indy and then made sure Vince saw me pick up the shelter register. Vince gave a wily smile and said, "Don't worry about taking that register, Mate. I have that all taken care of!"

"How so?" Indy asked, somewhat surprised.

"I retracted my original statement at the last shelter in the register, so there is nothing to worry about, Mate. There will no longer be any jinx on the Vince of Wales, Indy, or the Mountain Slayer!" And he was very serious.

August 21, Moxie Bald Lean-to to Maine 15 (Monson, Maine) (milepoint 2052.6 north)

I left the shelter early and headed north with a plan of staying overnight in Monson, Maine, where I hoped that my last maildrop was waiting for me. It was great to be able to carry a light pack, knowing I would be resupplying at the end of the day.

The terrain for the day's hike appeared to be level according to the maps, with the only obstacles being a couple of rivers to ford, although one was said to be waist-deep!

Arrived in Monson just past two o'clock after a little help from some friends. I was not having much success hitching a ride and was just about to start walking down Maine Highway 6 toward town when a small pickup slammed on its brakes and backed up. "Hey, Mountain Slayer!" came a call from the truck, as Tony and Docie, the couple whom I had met back at Horns Pond Shelter, recognized me and were good enough to give me a lift to town.

Indy, Vince, and I decided to stay at the Pie Lady's Hostel in Monson, where she served us dinner and also included a breakfast and ride back to the trail for a very reasonable price. I had picked up my mail and was busy repacking and meticulously searching my pack for things I no longer needed and could send home. After leaving Monson, I was entering the hundred-mile wilderness and knew with 114.5 miles left on the A.T., there would be no more town or post office opportunities.

August 22, Maine 15 (Monson, Maine) to Long Pond Stream Lean-to (milepoint 2068.4 north)

The Pie Lady dropped me off at the trailhead a little later than I liked, but I was feeling good and the section ahead appeared to be fairly level, so I was not particularly worried about making miles. I'd had a very nice stay at the Pie Lady's place. Dinner the evening before had been steak and mashed potatoes with all the fixings, and breakfast had been eggs, home fries, and bacon.

I was carrying four days of food with every intention of restocking at a hunting camp I had heard about called the "White House," located in the hundred-mile wilderness. Wasn't sure what I would do if that did not work out, but five months of hiking had instilled in me enough confidence that I was not worried.

Hiker tips: As I entered the last hundred miles of my thru-hike, I figured a review of my equipment and how it worked for me would be in order. My Nomad tent worked well: I really liked the ease of setup, its durability, and light weight. I should have packed the Nomad in a waterproof bag instead of the original pack bag it came in because of durability and weather. Carrying it on the bottom and outside of my pack caused a lot of wear and tear on the pack bag. I had gotten rid of the MSR Dromedary water bag with its hose attachment midway through my hike. I just did not need to carry that much water anymore. I also sent home my portable water bag. Even though it was only three ounces, I had not used it enough to warrant carrying it. For water I was carrying a Gatorade bottle and a squeeze bottle with filter. I would filter a little water into the Gatorade bottle, depending on the water supply ahead on the trail, and simply use my squeeze bottle filter at the different water sources along the way. Carrying very little water had reduced my pack weight significantly!

The Leki Poles proved invaluable: they really saved my knees on downhill stretches and doubled well as tent poles for my Nomad tent, saving the extra weight of tent poles. A key to packing lightweight was finding items that could serve more than one purpose.

My external pack served me well, but it was an inexpensive model; and there were probably more comfortable packs on the market that weighed the same or less. I would probably try to get a better quality pack – and a smaller one – the next time, but I would certainly look for a large number of pockets. I purchased an inexpensive pack cover out of Campmor and would probably look into a better one if I could find a lightweight one. I also would not do without the waterproof pouch that I added to my pack belt. It kept my maps and camera very handy at all times.

My Esbit stove was great. I appreciated the ease of using lightweight fuel tabs, and it certainly took care of my limited cooking needs. I had purchased a case of fuel tabs ahead of time and that worked out just about perfectly; I only had a box or so left by the time I finished my hike. For cooking, I only had my Esbit stove with a .85 MSR titanium kettle and spoon. I would not change anything about my cooking equipment. As for food, I would probably have added some hot chocolate packets (after getting one from Indy) and I found Crystal Lite being very light weight and helping flavor the drinking water.

I loved my Feather Friends 20-degree down sleeping bag and was very happy that I paid a little more and bought it with waterproofing. There was no way to keep a down sleeping bag from getting some moisture on it, especially with a Nomad tent, so the waterproofing was essential.

My Olympus Camera weighed ten ounces, was waterproof, and served me very well! I also carried a very small tripod that attached to the camera and could be set up or attached to small trees or even hiking poles. With the tripod and self-timer, I was able to literally take hundreds of pictures that included me.

I carried an all-polyester handkerchief for perspiration. It worked very well pinned on the pack so that I would not lose it. My other handkerchief was cotton, and I attached that to my pack during cold weather for my runny nose. It was the only piece of cotton with me on the hike! If I had it to do over again, I would probably have had that handkerchief be synthetic too, for faster drying.

As for clothing, I had three pairs of socks, two pairs of nylon pants, two light synthetic t-shirts, one long-

sleeved shirt, two pairs of underwear, a Puffball jacket for winter time, and a pair of camp shoes. I had a little more weight in clothing than most hikers, but I really appreciated the extra set of clothing for dry clothes in the evening and stops into town. I found it very important to have a dry set of clothes at night. I also liked to wear clean clothing to go into towns.

For rain gear, I used Frogg Toggs, which was very light and waterproof. I used my Frogg Togg jacket the entire trip, as it served both as a raincoat and as a jacket during cold weather. The pants I sent back home early in the hike.

I had the lightest Therm-A-Rest sleeping pad available: a three-quarter-length pad a half-inch thick. I also carried part of a Z-Rest sleeping pad (four sections) for sitting on in camp and placing at the end of my Therm-A-Rest at night for my feet. If I had it to do over again, I would probably go with a full-length Therm-A-Rest; the Z-Rest seemed to always slip out from under my feet during the night. It worked but was somewhat of a nuisance. Regardless, I would stay with the Therm-A-Rest sleeping pad, which is very popular on the trail.

It felt great to be hiking with clean clothing, probably the last time for a good clean-up before Mount Katahdin as we headed into the hundred-mile wilderness without much chance of getting clothing washed again. But I was looking forward to seeing the Maine wilderness. I had been told it was not as desolate as it once was, but time would tell.

I had not really heard much about the ponds in Maine but had been pleasantly surprised that the A.T. often took hikers right down to the ponds' edges to enjoy the wildlife and serenity.

I arrived at Little Wilson Stream and met up with Vince, who took the lead, jumping from rock to rock as he weaved his way across the stream. Midway through he ran out of luck, and in he went! The stream was no more than knee-deep, but he did get a couple of boots full of water. Fortunately, I was able to find another route that allowed me to make the crossing with dry feet.

I lunched with Vince and the Four Dutchmen. I had been reading about the Four Dutchmen for a long time in the shelter registers and enjoyed the opportunity to meet the four cousins from the Pennsylvania Dutch country. Not many groups of hikers could stick together long enough to make it all the way, but it looked as though they would defy the odds.

I passed the Dutchmen just before Long Pond Lean-to, my destination for the evening; and true to their reputation, they were taking a very cold swim in a stream. I could hear them well before I saw them.

August 23, Long Pond Stream Lean-to to West Branch of Pleasant River (milepoint 2083.0 north)

I left the Long Pond Stream Lean-to unsure of my destination for the day, but I looked for something like a fifteen-mile day. It was a pretty morning as I climbed Barren Mountain, still looking for that first view of Mount Katahdin.

The top of Barren Mountain was 2,660 feet, making it a good early morning climb. I had some great views from the mountaintop, but no Katahdin. As I looked south, there were some monster mountains. I couldn't imagine what went through southbounders' minds as they stood where I was standing and got their first glimpse of the mountains ahead.

I was back on the trail after a mile-long round trip on a blue blaze trail to get water; and to make matters worse, I had to get the water from a nasty pond. But at least I had water. My *Data Book* said that there was a spring near the shelter on the blue blaze trail, but I'll be damned if I could find it.

Ran into three hikers from England, and they informed me there would not be any water until the next shelter. So I was glad I got my water when I did. I told them there was a thru-hiker from Wales just a few miles behind me and they said, "Grand! We would like to talk to the bloke."

I met a section-hiker and his son from Long Island, New York, who had hired a guide to assist them in their hike. Surprised by the hiring of a guide, I said, "Hell, all you have to do is follow the white blazes!" A little less confident, the father shook his head and said, "Maybe for you, but it's not quite that easy for us." I talked with their guide Tree Hugger on top of Fourth Mountain. He had hiked the trail back in 1992 and currently worked as a guide. A friendly fellow, he just might have the greatest job on earth: hiking the A.T. and getting paid for it.

Amazingly, I met another father/son team as I headed down Fourth Mountain. Don, the father, was seventy-eight, and when I told him how impressed I was, he responded, "Seventy-eight isn't old." Then he rubbed his back and added, "Except at times!" I could only hope I had the health and spirit to be hiking the A.T. when I turned seventy-eight.

As I continued north through the wilderness, I met a young hiker wearing a Catholic Central football jersey. I asked, "Is that the Catholic Central in Springfield, Ohio?"

He just about fell over with surprise and answered, "Yes, how in the world did you know that?"

I told him I was from Versailles, which is not far from Springfield. In fact, the two schools are in the same athletic conference. We both laughed at the odds of the two of us meeting out in the middle of Maine's hundred-mile wilderness! For that matter, I had a hard time believing that I was hiking in the "wilderness," for I had met more hikers in one day than I had seen in weeks! I was a little disappointed in how the hundred-mile wilderness was being exploited.

We found a nice little campsite right next to a clean stream, and I quickly chowed down my mac and cheese as it began to rain. The following day appeared to be our last big day of mountains, and then it was said to be pretty level until Mount Katahdin. With 84.1 miles to go, we were on schedule to reach the base of Mount Katahdin on August 28. Although I was excited about the finish being so close, I was also experiencing a let-down that it would soon all be over. The goal was within reach, and I was already feeling some sadness that the hike would be coming to a close.

The three of us had a good time in camp as we shared plans for our post-A.T. adventures. Vince and I talked of doing more hiking, for me, possibly the coast-to-coast hike in England; and we had a good chuckle when Indy shared his agenda: "All I plan to do is shave and find a job!"

August 24, West Branch of Pleasant River to East Branch Lean-to (milepoint 2099.3 north)

I left a wet camp and was told by some southbounders that they'd had to ford the Pleasant River just north of our campsite. I kept hearing about having to ford rivers, but I had yet to take off my boots and wade across any river. I'd usually been able to find some type of a rock crossing.

As I hiked to Pleasant River, it looked pretty wide; and I didn't know if I would be able to make it across without getting my feet wet. Stretched to my limits in finding rocks, I did make it across, although some of the rocks I ended up using were actually under water an inch or so.

A conservancy district called the Hermitage was the next section I hiked through, a very popular area that appealed to hikers to "leave no trace" and did not allow camping.

The Hermitage was very well managed, but the trail markings were a little confusing. Apparently they had changed a few blue blazes by painting them white, and some of the blue blazing was leaching through the white. As a thru-hiker following the white-blazed A.T., seeing a blue blaze on the trail sent a cold chill through my body.

I crossed another bog on logs so slick that I would have sworn they had been greased!

I passed a sign that indicated White Cap Mountain was 9.5 miles away, and the outlook was looking good for my first view of what many hikers described as the "Holy Grail" – Mount Katahdin. I was running low on energy and felt sluggish. The toll of the trail continued to catch up with me.

But it was a great morning as the sun was coming out, and I already had a Snickers bar in my belly. What more can a thru-hiker want? My only concern was the wet rocks, the tree roots, and the mud, a lethal combination if one were not careful; and I was too close to the end now to risk any type of broken bone.

All of the hikers heading south were congratulating me, making me very nervous as I replied, "I'm not done yet," to which they normally smiled and said with confidence, "You've got it made!" But I kept reminding myself what Yogi Berra said: "It ain't over till it's over."

At White Cap Mountain Summit I took a picture, and no, I could not see Mount Katahdin. It was a little foggy, and with Mount Katahdin still more than seventy-two miles north, I guess I really shouldn't have expected to get a view.

During a lunch break at Logan Brook Lean-to, Indy was really getting on Vince about crossing the river earlier in the morning. Apparently Indy was in the process of removing his shoes and socks to ford the river when up came Vince, who as Indy put it, "just splashes through to the other side!" It looked as though Katahdin fever really had its grip on the Vince of Wales!

I could hear him well before I could see him, the southbound hiker with bells hanging from his pack that sounded like Santa's sleigh coming down the trail. I would think that the bells would drive a hiker crazy after a few days on the trail. I personally would rather contend with the bears than those damn bells!

I finally settled in for the evening a little after 6 p.m. at the East Branch Lean-to. It was a beautiful evening, and everyone seemed to have mellowed out as they relaxed and shared their post-A.T. plans. Being so close to the end probably had something to do with the melancholy attitude of the hikers.

Around 10 p.m., two hikers who had been night hiking in the rain came into camp using their headlamps. One ended up sleeping on the shelter picnic table while the other tented. The young hikers continued to amaze me with their unique hiking hours.

August 25, East Branch Lean-to to Pemadumcook Logging Road (White House Landing) (milepoint 2121.1 north)

It was a little before 6 a.m. as I left the East Branch Lean-to as quietly as possible, not wanting to wake the hikers who were still asleep. I had a big day planned, approximately twenty miles, with hopes of getting to the White House Wilderness Landing Camp. I was on schedule to finish on August 29, although a summit of Katahdin on the 28th was a real possibility, depending on the weather when I got to Daicey Pond Campground. The summit was about seven miles from Daicey Pond and five miles from Katahdin Campgrounds.

As for afterward, Indy had two friends driving in from Indianapolis to meet him for the summit climb, and they had offered me a ride to Brooklyn, New York, where I hoped to visit with my daughter and wait for my wife to pick me up.

Hiker tips: Park rangers at Daicey Pond asked that thru-hikers check in at their ranger station and they'd then be permitted to stay in the campsite reserved for thru-hikers. If hikers wanted to get closer, the rangers would call ahead to Katahdin Campgrounds at the foot of Mount Katahdin.

I crossed Little Boardman Mountain, the last "bump" on my profile map. It was an easy climb on a beautiful day, but still no view of Katahdin.

Some reflections on my A.T. thru-hike: As I prepared for a thru-hike from Georgia to Maine, many of my friends asked why I was doing it; and for lack of a better answer, I usually told them that if they were asking that question, no amount of explaining on my part would help them understand. But as I closed in on completing the trail, I believed I could answer the question why with a few simple questions of my own: Have you every set your tent up on top of Max Patch and watched in awe as the sun set over the Smokey Mountains? Have you ever walked down to a pond in Maine to filter water and looked up to see a big bull moose in all its splendor watching you? Have you ever sat on that perfect rock in the middle of the woods to eat a snack and glanced over your shoulder to see an enormous bear looking at you just a few feet away? To be able to see the mountains, trees, rivers, and wildlife in their natural settings was what the trail and hike was all about. Also, leaving thirty-plus pounds of my own excess weight somewhere along the rugged Appalachian Mountain chain was an added benefit I had not considered before the hike.

> *Hiker tips: The one question most asked as I got close to the end, "How did you do it?" My answer was simple: "Get out and hike." Although very obvious, it could not be overstated that thru-hikers needed to really love hiking and then hike the miles. I had met many hikers along the A.T. who enjoyed the outdoors but really did not like to hike, and they often ended up spending too much time in towns. Long town stays usually led to falling behind, getting discouraged, and leaving the trail. The bottom line is you have to hike the miles to get to Katahdin!*

By the time I reached Jo-Mary Road, I had hiked more than twelve miles and began to think that the White House Camp hamburgers were going to be a real possibility. It would require a big twenty-three-mile day, but I had a bad case of burger fever!

It continued to be a beautiful day as I headed north and had only seen two hikers, which is what I had expected the hundred-mile wilderness to be like. One hiker blurted out as he approached, "You're a northbound thru-hiker completing the trail!"

Surprised, I asked how he could tell and he replied; "You've got that look in your eye!"

I laughed and said, "You sure it's not the smell and skinny ass?"

To which he winked and said, "That, too!"

I hiked into the Potaywadjo Spring Lean-to, a nice new shelter maintained by the people of the L.L. Bean Company and where we had talked of staying for the night, so I left Indy and Vince a note that I was headed to the White House. I attempted to entice Vince to hike the extra couple of miles by writing "hamburgers," figuring that would do the trick.

When I passed by Pemadumcook Lake, I got my first view of Mount Katahdin. It was a beautiful day, and once again the Maine A.T. Club had come through with a sign directing hikers to a location just off the trail for a great view of Mount Katahdin. The mountain was about forty-eight miles away. I was able to have one of the Dutchmen take my picture with the "Big K" in the background. If that magnificent view did not get a thru-hiker's heart pumping, I don't know what would. I headed toward Mount Katahdin with an extra spring in my steps!

At a newly cut logging road that crossed the A.T., a sign read "White House Camp, food, cabins and supplies 3/4 mile." I was headed to the White House with food on my mind.

Next, I came upon another homemade sign pointing to the left into the woods off the logging road that read "White House Landing for pickup." It was getting interesting, and I was getting a little uneasy.

After a short hike through the woods, the trail I had been following suddenly disappeared into the lake! "What's going on?" I thought to myself. "Someone jerking me around?" I began to question my decision to get off the A.T. when I noticed another hand-written sign next to an air horn hanging on a string that read, "Sound air horn for pick up with motorboat, free. Please be patient – we may be in the middle of something!" Now I really began to question my decision as I thought, "OK, where's the candid camera?" as I scanned the water edge for some jokester hiding behind the bushes. No one was around, so I figured, "What's the harm?" and gave the air horn a somewhat embarrassed squeeze. The blast echoed through the woods and across the mirror smooth lake.

After what seemed like an eternity but I'm sure was only a few minutes, I heard the faint "put-put" of an outboard motor as a small motorboat headed my way from across the lake. Bill Ware, owner of the White House Camp, was on his way to pick me up in his small boat and take me over to his landing. What a great way to do business!

The camp was fantastic. Rustic, with no electric, only propane to run their appliances, but I would not have wanted it any other way. I heard someone ask Bill's wife Linda about electricity, and her response was quick and direct, "I hope we never get it!" I certainly understood her wanting to keep the homey landing just the way it was. I had a wonderful lunch of hamburgers and potato salad, along with ice cream, and I also had an opportunity to resupply. I was told we could look forward to a hearty breakfast in the morning before Bill took us back across the pond. Heaven, simply heaven! I had found a thru-hiker's paradise in the middle of the hundred-mile wilderness!

As I sat on the porch of their lodge with one of the Dutchmen, I watched in awe as a bald eagle swooped down on two loons out on the lake. Then, as nighttime closed in on the peaceful little camp, I headed to bed in the bunkhouse, a very contented thru-hiker ready to take on Mount Katahdin!

August 26, Pemadumcook Logging Road (White House Landing) to Rainbow Spring Campsite (milepoint 2140.8 north)

The call of a loon out on the pond awakened me, and I could not imagine a more pleasing wake-up call.

An ideal stop for thru-hikers, the White House Landing had been in full operation for thru-hikers since the previous July when the logging road was put through and crossed the A.T. on the other side of the pond. Bill and Linda operated the White House Landing Wilderness Camp year-round for ice fishing and snowmobiling as well. They also served as a bear camp for hunters but were not comfortable with that part of the business. As Linda said, "We hope that the additional income from thru-hikers will enable us to eliminate the bear hunting camp." Built in the early 1900s resembling the Washington, D.C. White House – hence the name – the landing had a turn-of-the-last-century atmosphere I absolutely loved, a wonderful experience. I hoped the Wares would continue to accommodate future thru-hikers, as the landing was definitely an oasis in the hundred-mile wilderness.

As I waited on the front porch swing for breakfast and listened to the loons, I could not see Mount Katahdin but felt I was close enough to smell it!

My boat ride back across the pond was captained by a young southbounder who told me, "I stopped by the landing for a night, fell in love with the place, and decided to spend the summer working for Bill and Linda."

> *Hiker tips: I believe the pickup point for the White House Landing was a bit farther than the three-quarters of a mile that the sign claimed, but it was certainly worth the hike!*

I had a full belly after breakfast, and with a twenty-mile day planned, I would need all the energy I could get. Although I knew I had lost some weight, I was surprised to see a weight loss of more than thirty-five pounds when I'd stepped on the scales at the lodge.

Back on the south side of the pond, I hiked along the edge of Nahmakanta Lake in clear and cool weather. Today's weather was fine, and more importantly was that Bill had said the weather forecast for August 28 at Mount Katahdin looked ideal.

By noon, when I was at Wadleigh Stream Lean-to, I had only hiked eight miles. With twelve miles to go, it looked to be a long day.

A plane landed on the lake right next to me on the trail. I assumed coming in to the backwoods of Maine by plane was probably the quickest and easiest method, as there were only a few logging roads that crossed the hundred-mile wilderness.

As I crossed Nesuntabunt Mountain at 1,520 feet, I had climbed one thousand feet in a half-mile.

I left Rainbow Spring Lean-to after finishing a snack with Indy and Vince. We decided that since we were making good miles and the weather was so great, we would go for a summit of Mount Katahdin on August 28 instead of the 29th and wanted to reach Rainbow Spring Campsite tonight, about three more miles. The forecast was good through the 28th, so we wanted the best shot at a good summit day.

With such beautiful weather, I was looking forward to tenting. I was getting a little tired of all the hiker talk in shelters. Hikers are great people, but I wanted some time to myself. Staying in the tent would give me just that.

When we arrived at the Rainbow Stream Campsite, we found a great spring and ideal campsite. With my tent up and my belly full, I took some time to read in my *Appalachian Trail Thru-Hikers' Companion* that "Katahdin" meant "greatest mountain." The mountain was considered a holy place to Native Americans, who said that the deity on Mount Katahdin would destroy any man who ventured too close to the mountain. The first ascent by a white man was in 1804.

Reflection time: As we sat around the camp someone asked, "What you going to miss most about hiking the A.T., Mountain Slayer?" Without hesitation, I replied, "I'm going to miss getting up in the morning and throwing my pack on for the day's hike!" My favorite part of the thru-hike had been just that, the opportunity to hike every day. The independence of the trail was something I would always cherish: the opportunity to hike when I wanted and stop when I wanted, to do what I wanted when I wanted had been a dream come true. Also high on my list were the new people and the many friends I had come to know along the way; and last, but by no means least, were the incredible views and the natural scenery on the trail.

Another interesting question was "What will you *not* miss?" That, too, was easy to answer, but resulted in a much shorter list: filtering water, laundry, and mac and cheese!

As darkness settled in over the campsite, the mosquitoes soon followed, so I quickly found shelter in my tent. It proved to be a wonderful night as I lay in my tent listening to the loons in full lunatic chorus on the pond.

August 27, Rainbow Spring Campsite to Daicey Pond Campgrounds (milepoint 2159.5 north)

I packed my gear to leave Rainbow Springs Campground a little after 6 a.m. as the mosquitoes continued to swarm.

Mount Katahdin was 26.3 miles away, but my goal for the day was to get to Daicey Pond, approximately nineteen miles, and report in to the ranger station. Indy hoped to find his two friends from Indiana who were planning to reach Abol Bridge Campground.

Hiker tips: More equipment thoughts. Throughout my thru-hike I had been able to share a lot of information on gear, but I don't think I mentioned the importance of my watch. Some people did not believe in having any kind of modern technology on the trail (they were usually the same people who asked me what time it was!) but to me a watch was invaluable. It helped me regulate my speed, distance and, on occasion, figure out where I was, or at least should be! I did not need, or for that matter, want an expensive watch; but it was extremely important that the watch be waterproof and visible at night, as there were not many lights in the shelters! I also had a very small Photon Micro-light hooked on my mini-Swiss knife. It worked very well and provided all the light that I needed. Although I did carry a mini-Mag Lite, the only times I really used it were for occasional reading at night. Again, I want to reiterate that my thoughts on equipment simply reflect what worked for me on my thru-hike along with occasional comments from fellow thru-hikers. But I am very confident that anyone reading this will go away with an excellent idea of what gear is best suited for the Appalachian Trail.

I passed a sign that indicated Abol Bridge was six miles and Mount Katahdin 20.5. I planned on stopping at Abol Bridge Campground to get a few snacks for the night and, I hoped, a Guinness for a Mount Katahdin summit toast. Then off to Daicey Pond Campground for the final night on the trail.

As I closed in on Abol Bridge, I heard some automobile traffic, the first traffic noise I had heard in weeks. There was also a warning sign for southbounders that read: "Caution: It is 100 miles south to the nearest town at Monson. There are NO places to obtain supplies or help until Monson. Do not attempt this section unless you have a minimum of 10 days supplies and are fully equipped. Do not underestimate its difficulty."

Of course, when the sign was posted, the White House Wilderness Landing Camp had not been available to hikers, and in any case, probably should not be totally relied on as a supply opportunity.

I left the Abol Bridge Campstore, where I'd had a mysterious sandwich called a double cheeseburger and several other snacks. I had no idea what kind of meat was on the burger they put in the microwave; and it was probably just as well that I didn't know, but it surely didn't taste like beef!" I had been hoping for a Guinness to toast my summit, but it looked like a Miller Lite would have to do.

The Four Dutchmen were at the store having a great time. They were real characters! Two were throwing a Frisbee around, while another was getting some fishing gear together for some trout fishing. The four were continually pulling tricks on each other and could be very entertaining at times, as long as you were not part of their shenanigans. Back at the White House Landing, I'd observed one of the Four Dutchmen pouring water in another's boot as a prank – only a really good friend could get away with that!

Entered Baxter State Park, where a sign read that the shelters at Daicey Pond were reserved for A.T. thru-hikers only. It was nice to know someone was looking out for the thru-hikers, who had limited options.

I was hiking along the Penobscot River with my head down and my mind somewhere up on Mount Katahdin when I came head to horns with an enormous ten-point buck! What a surprise! It was obvious I was back in a state park as the buck totally ignored me, being much more interested in the grass it was eating.

A short time later, I arrived at Daicey Pond Campground and went directly to the ranger station, where I waited a half-hour for an overly talkative ranger to check me in. As I was waiting, two young fellows rode up on bikes and asked, "Are you hiking with Indy?" Now how lucky was that? They had a backpack full of food and beer with them. We would be eating and drinking like kings on our last night on the trail!

It was 5 p.m. when I arrived at Daicey Pond Lean-to, where I found a shelter and laid out my sleeping pad and bag for the final time on the Appalachian Trail.

Woodchip had stayed in the same shelter the night before her summit of Mount Katahdin and had left a poem in the shelter register. Not only was Woodchip an outstanding hiker, but also a poet, a lady of many talents. It was so well done and put into words the feeling and thoughts of so many thru-hikers, I felt it needed to be shared:

"It starts with a yearning
Then turned into reality
And my life goes on
The thoughts return of the A.T.
Spring's early showers
Then bushes of pink and white laurel
The smell of the earth
Hiking in a foggy haze
The roots and the rocks
The wind in the trees
The mossy covered logs
The smell of the earth
The trail with quagmire
Many a steep incline
The hoot of the owl
Along with the whippoorwill
And others join in from the forest
The call of the loon
The sight of a wild creature
Skeeters, ticks and the fly
Folks that we meet
Alas, cold early spring snow
The sunset serene
To follow the white
Then take our rest
142 days from GA to Me
Trail angels are caring
The towns on the way
May offer a treat
The rivers and lakes
Enduring the pain
And SO much more
Bring forth in my reverse
That will live to the end

The spark kept on burning
And now becomes a memory
But just like an old song
To always be a part of me
Below leafless bowers
Azaleas of pink white red and coral
The grassy field turf
Also bright sunny days
Silent needled walks
Whoops fell on my knees
The boards in the bogs
The grassy hills turf
Certainly not a desire
Dawn again time after time
A nighttime fowl
By day the thrush trill
Frogs make up the chorus
Is part of the tune
Is a wonderful feature
A nuisance I must decry
With a trail name we greet
Ah, but the moon glow
Is part of the scene
From dawn to dusk light
For the morrows guest
With me will remain
Their magic are sharing
Where a food package lays
From trail food to eat
The many snack breaks
The guts to remain
In my memory store
Forever a part of me
Till I say my last Amen"

Woodchip 8-19-00 Mass."

At Daicey Pond Camp on my final night on the Appalachian Trail were Indy, Vince of Wales, Duke-Nuk'em, the Four Dutchmen, Puddin', and a flip-flopper whose trail name escaped me. We had a great evening, full of exhilarated talk around an inviting fire with lots of food, drinks, and merriment.

The Maine nights continued to mesmerize me with the bright stars and moon lighting up the evening sky, and my final evening on the trail had been no exception. When I got up around 1:30 a.m., the night sky was so bright and clear I just sat down and took it all in. I noticed Duke-Nuk'em lying out in the field next to the camp in only his sleeping bag, also enjoying his last night under nothing but the brilliant Maine sky.

August 28, Daicey Pond Campgrounds to Mount Katahdin Summit (milepoint 2167.1 north)

I left for Mount Katahdin a little after 6 a.m. with 7.6 miles remaining to the 5,268-foot summit of Mount Katahdin. It was a beautiful day, with not a cloud in the sky. We had a great day for a summit.

Indy left earlier in the morning to meet his friends, Craig and Dave, at Katahdin Springs Campground, knowing they would probably need a little extra time.

I felt a little sorry for the flip-flopper, as we all had talked with excitement throughout the evening about completing our A.T. journey. He would be just halfway done when he reached the summit of Mount Katahdin, where he would turn south to complete the trail in Maryland. There's nothing wrong with Maryland, mind you, but there is something special about ending your A.T. thru-hike at Mount Katahdin. He'd run into some physical problem on his way north and had to get off the trail for an extended time, which resulted in his flip-flop to Katahdin and then south. He was a really nice fellow with a lot of questions about the White Mountains he had heard so much about. I wished him the best.

As Indy's friends had volunteered to drop me off in the New York City area, I was eagerly searching for a telephone to call my daughter Elizabeth to find the best way to get to her place in Brooklyn. But much to my dismay, there were no telephones in the hundred-mile wilderness or in Baxter State Park. In the early 1900's, Maine's Governor Baxter purchased the area after his term in office and donated it back to the state with the rules that it remain an undeveloped wilderness. In other words, no modernization – no telephones, no electricity, and so on. But the lack of modern conveniences certainly had not deterred people from using the park, as it was booked months in advance.

The rangers at Katahdin Stream Campground had daypacks for thru-hikers who wanted to summit without their heavy packs, but my old Jansport had been with me every step of my hike; I would not feel right leaving it in the ranger station as I made my final ascent up Mount Katahdin.

There was another beautiful sunrise as I made my way toward the foot of Mount Katahdin. I was really excited about the summit but also felt a little nostalgic, knowing that my hike was almost over. Being on the trail for five months and finishing was akin to leaving an old friend. So as I hiked my last few miles on the Appalachian Trail to Mount Katahdin, I felt torn: part of me couldn't wait to get to Katahdin, while the other part of me wanted to stop and not let it end.

The perfect day for a summit would also be a perfect day to yo-yo. "Yo-yo" was thru-hiker jargon for turning around at Mount Katahdin and heading back to Georgia. But my body cried "Enough for now," and I was sure my wife would have something to say about that as well! At the base of Mount Katahdin, a plaque read:

"Man is born to die, his works are short-lived, buildings crumble, monuments decay, wealth vanishes, but Katahdin in all its glory forever shall remain the mountain to the people of Maine."

I met up with Indy, Craig, and Dave, and placed some unneeded equipment in their car for the final leg of my journey. We passed a sign reading that hiking on Mount Katahdin after October 15 was prohibited without special permission and that violators would be prosecuted. I had heard many stories about people getting stuck up on the mountain in the late fall due to bad weather, so the warning certainly had merit.

With Indy and his friends taking their time, I continued ahead on my own. The mountain climbing was tough for new people on the trail. They were doing great, but I was all pumped up with the emotion of finishing the trail and did not want them to think I was pushing, so I decided to hike ahead. Besides, I liked finishing the Appalachian Trail the way I started one-hundred-and-fifty-three days earlier: alone and full of excitement and anticipation.

I stopped for a break and put on my raincoat for a windbreaker as it was getting cool. I could only imagine what the mountain was like in bad weather. Even on a beautiful day, it was windy and cool and tough going. I had my hiking poles put away and was doing some major boulder climbing at the three-mile mark to the summit. My wife had been correct to turn down my suggestion that she join me for my summit of Mount Katahdin. After looking at the map and knowing she was not in hiking shape, she thought it best not to attempt Mount Katahdin. It was a wise decision.

At the two milepost, the wind continued to really blow hard, making Mount Katahdin much more of a challenge than I had anticipated.

I reached a plateau called the Tableland, which included a spring named after Henry David Thoreau, who explored the area in 1846. The wind had died down, and it was actually comfortable hiking.

11:00 a.m. - Mount Katahdin Summit

To the reader: Stop, put the book down, go to the refrigerator and get yourself a nice cold drink of your choice. I'll wait! OK, back now? I want you to raise that drink you have, as I do the same, and toast the summit of Mount Katahdin with me. To each and every one of you who have traveled the 2,167.1 miles of Appalachian Trail with me as my hiking partner, Cheers! Although you were not physically on the trail, I know you were with me in spirit. And I hope that by reading my book and experiencing the trail through me, you have shared in the joy I experienced during my five months of hiking.

To avoid leaving someone out, I resisted the urge of personally thanking the many people who had helped me along the way, but I did need to mention a few very important people in my life who really made my thru-hike possible. A person I had not mentioned throughout the hike but to whom I dedicated my hike in her memory was my mother. She left us way too soon, but the ideals and faith she instilled in me have been the driving forces that enabled me to complete the journey. She was often in my thoughts as I walked the mountains and valleys of the A.T., and I can say without reservation that I felt as close to her on Mount Katahdin as I had at any other time since she passed away.

Also, to the family members and friends who hiked with me in preparation for the A.T. and on the A.T. – thank you! And to those friends who assisted me and my wife directly or indirectly while I was on the trail – thank you!

Finally, there is the one special person who made it possible for me to share my hike and was always there with help and encouragement when I needed it: my wife Connie. I could not have made it without her.

All the thru-hikers who had reached the summit at that time gathered for a group picture. It included Vince of Wales, Indy, the Four Dutchmen, Puddin', Duke Nuk'Em, Never Again (and she meant it), Camo, and the flip-flopper.

It was especially nice to summit with the Vince of Wales; Vince and I met the very first day on the trail, and who would have ever thought we would summit Mount Katahdin together 153 days later?

We saw the Knife-Edge Trail north of the summit, and wanting a different trail down decided to take it. What a trail! It was as much a challenge as any on the entire A.T. and certainly lived up to its name! A sign read "Knife Edge, do not take this trail in bad weather." That was a no-brainer.

Vince and I finally made it back to the Katahdin Stream Campground, about twenty miles by road back to the campground from the end of the Knife-Edge Trail. Fortunately, we got a quick hitch back to the campground and were just waiting for Indy and his friends so we could head home.

Indy and his friends Craig and Dave eventually came in. The last couple of miles coming off Mount Katahdin on the Knife-Edge just about did Dave in. To his credit, it was an extremely tough section and probably too much for non-seasoned hikers to attempt, but he made it.

With the five of us and all our gear stuffed to the top of Dave's Blazer, we headed south, first to Millinocket, Maine, for a quick shower at the Appalachian Trail Lodge run by Don Cogswell. A great fellow, he took just a few dollars to allow us to clean up for the ride home even though we did not intend to stay overnight. Then we grabbed a quick bite to eat and headed south to Bangor where we left Vince off around 2 a.m. to catch a bus to Canada. We all hated dropping Vince off at a closed bus station that early in the morning, but he insisted he would be OK. I guess if you can handle five months on the trail, a layover in Bangor, Maine, is not a problem. Even though Vince was down to his last eight dollars in cash, he would not take any money -- still the headstrong Welshman I had come to know!

At 8 a.m. on August 29, Indy and his friends dropped me off at a commuter train station just south of Poughkeepsie, N.Y. off Interstate 84 to catch a ride to Grand Central Station in New York City, where I planned to meet up with my daughter. They all laughed when Indy joked, "Well, Mountain Slayer, you thought your adventure was over at Mount Katahdin; but headed to New York City with a backpack, it may just be starting!"

So ended my one-hundred-and-fifty-three-day journey on the Appalachian Trail. I left the solitude of the Maine backwoods, where everyone I met had a smile on his or her face and an eagerness to talk, for a jam-packed commuter train headed for Grand Central Station, where nothing but blank stares greeted me. Once a celebrity of sorts on the Appalachian Trail as a thru-hiker, I found I was nothing but a nuisance carrying a backpack for those wanting a seat on a full commuter train headed toward New York City!

A

Ace and Alias, 136
Addis Gap, 32, 33
**American Youth Hostel (Harpers
  Ferry, West Virginia**, 144
Amicalola Falls State Park, 11
Appalachian Trail Conference Center,
  13, 145
Appalachian Trail Data Book, 13
*Appalachian Trail Thru-Hikers'
  Companion*, 13
Atkins, Virginia, 97

B

Badger, 91, 168
Bald Mountain Shelter, 72, 74
Bear Mountain Inn, 191, 192
Bearfence Mountain Hut, 129, 130
Beaver Brook Shelter, 234, 236
Bemis Mountain Lean-to, 261, 263
Benton MacKaye, 193, 271
Big Branch Shelter, 219, 221
Blackburn Trail Center, 141, 144
Bland, Virginia, 101, 102
**Blue Mountain Lakes Road, New
  Jersey**, 177
**Blue Mountain Summit,
  Pennsylvania**, 168
Blue Ridge Summit, Pennsylvania,
  149, 151
Bob Illi, 59
Boiling Springs, Pennsylvania, 155,
  157
Braemar Castle Hostel, 84, 85
Brown Fork Gap Shelter, 48, 50
Buena Vista, Virginia, 119

C

Calf Mountain Shelter, 126, 127
Carter Gap Shelter, 37, 39
Catawba Mountain Shelter, 110,
  111
Cherry Gap Shelter, 75, 77
Chimney Mirror Motel, 214
Cloverdale, Virginia, 111, 113

Cold Spring Shelter, 43, 46
Congdon Shelter, 214, 215
Cove Mountain Shelter, 114, 116
Crocker Cirque Campsite, 267, 269
Cruise Control and Shadow, 235

D

Daicey Pond Campgrounds, 288,
  292
Damascus, Virginia, 91
Dan Bruce (Wingfoot), 67
Davenport Gap, 62
Dead Horse, 37, 64
Delaware Water Gap, Pennsylvania,
  173, 177
Dennytown Road Campsite, 192,
  194
Dicks Creek Gap, 33, 35
Double Spring Gap Shelter, 55, 57
Double Springs Shelter, 85, 87

E

Eagle's Nest Shelter, 164, 166
East Branch Lean-to, 282, 284
Eckville Shelter, 166, 168
Egermont Inn, 204
Elk Park, North Carolina, 80
Erwin, Tennessee, 74
Ethan Pond Campsite, 243, 244
Etna, New Hampshire, 231, 232

F

Firewarden Cabin, 232, 233
Flint Mountain Shelter, 70
Fontana Dam, North Carolina, 50
Four Dutchmen, 280
Franklin, North Carolina, 39, 42, 43
Full Goose Shelter, 255, 257
Fullhardt Knob Shelter, 113, 114

G

Gall Pond Lodge, 263
Garfield Ridge Campsite, 240, 243
Gaslight Motor Lodge, 206, 208
Gathland St. Park, 147